Word 365 - Building Professional Documents

Microsoft Word is a full-featured **Word Processor** used to create and design documents such as letters and memos. Since it is a tool we use on a daily basis, it is important to take advantage of time-saving tips and ways to improve efficiency. Using **Microsoft Word** to its fullest extent can provide a professionally structured layout to communicate messages with creditability and accuracy. Furthermore, effective documents must have a professional look and layout. Therefore, if you are building a large document containing **Chapters**, **Table of Contents**, **Index**, and **Legal Citations**, this **Step-By-Step Workbook** will provide the knowledge necessary to implement capabilities for communicating effective messages.

Creating A Document

Chapters 1-14 will help you understand features needed to enhance a document. This manual will cover in-depth how to manipulate text using **Characters**, **Paragraphs**, **Indenting**, **Date**, **Time, Number,** and **Bullets**. You will also be able to edit documents, as well as enhance their appearance and print them in a variety of formats. Additionally, creating a new document using a **Template** is a quick method to get started. Plus, using different viewing layouts and methods of navigating will increase productivity and learning. This manual will also demonstrate diverse ways to insert and use graphic images within a text. Applying **Word Wrap** features will also allow text to flow around images. Finally, you can use **Spell Check**, **Grammar**, **Contextual**,  **Smart Lookup** spelling tools to find and correct wording and spelling issues.

Large Documents

Because there are unique challenges faced with very large documents due to the consistency of **Headers**, **Footers**, **Chapter Names**, **Indexes**, **Table of Contents**, and many other **Large Document** challenges. Chapters 15-24 will allow you to enter special commands and build a long document structure. You will also learn how to create **Tables,** insert rows/columns, add borders, backgrounds, merge cells, combine cells, and convert text to a **Table**. As text is entered, a **Page** will **Break** automatically, or you can insert a specific code to **Break** the **Page** such as **Section Break, Odd Page Break**, and **Column Break**. Placing **Headers** and **Footers** on each page can finalize a document for printing, but you may want the chapter header to be different for each chapter. Therefore, this manual will cover how to use **Page Breaks** to stop formatting between pages to allow one page for **Landscape** and the next page to switch back to **Portrait**. We will also explain how to use the **Draft View** and **Show/Hide** marks to see hidden codes such as **Page Breaks** and **Index** markers. Furthermore, **Styles** will allow you to define a specific format in order to create titles, generate a **Table Of Contents**, and provide consistency for text. We will also cover adding an **Index** and other **References** for legal documents at the end of a document. Finally, the final project will focus on creating **Large Documents** including a **Table Of Contents**, **Index**, **Section Breaks**, etc. We have also added several optional special topics to the **Appendix** such as **Forms**, **Macros**, and **Mail Merge**.

About the Author

Jeff Hutchinson is a computer instructor teaching a variety of classes around the country. He has a BS degree from BYU in Computer-Aided Engineering and has worked in the Information Technology field supporting and maintaining computers for many years. He also previously owned a computer training and consulting firm in San Francisco, California. After selling his business in 2001, he has continued to work as an independent computer instructor around the country. **Jeff Hutchinson** lives in Utah and also provides training for Utah Valley University Community Education system, offering valuable computer skills for the general knowledge of students, career development, and career advancement. Understanding the technology and the needs of students has been the basis for developing this material. **Jeff Hutchinson** can be contacted at JeffHutch@elearnlogic.com or **(801) 376-6687.**

Workbook Design

This workbook is designed in conjunction with an **Online-Instructor-Led course** (for more information see: **www.elearnlogic.com**). Unlike other manuals, you will not need to review lengthy procedures to learn a topic. All that is needed are the brief statements and command paths located within the manual that demonstrate how a concept is used. Furthermore, you will find that this **Workbook** is often used as a reference to help understand concepts quickly, and an index is provided on the last page to reference pages as necessary. However, if more detail is needed, you can always use the Internet to search for a concept. Also, if your skills are weak due to lack of use, you can refresh your memory quickly by visually scanning the concepts needed and then testing them out using the application.

Manual Organization

The following are special formatting conventions:

- **Numbered Sections** on the left are the **Concepts** covered.
- **Italic Text** is a Step-By-Step procedure to better understand a concept.
- **Practice Exercises** are a **Step-by-Step** approach to demonstrate the **Concept**.
- **Student Projects** are a more comprehensive approach to demonstrate the **Concept**.
- **Dark, Grayed-Out Sections** are optional/advanced **Concepts**.
- **Bolded** items are important points, terminology, or commands.
- **Tips** are additional ideas to help better understand the **Concept**.

Table of Contents

Exercise Download

Exercises are posted on the website and can be downloaded to your computer. Please do the following:

Open Internet Explorer. Or Google Chrome:

Type the web address:

elearnlogic.com/download/word365-12.exe

You might get several security warnings, but answer yes and run through each one. When you click "**Unzip**," the files will be located in **C:\Data\Word365-12 folder**.

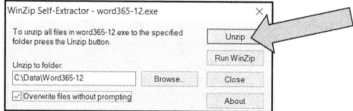

If there are any questions or problems, please contact Jeff Hutchinson at:

JeffHutch@elearnlogic.com

Note: For **Mac** users, download the file at:

elearnlogic.com/download/word365-12.zip

Alternate Google Download Folder:

https://drive.google.com/drive/folders/1IW0y5dxJsrbRq3GmvF2WDm6DZO7leiki?usp=sharing

Copyright and Release Information

This document was updated on **4/1/2022 (Version 1)** and combines both Level 1 and Level 2. Special features have been added, where appropriate, for **Word 2010, 2013, 2016, and 2019**. This guide is the sole property of Jeff Hutchinson and **eLearnLogic**. Any emailing, copying, duplication, or reproduction of this guide, must be approved by Jeff Hutchinson in writing. However, students who take a class or purchase the guide are free to use it for personal development and learning.

Paperback Book ISBN: 9798730219151

Chapter 1 - Interface/Overview

Microsoft Word is a full-featured word processor in which you can create and design documents such as letters and memos. When you open **Microsoft Word**, a blank document appears in the application window. You can start typing in the blank document window or select an option in the **File Tab** button to open an existing document or create a new document using templates.

In a new document, you will notice a blinking vertical character in the upper, left corner of the document. This blinking character indicates the position of the next typed character and is known as the insertion point. Press the **Enter** key to move the insertion point for typing a new paragraph, creating a blank line between paragraphs, or ending a line of text (such as the individual lines of an address).

When typed text fills a line, **Microsoft Word** automatically moves to the beginning of the next line. This feature is called word wrap. You press the **Enter** key only when you want to begin a new paragraph or insert a blank line. The following will indicate some of the features:

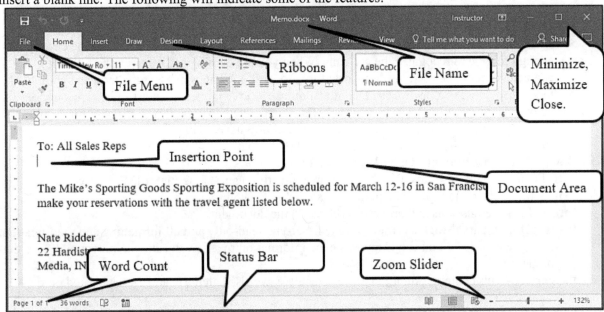

Practice Exercise 1 - Entering Text

1. **File** *Tab* → **New** → *Blank document.*
2. *Type To: All Sales Reps.*
3. *Press* **Enter** *key twice.*
4. *Type "The Mike's Sporting Goods Sporting Exposition is scheduled for March 12-16 in San Francisco. Please make your reservations with the travel agent listed below."*
5. *Press* **Enter** *key twice and type the following text, pressing* **Enter** *key after each line:*
   Karl Ritter
   34 Elm Street
   Media, PA 19107

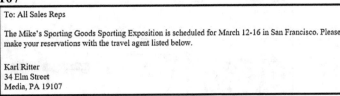

1.1 File Tab

The **File** **Tab** is located at the top, left-hand corner. It includes most of the commands traditionally found in the **File** menu in older **Microsoft Word** versions.

New - A **New Microsoft Word** document is based on the **Blank Document** template (also referred to as the Normal template). Templates are available to get you started more quickly because you can then reduce the time it takes to manually create a new document. Templates also provide a more professional look.

Open - **Open Microsoft Word** by selecting it from this menu. You do not need to remember the file name because the **Open Dialog Box** displays a list of folders and files in the current drive and folder. You can then select a desired document from the list, or you can type the name of a document you want to open. When you choose a different file type in the **Open Dialog Box,** you will be able to open files created in other programs. **Tip**: In **Word 2010,** there was a menu called **Recent.** It listed the previously opened files similar to the **Open** menu in newer versions.

Save - This will **Save** the active file that is currently opened.

Save As - A file name can consist of multiple words (up to 255 characters) and should be descriptive enough for you to recognize the contents. When you are naming a document, the following characters cannot be used in file names: forward-slash (/), backslash (\), greater than symbol (>), less than symbol (<), an asterisk (*), quotation marks (", "), question marks (?), pipe symbol (|), colon (:), or semicolon (;).You can easily **Save** an opened document to a different file format by choosing the option. The following are a few file formats available:

Word Document - This is the new Office XML File format.

Word 97-2003 Document - Older **Word** file format.

PDF Format - You now have the ability to save directly to an Adobe PDF file.

Print - Many **Printing Options** will now be available for you to print.

Info - This is permissions and properties related to the document.

Protect Document→Mark as final - File will become read-only and all formatting and modification tools are disabled. You can Copy/Paste the information to a new document, but you will lose the properties.

Properties - This contains Author, Title, Subject, Keywords, Category, and Status located on the right side of the document.

Check for issues→Inspect Document - Inspects document for hidden metadata, personal information, Custom XML code, information in headers, footers, watermarks, and formatted hidden text.

Practice Exercise 2 - File Tab

1. *Open a new workbook if necessary.*
2. **File** *Tab →* **Save** *→* Browse *→File name: C:\Data\Word365-12\Test.docx →* Save .
3. *Click the* **File** *Tab →Click* Close .
4. *Create New Blank Document: Click* **File** *Tab →* New *→* Blank Document.
5. *Click the* **File** *Tab →Click* Open *→* Browse *→ C:\Data\Word365-12\Test.docx →* Open .
6. **File** *Tab →* New *→(Choose a Template):* New .

1.2 The Ribbon

The **Ribbon**, located under the application title bar, is a band of functional **Tabs** that replace the menu system used in older versions of **Microsoft Word**.

Home Ribbon Tab - This brings together the most frequently used commands in one easily accessible place. While some buttons in the **Ribbon** immediately apply a command, such as the **Bold** button, other buttons offer a large range of choices.

Down Arrows - When you see a button with a **Down-Pointing Arrow**, it indicates that the button offers several options. Generally, clicking this type of button displays a **Gallery**, although some buttons display just a menu, while others show both a gallery and a menu. A **Gallery** is a graphic display of the options available from the button. If a button appears dimmed, it indicates that the command is not available for the current task.

Ribbon Groups - The buttons are arranged in named **Groups** within each tab. The **Group Names** appear below the buttons. A **Launcher Arrow** to the right of some **Group Names** opens either a dialog box or a task pane providing additional options not available from the buttons.

KeyTips - Press alt to display the **KeyTips** letter and use the arrows or press the letter displayed to choose a command, and the **Enter** key to select the command.

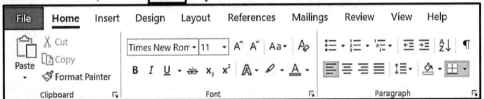

The following are some of the **Ribbon Tabs** that appear on top of the interface:

File Menu - This is located in the upper left corner and contains file-related commands.

Home Ribbon Tab - This contains most of the format-related concepts.

Insert Ribbon Tab - This is used to insert objects such as graphic items.

Layout Ribbon Tab - This is used to define page settings or things that will affect page layout. Many of the printing-related features are contained here.

> Tip: **Excel 2010** the name was **Page Layout Ribbon Tab**.

References Ribbon Tab - This includes references such as a table of contents, index, etc.

Mailings Ribbon Tab - This allows you to merge addresses on envelopes, form letters, and send mass e-mails to a specific person.

Review Ribbon Tab - This includes spell check and tools that analyze the document.

View Ribbon Tab - This includes Zoom, Print Layout, and window layout tools.

Practice Exercise 3 - Ribbon

1. ***Create New Blank Document:*** File *Tab→* New *→* *Blank Document.*

2. ***View Ribbon Tab → Views Group →*** *Print Layout.*

3. ***Type the word: TEST***

4. ***Select the word test by highlighting it.***

5. ***Home Ribbon Tab →Font Group →Click the arrow*** *on the right-hand part of the Text **Highlight Color button*** .

6. ***Click Bright Green*** *in the Fill Colors gallery.*

7. File *Tab →* Close *→* Don't Save *when prompted whether to save the changes.*

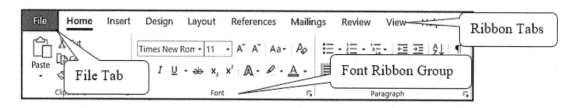

1.3 Contextual Ribbon Tabs

These are **Ribbon Tabs** that remain hidden until needed. When you select specific objects, the **Contextual Ribbon Tab** appears and the **Design Ribbon Tab** is available. The term Context-based feature provides options pertinent to the type of entity you select.

In addition to the standard tabs in the **Ribbon**, there are **Contextual Tabs** that appear when you create or select certain types of objects such as pictures, tables, or charts. These **Contextual Tabs** always display to the right of the standard tabs, have a different highlight color, and contain commands related to the selected object. All **Contextual Tabs** display a heading. Depending on the object type inserted or selected, more than one **Contextual Tab** may appear under the heading. When you deselect the object, the **Contextual Tabs** automatically disappear.

Types of Contextual tabs

Depending on the object selected three different **Contextual Tabs** may appear.

Format - This tab appears when you choose Textbox, shapes, WordArt, SmartArt graphics, pictures, and Clip Art. **Example: *Insert Ribbon Tab→Illustrations Group→Clip Art→Place Clip Art.***

Design - This tab appears when you choose Tables in **Microsoft Word**, Headers/Footers, and SmartArt graphics. **Example: *Insert Ribbon Tab→Header & Footer Group→Header→Blank.***

Layout - This tab appears when you insert tables in **Microsoft Word**.

  Example: *Insert Ribbon Tab→Tables Group→ ⊞ Table*

Practice Exercise 4 - Contextual Ribbons

1. ***Create New Blank Document:*** File *Tab→* New *→* *Blank Document.*
2. ***Insert Ribbon Tab→Illustrations Group→*** Shapes ▾ *Shapes down arrow→(Choose any shape).*
3. ***Observe the Format Ribbon Tab (Contextual Ribbon).***
4. ***Select/Unselect the object to see the Contextual Ribbon turn on and off.***

Tip: You may need to **Double-click** on the chart to see the **Contextual Ribbon**.

1.4 Galleries

Many icons have a down arrow next to them that displays a menu, **Galleries**, or both. Clicking on a **Gallery** object will insert it into a document.

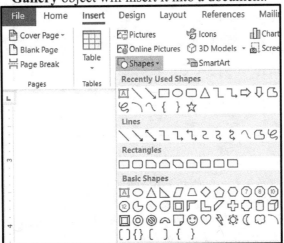

Practice Exercise 5 - Galleries

Continue from the previous practice exercise.

1. *Insert Ribbon Tab → Illustrations Group → Shapes.*
2. *Choose ⬜ Callouts Shape.*
3. *Draw the Callout shape on the document.*
4. *Drag the yellow dot on top of the Callout.*
5. *Use the ⟳ Rotation handle to rotate the shape.*
6. *Use the white dots to increase the size of the Callout.*
7. *Type the text: This is a callout.*

1.5 Dialog Box Launcher

The result of some commands will open a **Dialog Box** in order to show more detailed options. This feature is similar to **Office 2003 Dialog Box**.

Tip: When you click a ⌐ small arrow in the lower-left corner of most **Ribbon Groups**, a **Dialog** box will be displayed containing additional options.

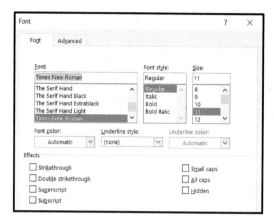

Practice Exercise 6 - Dialog Box

1. *Type the text "Dialog Box Launcher" and select it.*
2. *Home Ribbon Tab →Font Group.*
3. *Click the small arrow in the lower right corner.* 🔲. *Tip: A dialog box is displayed.*
4. *Click on the Font tab→Font Styles: Bold Italic.*

1.6 Quick Access Toolbar

This is a feature that is available in **Microsoft Office 2010/2013/2016/2019** applications. It appears at the top left of the application window just above the 🔲File Tab. It is a quick and easy way to access some of the regularly used features without using the other **Ribbon Tabs**. You can choose to display the **Quick Access Toolbar** below the **Ribbon**. You can customize the **Quick Access Toolbar** to add more commonly used commands, such as **New, Open,** and **Quick Print**. The following are some of the **Quick Access Toolbar** features:

More Commands - This allows you to place any command in this area.

There are 3 commonly used options to add commands:

Popular Commands

Commands Not In The Ribbon

All Commands

Example: *Select the small arrow to the right of the Quick Access Toolbar→ Choose Mor Commands→Choose Commands from: All Commands → Choose* 🅱 *Bold→Add.*

Show Below Ribbon - This is used to move the **Quick Access Toolbar** below the ribbon.

Example: Select the ▾ small arrow to the right of the *Quick Access Toolbar→Choose* Show Below the Ribbon .

Minimize the Ribbon - This saves screen space. Example: *Double-click on the Home Ribbon Tab to minimize the ribbon→Double-click on the Home Ribbon Tab to Maximize the ribbon.*

Add to Quick Access Toolbar - By right-clicking on any ribbon command, you can add it to the **Quick Access Toolbar. Example:** *Review Ribbon Tab→Proofing Group→Right-click on the Spelling and Grammar button→Choose Add to Quick Access Toolbar.*

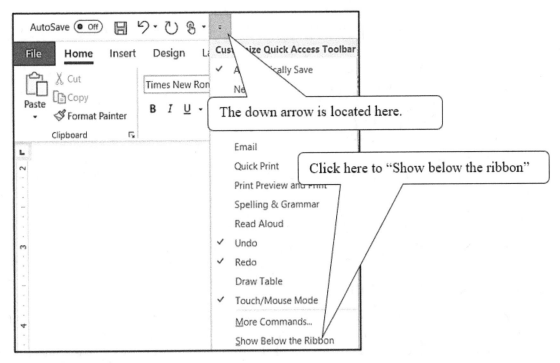

Practice Exercise 7 - Quick Access Toolbar

Continue from the previous practice exercise.
1. ***Locate the Quick Access down arrow in the upper left corner on the top of the screen.***
2. ***Click*** Located in the upper left corner on the top of the screen.
3. ***Click More Commands***

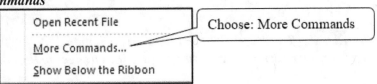

4. ***Click All Commands.***

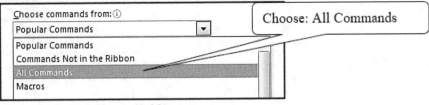

5. ***Review the many commands available.***
6. ***Click the "5-Point Star"*** 5-Point Star →*Add*→ OK .
7. ***Test it: Click the 5-Point Star in the Quick Access Toolbar→***
   Then draw the 5-Point Star on the document page.

1.7 Min/Max Buttons

The entire workbook can be **Minimized** to the **Windows** status bar on the bottom of the **Windows** screen. It can also be **Maximized** to encompass the entire screen. The restore button will partially shrink the screen and clicking it again will **Maximize** it. The last option available is to Close the screen.

Word 2010 Buttons

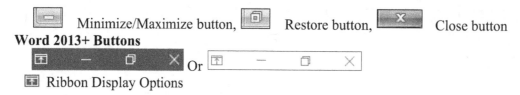 Minimize/Maximize button, Restore button, Close button

Word 2013+ Buttons

Or

Ribbon Display Options

Practice Exercise 8 - Min, Max, Restore

Continue from the previous practice exercise.
1. *Click on the Minimize button.*
2. *Click on the Microsoft Word document on the bottom of the screen to maximize Microsoft Word.*
3. *Click on the restore button.*
4. *Click on the restore button again to maximize the document.*
5. *Close the file without saving it:* File *Tab →* Close *→* Don't Save.

1.8 Exiting/Closing Word

When you are finished using **Microsoft Word**, you should **Exit** the application properly because **Microsoft Word** performs necessary housekeeping before it **Closes**. If the current document has been modified but not saved, a **Microsoft Office Word Dialog Box** prompts you to save the changes before **Exiting**.

Tip: Microsoft Word does not have an **Exit** button because it was redesigned to support dual monitors. So, you can now open different documents and place them on different monitors. Because **Microsoft Word** uses a separate memory image for each opened file, you must close each opened file one at a time.

Practice Exercise 9 - Close

1. File *Tab →* Close. *Tip: Excel 2010 will have an Exit option.*
2. *If a message box opens asking if you want to save the changes to the current document, select No.*

1.9 Pinning Files

This is used to **Pin** the **Files** you need to reopen in the future such as **Status Reports**, etc.

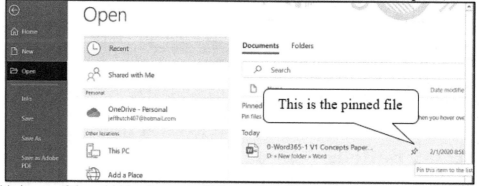

This is the pinned file

Tip: This is one of those hidden features of **Microsoft Office** used to permanently remember previously opened files.

Practice Exercise 10 - Pin Files

Continue from the previous practice exercise.

1. **File** *Tab →Recent button.*
2. *Click the pin on the right of the filename.*

1.10 Using Live Preview

Live Preview is a new feature in **Office 2013/2016+**. You can try out different styles, effects, and colors to visualize their effects before applying them. To see the change in your document, hover the mouse pointer over the thumbnail images or list items in the galleries.

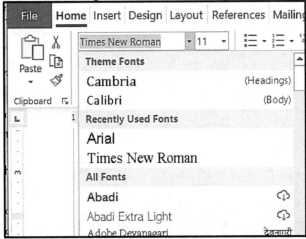

The **Live Preview** feature will temporarily display the changes to the selected object. When you finish previewing the styles, click to select your preferred option.

1.11 Using the Mini Toolbar

When you select some text and **Right-click**, the **Mini** toolbar and a **Shortcut Menu** appear beside the mouse pointer. The **Mini** toolbar contains a selection of popular formatting command buttons so that you do not have to move away from the cell to format it.

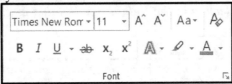

Practice Exercise 11 - Mini Toolbar

Continue from the previous practice exercise.
1. *Select some text and Right-click.*
2. *Click the Bold button* [B] *in the Mini toolbar.*
3. *Click the Increase Font Size button* [A^] *in the Mini toolbar.*
4. *Italicize the text using the Mini Toolbar.*

1.12 Status Bar

Right-click on the **Status Bar** to customize its layout. If the options are checked, they will be displayed in the **Status Bar**. They will not be displayed if the option is unchecked.

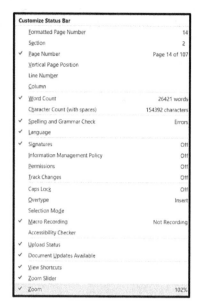

Practice Exercise 12 - Status Bar

Continue from the previous practice exercise.
1. ***Right-click on the Status Bar→ UnCheck Zoom Slider.***
2. ***Right-click on the Status Bar→ Check the Zoom Slider.***
Tip: The **Status Bar** along the bottom of the **Microsoft Word** application window provides information about the status of a variety of features as you work.

Student Project A - Exploring Word

1. ***Start Microsoft Word, if necessary, and open a blank worksheet.***
2. ***Display the*** File ***Tab.***
3. ***Open the Microsoft Word Options Dialog Box:*** File ***Tab→*** Options **.**
4. ***Under the Save options section in the Default file location and change it to C:\Data\Word365-12.***
5.
Default local file location:	C:\Data\Word365-1
6. ***Customize the Quick Access Toolbar by adding the Quick Print command icon.***
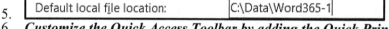
7. ***Remove the Quick Print command from the Quick Access Toolbar.***
8.
9. ***Exit Microsoft Word without saving changes to the document.***

1.13 Scrolling Using The Mouse

To view areas of the document that are not visible on the screen, you can scroll the document using the **Mouse** and **ScrollBars**. The **Vertical Scrollbar** is located on the right side of the document window and is used to **scroll** the document up or down. You can click the up or down arrow in the **Vertical Scroll Bar** once to move the document up or down one line. If you click and hold the mouse button on an arrow, the screen continues to scroll up or down until you release the mouse button. When you drag the **Vertical Scroll Box**, a **ScreenTip** indicates the relative page location of the window display.

The **Horizontal Scrollbar** is located at the bottom of the document window and scrolls the document to the left or right.

Scrolling does not change the location of the insertion point. Although you may be viewing page 3 of your document, the insertion point can be located on page 1. Any text you type is entered at the insertion point, regardless of the window display. To reposition the insertion point, you can click on the desired location.

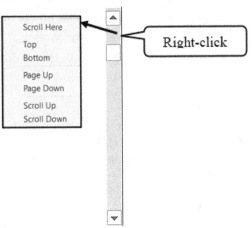

Practice Exercise 13 - Scroll / Arrows

1. File *Tab* → Open → Browse → *C:\Data\Word365-12\Find Replace.docx*
2. *Click the scroll down arrow ▽ to scroll down one line in the document text.*
3. *Click the scroll up arrow △ to scroll up one line in the document text.*
4. *Click on the vertical scroll arrow ▷ to scroll to the right.*
5. *Click on the vertical scroll box ◁ to scroll to the left.*
6. *Click the Page Number box in the lower-left corner on the status bar to navigate to a specific page.*
7. *Tip: Right-click on the vertical scrollbar.*

1.14 Moving Using The Keyboard

The easiest way to move the insertion point (the blinking vertical character) short distances is to use the Arrow **keys**. You can also use additional keys to move the insertion point longer distances. When entering text, you must first position the insertion point where you want to insert the text. You must position the insertion point either to the left or right of an existing character. You cannot place the insertion point directly on a character, past the end of the document, or in an area that does not contain text or codes.

Practice Exercise 14 - Keyboard

1. *Press* Ctrl Home *keys to move the insertion point to the beginning of the document.*
2. *Press the* Down Arrow *keys* ↓ *to move the insertion point down one line.*
3. *Press the* Up Arrow *keys* ↑ *to move the insertion point up one line.*
4. *Press the* Right Arrow *keys* → *to move the insertion point one character to the right.*
5. *Press the* Left Arrow *keys* ← *to move the insertion point one character to the left.*
6. *Press* End *key to move the insertion point to the end of the current line.*
7. *Press* Home *keys to move the insertion point to the beginning of the current line.*

8. *Press* `Ctrl` `Right Arrow` *keys (* `Ctrl` `➜` *) to move the insertion point to the next word.*
9. *Press* `Ctrl` `Left Arrow` *keys (* `Ctrl` `⬅` *) to move the insertion point to the previous word.*
10. *Press* `PgDn` *keys to move the insertion point down one screen.*
11. *Press* `PgUp` *keys to move the insertion point up one screen.*
12. *Press* `Ctrl` `PgDn` *keys to move the insertion point to the top of the next page.*
13. *Press* `Ctrl` `PgUp` *keys to move the insertion point to the top of the previous page.*
14. *Press* `Ctrl` `End` *keys to move the insertion point to the end of the document.*
     Tip: Refer to the **Appendix** of this manual for a list of other shortcut keyboard commands.

1.15 Selecting Text

There may be times when you want to perform a function (such as deleting or spell checking) on a word, sentence, paragraph, or particular area of text. In order to perform this function, you must first select the text. **Selecting Text** expands the insertion point to highlight a block of text. You can use the mouse or key combinations to select text.

Another method of **Selecting Text** is to use the white area in the left margin called the **Selection Bar**. The number of times you click in this area determines the amount of text that is selected.

Selecting a new **Text** block or repositioning the insertion point deselects the original selection unless you use the `Shift` or `Ctrl` keys. The `Shift` key extends a selection in a continuous block, whereas the `Ctrl` key allows you to select multiple, non-contiguous **Text Selections**.

In summary, the following are ways to select text:

1. *Double-click on a word to select or highlight the word.*
2. *Triple-click on a word to select a paragraph.*
3. *Click on the left margin to select one row of text or drag to select multiple rows.*
4. *Place your cursor at the starting point, hold the* `Shift` *key down, then click the endpoint to select between the two points.*
5. *Double-click in the left margin to select a paragraph.*
6. *To select text using your mouse, hold the* `Ctrl` *key down, then select a different area to select non-adjacent areas.*
7. *Hold the* `Shift` *key and press one of the* `Arrow` *keys to select characters or rows up/down.*
8. *Hold the* `Ctrl` *key down and click on a word with your mouse. It will select the current sentence.*
9. `Ctrl` `A` *keys will select the entire document.*
10. *Place your cursor at the start of the text to be selected, hold the* `Ctrl` *key down, and press the* `PgDn` *or* `PgUp` *keys to select from the starting point to the end or the beginning of the page.*
11. *Click in the beginning or middle of a word and* `Ctrl` `Shift` `Right Arrow` *or* `Left Arrow` *keys will select to the End or Beginning of the word.*
12. *Place the cursor on a word, then press* `Ctrl` `Shift` `Up Arrow` *or* `Down Arrow` *key will select from the current position to the beginning or end of the paragraph.*
13. *Place the cursor on any word, click the* `Home` *key, hold the* `Shift` *key, then press the* `End` *key in order to select the row of text.*
14. *Press the* `End` *key, then press the* `Shift` `Up Arrow` *or* `Down Arrow` *keys to select the current line or the line below.*
15. *Press the* `Home` *key, then press the* `Shift` `Up Arrow` *keys to select the row above.*

16. *Place the cursor on a word, then press* Ctrl Shift Home *or* End *key which will select from the current position to the beginning or end of the document.*
17. *Place the cursor on a word, then press* Alt Ctrl Shift PgDn *or* PgUp *and the keys will select from the current position to the beginning or end of the visible viewed window.*

Practice Exercise 15 - Selection

1. *Scroll as necessary and Double-click the word "following" in the first sentence of the body of the letter.*
2. *Click anywhere in the document.*
3. *Hold* Ctrl *key and click on the sentence beginning with "The following."*
4. *Triple-click in the paragraph beginning "The Following."*
5. **Select using the** Shift **key:**
   5a. *Click before the letter T in the text "The" in the first sentence of the first paragraph.*
   5b. *Hold* Shift *key and click after the second letter G in the last word of the second sentence of the first paragraph.*
6. *Hold the* Ctrl *key and drag to select letters in any sentence.*
7. *Press* Ctrl A *keys.*
8. *Click anywhere in the document.*
9. *Click in the selection bar (blank area in the left margin) to the left of and text.*
10. *Click in the selection bar to the left of any line in the second paragraph.*
11. *Click in the selection bar to the left of any line and triple-click.*
12. *Click anywhere in the document to deselect the text.*
13. **Close the file without saving it:** File *Tab* → Close → Don't Save .

1.16 Click And Type

If you start a new document or page down to the very bottom of an existing document, you will see a white screen. An area where no information exists is called white or dead space. If you hold your cursor over that area, you will see 3 different icons in the cursor. If you double click in this white space, you will be able to start typing using one of the following 3 methods:

- If you move your cursor to the **left** of the white space and **Double-click**, the paragraph will be **Left Justified**.

- If you move your cursor to the middle of the white space and **Double-click**, the paragraph will be **Center Justified**.

- If you move your cursor to the **right** of the white space and **Double-click**, the paragraph will be **Left Justified**.

1.17 Using Overtype Mode

Most editing is performed in **Insert Mode**. When typing in **Insert Mode**, the existing text is pushed to the right of the insertion point as you type. This mode is called the default typing mode.
When typing in **Overtype Mode**, each character typed replaces the character to the right of the insertion point. Since the advent of **Windows**, the ability to select unwanted text and replace the selection with the desired text has made **Overtype Mode** redundant.
Perhaps in recognition of this, **Microsoft Word**, by default, disables the **Insert** key, so **Overtype Mode** is less accessible unless you make the effort to change the default settings.

Practice Exercise 16 - Overtype Mode

Continue from the previous practice exercise.

1. **File** *Tab* → Options .
2. **Click Advanced.**
3. **Click ☑ Use overtype mode.**
4. **Click** ☐ OK ☐.
5. **Right-click anywhere on the Status bar at the bottom of the Microsoft Word window.**
6. **Click on Overtype.**
7. **Enter some text and then edit it.**
8. **Change the mode back from Overtype mode to Insert mode by deselecting the Use overtype mode checkbox in Microsoft Word Options and try editing the text again.**
9. **When you have finished, ensure Overtype mode is deactivated and turn off the mode status display on the Status bar.**
10. **Do not save the document.**

Student Project B - Overtype Mode

1. **Create a new document.**
2. **Type the following information in the document:**

> *Breakfast 9:30 - 10:30*
> *Keynote Speaker 10:30 - 11:00*
> *Exhibitions 11:00 - 1:30*
> *Lunch 1:30 - 2:30*
> *Workshops 2:30 - 4:30*

3. **Save the document to the student data folder (C:/Data) with the name Agenda:** **File** *Tab* → Save As → 🗁 Browse →*C:\Data\Word365-12\Agenda.docx.*
4. **Close the document:** **File** *Tab* → Close .
5. **Open Agenda:** **File** *Tab* → 🗁 Open →*C:\Data\Word365-12\Agenda.docx.*
6. **Add the following title to the top of the document: Tomorrow's Agenda. Enter a blank line below the title. (Tip: Press Enter key at the top of the document to push the text down.).**
7. **Turn off the overtype mode to change the exhibition times to:11:30 - 4:30:**
   7a. **File** *Tab* →Options →Advanced Tab →Turn on the following:

   > ☑ Use the Insert key to control overtype mode
   > ☑ Use overtype mode

   7b. *Press the* **Insert** *key until the status bar says the following.*

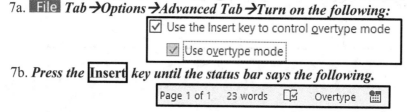

7c. *Click in front of the 11 in Exhibitions →and type: 11:30-4:30.*
7d. **Set the options back to the system default:**
     File *Tab →Options →Advanced Tab →Turn on the following:*

☐ Use the Insert key to control <u>o</u>vertype mode

☐ Use o<u>v</u>ertype mode

8. *The final results will look like the following.*
9. **Close the document:** File *Tab →* Close .

> Tomorrow's Agenda.
>
> Breakfast 9:30 - 10:30
> Keynote Speaker 10:30 - 11:00
> Exhibitions 11:30 - 4:30
> Lunch 1:30 - 2:30
> Workshops 2:30 - 4:30

1.18 Design Tab

(Word 2013+ Feature)

Microsoft Word has added the **Design Ribbon Tab** to the ribbons. You can change the color theme, format the document using standard document formatting, change paragraph spacing, add watermarks, change page color, and add page borders.

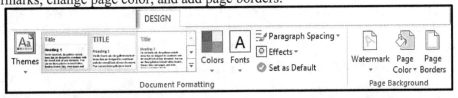

1.19 Resume Reading

(Word 2013+ Feature)

This feature works in **Microsoft Word** and **PowerPoint.** The **Resume Reading** function will automatically bookmark your document and return you to the previous location when you choose to finish reading. You can even use **Resume Reading** on a different device (such as a **PC** or a **Tablet**).

Practice Exercise 17 - Resume Reading

1.   File *tab →* 🗁 Open *→* 🗁 Browse *→ C:\Data\Word365-12\Find Replace.docx→Page down several pages →* File *Tab →* Close .

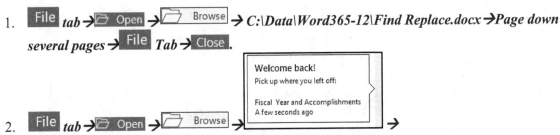

2.   File *tab →* 🗁 Open *→* 🗁 Browse →   →
     C:\Data\Word365-12\Fine Replace.docx.
3.   *Click on the following message and you will go back where you left off:*

1.20 Screen Layout

(Word 2013+ Feature)

The **Screen Layout** feature allows you to **Autohide Ribbons, Show Ribbon Tabs,** or **Show Tabs/Ribbons.** Another way to **Hide/Unhide Ribbons** is to **Double-Click** on any **Ribbon Tab** located on the top of the interface.

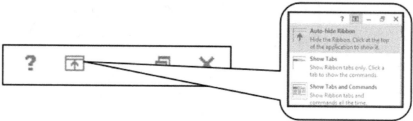

The **Autohide** feature temporally removes the **Ribbons.** You will need to use the [···] to restore it. This feature is designed for **Tablet Devices.**

Practice Exercise 18 - Collapse Ribbon

Click the [⬆] *button to test this feature.*

1.21 PDF Reflow

(Word 2013+ Feature)
The **PDF Reflow** function allows you to open a **PDF** directly into **Microsoft Word**, make edits and changes, and then resave it as a **Microsoft Word** document or a new PDF.
Edit PDF files - This converts the **PDF** file to an editable **Microsoft Word** document.
Test It: [File] *Tab →* [Open] *→* [Browse] *→Example PDF File.pdf.*

1.22 Read Mode

(Word 2013+ Feature)
This was formerly called **Full-Screen Reading in 2010.** There is a common problem that occurs when opening an attachment from an email: it opens the file in the **Read Mode.** To fix this, you can turn it off in **Options.** Scrolling the page has also been eliminated with a simple click required to compress the portions you've read and brought up the next section.
Tip: When a **Word** attachment is opened in **Microsoft Outlook**, it is displayed in the **Read Mode.**

This can be changed in the **Word** system **Options:** [File] *Tab →Options →General tab →*
Office 2013+ Option:

☑ Open e-mail attachments and other uneditable files in reading view

Office 2010 Option:

Start up options

☐ Open e-mail attachments in Full Screen Reading view

Page Color - While in **Reading Mode**, you can toggle the page color between the standard white background, **Sepia,** and inverse mode.
Test It: In Microsoft Word: *View Ribbon Tab →Views Group →*
[📖] *Read Mode.*
In Read Mode: *View Tab →Page Color →(choose page color).*
Object Zoom - This is a new feature that works in **Read Mode** only. It is used for viewing charts, tables, images, or videos.

Chapter 1 - Introduction/Interface

In Microsoft Word: *Insert Ribbon Tab→Illustrations Group→*

Picture→(Choose a picture)→View Ribbon Tab→Views Group→Read Mode.

In Read Mode: *Double-click on the picture until you see the magnifying tool.*

Chapter 2 - Basic Text Editing

2.1 Removing Characters

You can use the $\boxed{\text{Backspace}}$ key or the $\boxed{\text{Delete}}$ key to remove one character at a time. The $\boxed{\text{Backspace}}$ key removes the character to the left of the insertion point, and the $\boxed{\text{Delete}}$ key removes the character to the right of the insertion point.

Practice Exercise 19 - Remove Characters

1. *Open Text Editing.docx from the student data folder C:\Data\Word365-12.*
2. *In the first sentence, click to the right of the letter "w" in the word "listed below.*

> ### Terms and Conditions of Sale
> The following terms and conditions listed below| govern all

3. *Press* $\boxed{\text{Backspace}}$ *key to Remove Listed below and type the word "to."*

> ### Terms and Conditions of Sale
> The following terms and conditions to| govern all transactions

4. *Undo action: Press* $\boxed{\text{Ctrl}}$ $\boxed{\text{Z}}$ *keys several times.*
5. *In the first sentence, click to the left of the letter l in the word listed.*
6. *Press* $\boxed{\text{Delete}}$ *key several times to remove the word listed below" and replace it with the word "to."*

> ### Terms and Conditions of Sale
> The following terms and conditions to| govern all transactions

2.2 Deleting Selected Text

There may be times when you need to **Delete** a word, sentence, paragraph, or block of text. To accomplish this task, you must first select the text you want to **Delete**. Once the text has been selected, it can be **Deleted** with a single keystroke.

Practice Exercise 20 - Delete Text

1. *Double-click the second occurrence of the word Mike's in the first sentence under the Delivery heading.*
2. *Press* $\boxed{\text{Delete}}$ *key.*

> Any change in terms and/or conditions, whether oral or written, must be approved by the management of |Sporting Goods.

2.3 Replacing Selected Text

You can **Replace** the **Selected Text** simply by typing new text. This option eliminates the need to first delete text.

Practice Exercise 21 - Type Over Text

1. *Double-click the word govern in the first paragraph.*

> The following terms and conditions listed below govern all

2. *Type the word "cover."*

> The following terms and conditions listed below cover|all

2.4 Cutting/Copying And Pasting Text

When editing a document, you may want to **Move** or **Copy Text**, either within the same document or between documents.

When you **Move Text**, it is deleted from its original location and placed into the new location. The **Cut** and **Paste** features make it easy to **Move Text**.

If you want to duplicate text in another location, you can **Copy** the **Text** rather than retype it. To duplicate text, you can use the **Copy** and **Paste** features. The **Copy** feature is similar to the **Cut** feature, except that the **Copy** feature does not remove the text from the original location.

When **Moving** or **Copying Text** using the **Cut**, **Copy**, and **Paste** features, **Microsoft Word** automatically adds or removes spaces as needed, provided that the Use "**The Smart Cut And Paste**" option is enabled. (This can be found by selecting the *File Tab →Options →Advanced Tab*. It is the last option listed under **Cut, copy, and paste**, and is selected by default.) It is a good idea to display all the formatting marks when moving and copying text.

(*Home Ribbon Tab →Paragraph Group →¶ Show/Hide*).

Cut or **Copied Text** is placed on both the **Windows Clipboard** and the **Office Clipboard**, where it is saved until you **Paste** it into a new location. While the **Windows Clipboard** can only hold a single item, the **Office Clipboard** can hold multiple items for **Pasting**. If you need to **Cut**, **Copy**, and **Paste** multiple items, you can use the **Office Clipboard.**

(**Located at:** *Home Ribbon Tab →Clipboard Group*).

After an item has been **Pasted**, the **Paste Options** button appears in the document just below the **Pasted Text**. You can use **Paste Options** to choose whether the source or destination formatting should be applied, or you can press the **Esc** key to hide the button. This can be obtained by pressing the ⌄ down arrow under the Paste button. You can also **Move** and **Copy Text** using the keyboard. Press **Ctrl** **X** to cut, **Ctrl** **C** to copy, and **Ctrl** **V** to paste the text.

Practice Exercise 22 - Cut Copy Paste

1. *Display the Home Ribbon Tab.*
2. *Hold* **Ctrl** *key and click the last sentence Worldwide Sporting Goods has in the first paragraph under the Returns heading (make sure the paragraph mark is not included).*

> returned to Mike's Sporting Goods without an authorization label are the responsibility of the customer. Mike's Sporting Goods has the right to refuse authorized returns and is not responsible for the shipping costs of such returns.

3. *Click* ✂ *Cut.*
4. *Click to the right of the period (.) after the word defective at the end of the second paragraph under the heading Returns.*
5. *Click* 📋 *Paste.*

> returned because they were received by Specialty Sports in damaged condition or were defective. Mike's Sporting Goods has the right to refuse authorized returns and is not responsible for the shipping costs of such returns.

6. *Hold* `Ctrl` *key and click the second sentence No exceptions. in the first paragraph under the heading Returns.*

> Prior to returning merchandise, obtain a return authorization label from your Mike's Sporting Goods sales representative or from the Mike's Sporting Goods Customer Service department. No exceptions will be made to this rule. Shipping costs for merchandise returned to Mike's Sporting Goods without an authorization label are the responsibility of the customer.

7. *Click* Copy.
8. *Click to the left of the text Specialty in the first sentence of the second paragraph under the Returns heading.*

9. *Click* Paste.

> Authorized returns must be sent prepaid. Specialty Sports (No exceptions will be made to this rule) will be reimbursed for shipping costs, provided the merchandise is returned unopened and in its original packaging. It is the responsibility of Specialty Sports

10. *Press* `Esc` *key to hide the Paste Options button.*

2.5 Using The Paste Options Button

The **Paste Options** button, which appears after you have **Pasted** a **Cut** or **Copied** item, allows you to apply the desired formatting to the **Pasted** item. For example, if you are **Copying** bolded text, you may want to **Paste** the text without the bolding.

> Paste | ✂ Cut
> | 🗈 Copy
> ▾ | ❖ Format Painter
> Clipboard

If you select the **Keep Source Formatting** option, the text is **Pasted** with its original formatting. When the **Match Destination Formatting** option is selected, the formatting in the **Paste** location is applied to the **Pasted** text. The **Keep Text Only Option Pastes** the text without its original formatting.

Tip: You can hide the **Paste Options** button by pressing the `Esc` key.

Practice Exercise 23 - Keep Source Formatting

1. *Drag to select the text "Mike's Sporting Goods" under the Delivery heading*

> **Delivery**
>
> All shipments are FOB Mike's Sporting Goods regional warehouse. Unless previous arrangements have b

2. *Click* ⬛ *Copy.*
3. *Scroll as necessary and click at the beginning of the word orders under the Payment heading.*
4. *Click* 📋 *Paste.*
5. *Click the* ⬇ *dropdown arrow under the Paste button.*
6. *Click* Keep Source Formatting (K).

> **Payment**
>
> *Net payment for all Mike's Sporting Goods orders is due in 45 days.*

7. *Press* Esc *key.*

2.6 Using The Clipboard Pane

The **Office Clipboard** can store multiple items (including graphics) cut or copy from other documents or Windows programs. The cut or copied items are then available to be pasted into any open **Office** file.

The **Office Clipboard** is accessed by opening the **Clipboard** task pane. When you first open the **Clipboard** task pane, it displays the last item(s) cut or copied to the **Windows Clipboard**. As you continue to cut or copy items, they are collected in the **Clipboard** task pane and remain available to all **Office 2007** products.

For each of the cut or copied items, the **Clipboard** task pane displays an icon, and a description of the item or a portion of the text, as applicable. You can click any item to paste it at the insertion point, or you can use the **Paste All** button to paste all the items at one time. Pointing to an item and clicking the drop-down arrow displays a shortcut menu containing options to paste or delete the item.

After pasting the text, the **Paste Options** button appears in the document, allowing you to control the formatting of the pasted item.

Once you have finished a particular copying sequence, you can clear the **Office Clipboard** of all items by clicking the 🅰 **Clear All** button in the **Clipboard** task pane. In addition, the **Office Clipboard** clears automatically when you close all **Office 2007** programs.

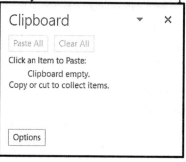

Practice Exercise 24 - Clipboard

1. *Home Ribbon Tab →Clipboard Group →Click* ▣.
2. *Click* Clear All.
3. *Move to the top of the document. In the first sentence of the first paragraph, copy the text Mike's Sporting Goods and then copy the text Specialty Sports.*

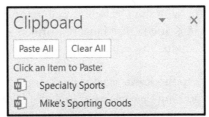

4. *Scroll to the bottom of the document heading Cancellation.*
5. *Click the Specialty Sports item in the Clipboard task pane.*
6. Enter *key.*
7. *Click Mike's Sporting Goods item in the Clipboard task pane.*

Cancellation

Order cancellations n
promotional items, personali
Specialty Sports
Mike's Sporting Goods

2.7 Using Drag-And-Drop Editing

Drag-And-Drop Editing allows you to move and copy text by using the mouse to drag the text to the desired location. The results are the same as cutting or copying and pasting, except that the cut or copied items are not saved to the **Clipboard**.

This feature is most useful when the text you want to cut or copy and the destination location are both visible in the document area.

Tip: If you hold the Ctrl *key* down when you **Drag n Drop**, it will make a copy of the selected text.

Practice Exercise 25 - Drag n Drop

1. *Drag to select the Breakage and Loss heading and body text.*

Breakage and Loss

If goods become damaged en route from the regional Mike's Sporting Goods warehouse to Specialty Sports site, claims should be made against the carrier. It is the responsibility of Specialty Sports to report such damage to the carrier, usually within 30 days of shipment.

2. *Point to the edge of the selected text, and drag it to the beginning of the*
3. *Prices heading.*

Breakage and Loss

If goods become damaged en route from the regional Mike's Sporting Goods warehouse to Specialty Sports site, claims should be made against the carrier. It is the responsibility of Specialty Sports to report such damage to the carrier, usually within 30 days of shipment.

Prices

4. *Click anywhere in the document to deselect the text.*

2.8 Using Undo And Redo

The **Undo** feature allows you to reverse the results of the previous command or action.

Once you have used the **Undo** feature, the **Redo** feature becomes available. The **Redo** feature allows you to restore the results of the command or action you reversed with the **Undo** feature. Both features can be accessed on the **Quick Access Toolbar**.

The task to be undone or redone appears as part of the **ScreenTip** for the **Undo** and **Redo** buttons.

For example, if you have just deleted text, the **ScreenTip** for the **Undo** button reads **Undo Clear**.

You can also use the list arrow with the **Undo** button to undo multiple actions. This feature is useful if you want to reverse a previous action, but have performed a number of actions subsequent to it. When you select an action to undo, however, all the items performed after the selected action in the list are also reversed.

The **Repeat** feature is related to the **Redo** feature but is only available when the **Redo** feature isn't available (i.e. when there is nothing that has been undone). You can use the **Repeat** feature to duplicate the previous action.

You can **Undo** and **Redo** actions by using **Keyboard Shortcuts**. Press Ctrl Z keys to **Undo** or Ctrl Y keys to **Redo** or repeat an action. Also, pressing Esc key will cancel a current action, without needing to complete and then undo it.

AutoSave ● Off

Practice Exercise 26 - Undo Redo

1. *Click ↺˅ to undo the last deletion.*
2. *Click ↻ to redo the last deletion.*
3. *Click ⤓.*
4. *Click the second Clear option to undo both deletions.*
5. *Click ↻ twice to redo both deletions.*
6. *Press the Ctrl Z keys to undo the previous steps.*
7. *Close the file without saving it: File Tab → Close.*

Student Project C - Using Basic Text Editing

1. *File Tab → Open → Browse → C:\Data\Word365-12\Text Editing Practice1.docx.*
2. *Change the interview date in the second paragraph to December 8.*
3. *Undo the change.*
4. *The last paragraph uses the word "Mike's" instead of the entire company name, Mike's Sporting Goods. Add the text Sporting Goods by copying the phrase from the first paragraph and pasting it after the word Mike's in the last paragraph. Tip: Be sure to use Paste Options → Source Formatting.*
5. *Change 7 AM to 8 AM in the third paragraph.*
6. *Use cut and paste to move the fourth paragraph, As you know, before the third paragraph, If you have. Use Cut n Paste or Drag n Drop*

> As you know, Mike's Sporting Goods is one of the most rapidly g|
> sporting goods for the active sportsman and plan a major marketin|
> Southern region within the next quarter.
>
> If you have any questions, or if the above day and time are not co|
> 1234, ext. 3434 between 8 AM and 5 PM.

7. *Use drag-and-drop editing to move the "Three Weeks Paid Vacation" paragraph to the beginning of the "Paid Holidays" line in the benefits list.*
8. *Tip: Be sure to use Paste Options → Source Formatting.*

> *Tuition reimbursement*
> Three Weeks Paid Vacation
> *Paid Holidays*

9. *Open the Clipboard task pane.*

10. *Copy both Mike's Sporting Goods and Southern Division, from the first paragraph.*

11. *Use the Clipboard task pane to paste the Mike's Sporting Goods text below the text Personnel Director at the bottom of the document.*
12. *Press* **Enter** *key and paste the text Southern Division below "Mike's Sporting Goods." Then hide the Paste Options button.*

> John O'Donnell
> Personnel Director
> Mike's Sporting Goods
> Southern region

13. *Create a new document.*
14. *Paste the text Mike's Sporting Goods into the new document.*

> Mike's Sporting Goods

15. *Close both open documents without saving the changes.*
16. *Clear the Clipboard task pane, and then close it.*

Chapter 3 - Document Views

3.1 Switching Document Views

Microsoft Word provides several different ways in which you can view your document. These views can be changed using the **Document Views Group** in the **View Ribbon Tab** on the **Ribbon**. You should select the view that allows you to work best with your document.

Print Layout ▤ - This will allow you to use commands, such as inserting text or working with headers and footers, which require you to work with this view. This is the default view for a new installation of **Microsoft Word**.

Draft View ▤ is the best for viewing page codes such as page, next page, etc.

Web Layout ▤ **View** is used for creating and editing web pages. Documents in **Web Layout View** behave like browsers in that the text wraps to fit the window.

Outline ▤ **View** is useful in long documents that use a heading style. **Outline View** allows you to expand and collapse outline levels so that only certain heading levels appear. This view is helpful in a document containing many heading levels. The **Outlining Tab** automatically appears on the **Ribbon** in this view. The functions available on this tab allow you to easily reorganize a document by moving information and adjusting indent levels.

Read Mode ▤ You can read or edit a long document in **Read Mode**. This feature removes the **Ribbon** so that you can see more of the document. It is designed to make the task of reading documents onscreen much easier.

Practice Exercise 27 - Document Views

1. **File** *Tab →* **Open** *→* **Browse** *→ C:\Data\Word365-12\Document Views.docx.*
2. *View Ribbon Tab →Views Group.*
3. *Click* **Draft***.*
4. *View Ribbon Tab →Show Group →* **☑ Navigation Pane** *Navigation Pane.*
5. *Scroll down the page using the keyboard* **PgDn** *key.*
   Tip: *Notice that the text is presented with full formatting, but without any white space, and the page break is marked. Also, notice that the highlighted headings in the Document Map change based on the current position of the insertion point.*
6. *Close the Navigation Pane: View Ribbon Tab →Show Group →* **☐ Navigation Pane**
7. *Test out the Document View buttons in the status bar*
   (Located in the lower right corner of the interface).
8. *Close the Outline View, then select the* ▤ *Print Layout View, if necessary.*

3.2 Read Mode

Read Mode is designed to make the task of reading documents onscreen much easier using **ClearType** technology. When a document appears in **Read Mode**, the layout of the document text does not appear as printed; rather it is adjusted to fit the screen. Instead of displaying pages, the document is divided into screens. If the document text is too difficult to read, you can enlarge or decrease the size of the screen text. Resizing the screen text does not change the size of the document text. Some editing options are available in **Read Mode View**, though not all. The **Read Mode View** provides a convenient view for tracking revisions.

Tip: In **Excel 2010** the feature was called **Full-Screen Reading View.**

In **Excel 2003** the feature was called **Reading Layout View.**

Tip: You can press the **Esc** key to drop back to the **Edit** view.

Tip: The default when reading email is **Read Mode.** To change this, uncheck the following option.

File *Tab →Options →General →*

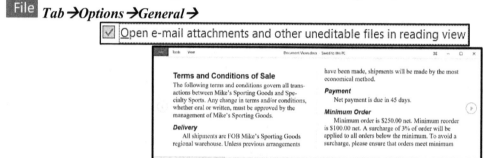

Practice Exercise 28 - Read Mode

1. *View Ribbon Tab→Views Group.*

2. *Click* **Read Mode**

3. *Click* 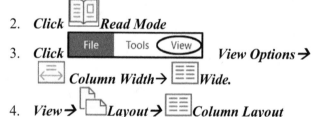 *View Options →*
   Column Width→ *Wide.*

4. *View→* *Layout→* *Column Layout*

5. **To close the Read Mode:** *Select the View Tab →* **Edit Document**

Tip: *This will return to the document's default view.*

Tip: You can press the **Esc** key to drop back to the **Edit Document** view.

3.3 Changing Document Magnification

You can a **Magnify** document to make the text easier to read, or you can reduce the **Magnification** in order to see more of the document.

The **Magnification Level** can be set to a percentage of the actual size, or you can choose to view the entire width of the page. **Changing** the **Magnification** does not change the document; it only changes how the document appears on the screen.

You can also use the **Zoom** controls on the status bar in the lower right corner to change the **Magnification** of a **Document**.

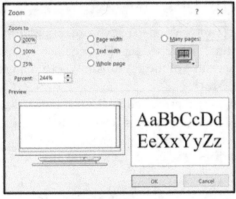

Zoom Dialog Box   *Zoom Slider*

Practice Exercise 29 - Zoom

1. *View Ribbon Tab→Zoom Group.*

2. *Click*  *Zoom.*

3. *Click ⊙ Text width→* OK .

4. *Change the Zoom to 140% using the Zoom Slider located in the lower right corner of the screen.* ⎯ ⎯ + 140%

5. **Return the Zoom to 100%:** *View Ribbon Tab→Zoom Group→* 100% *100%.*

3.4 Displaying/Hiding The Rulers

When you first create a new document in **Microsoft Word**, you will find that the document area is relatively uncluttered. The default settings show the whole page in ▤ **Print Layout View** with a vertical scroll bar down the right side. The **Horizontal** and **Vertical Rulers** are not displayed. However, you can choose to **Display** the **Rulers** and then hide them again when they are no longer needed. The **Horizontal Ruler** appears along the top of the document area and the **Vertical Ruler** appears down the left side.

You can use the **Vertical Ruler** to set-top and bottom margins and place items at specific locations in the document. You can use the **Horizontal Ruler** to set left and right margins and indents, as well as add and remove tab stops.

```
┌─────────────────────────┐
│  ☑ Ruler                │
│                         │
│  ☐ Gridlines            │
│                         │
│  ☐ Navigation Pane      │
│                         │
│         Show            │
└─────────────────────────┘
```

Practice Exercise 30 - Rulers

1. *View Ribbon Tab→Views Group.*
2. *Make sure you are in* ▤ *Print Layout View.*
3. *Show / Hide the ruler by checking and unchecking the Rulers checkbox.*
4. *View Ribbon Tab→Show Group→* ☑ Ruler *(Make sure the ruler is on).*

3.5 Viewing/Hiding The Formatting Marks

Each time you press the **Enter**, **Spacebar**, or **Tab** keys on the keyboard, or perform other actions such as inserting a line break, a **Formatting Mark** is inserted into the document. You do not usually see these **Formatting Marks;** you only see the results of the keystroke. When editing a document, it is sometimes useful to display the **Formatting Marks.**

The keystrokes **Enter**, **Spacebar**, or **Tab** keys are represented by the paragraph character, a dot, and a right arrow respectively. Any paragraph formatting such as **Keep with next** (often used in headings) is indicated by a small square box in the left margin.

You can view all of the **Formatting Marks** or display selected marks only.

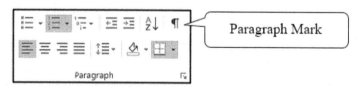

Paragraph Mark

Practice Exercise 31 - Paragraph Mark

1. *View Ribbon Tab→Views Group.*
2. *Make sure you are in* ▤ *Print Layout View.*
3. **Show / Hide the formatting marks** ¶ **by checking and unchecking the formatting marks button:** *Home Ribbon Tab→Paragraph Group→* ¶ *Show/Hide Paragraph Mark.*

3.6 Opening Multiple Documents

You may want to open several documents at one time to copy and paste text between them or to compare their contents. This is a **Single Document Interface (SDI),** meaning that each open document appears in its window and has its **Ribbon**. In addition, each document has a button on the taskbar. If a large number of documents are open, they may display as a single button on the taskbar; as you move your mouse pointer over this button, a list of open document names will display for you to choose from.

You can use the **Shift** or **Ctrl** keys in the **Open Dialog Box** to select and open **Multiple Documents**. When you use the **Shift** key, all files between the first and last selected files are selected. When you use the **Ctrl** key, you can select non-adjacent files.

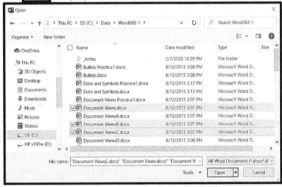

Practice Exercise 32 - Multiple Documents

1. *Make sure files Document ViewsA.docx, Document ViewsB.docx, and Document ViewsC.docx are open.*
2. **To Switch between documents:** *View Ribbon Tab→Windows Group.*
3. *Click* **Switch Windows.**

Tip: Another technique is to Hold the **Alt** key down and press the **Tab** key multiple times.

3.7 Comparing Side By Side Documents

It is often helpful to **Compare Two Documents** visually side by side. You may want to compare the text and formatting between two versions of the same document or that of different documents. The **View Side by Side** command places two open documents vertically in a side-by-side arrangement and displays both **Ribbons**.

You can return to a single-window view by re-selecting the **View Side By Side Button** on either of the two **Ribbons** displayed.

Practice Exercise 33 - Comparing Side By Side

1. **File** *Tab→* Open *→* Browse *→C:\Data\Word365-12 folder→Select files Document ViewsD.docx and Document ViewsE.docx. using the* **Ctrl** *key→Open.*

2. *View Ribbon Tab→Windows Group→* *Switch Windows→Document ViewsD.docx.*
3. *View Ribbon Tab→Windows Group→Click* [⊞⊞View Side by Side] *.*
4. *Choose Document ViewsE.docx→Ok.*
5. *Review the documents and notice the Payment section differences.*
6. *Turn the Synchronous Scrolling off. View Ribbon Tab→Windows Group→* *Synchronous Scrolling.*
7. *Review the documents and notice they are not Synchronized.*
8. **Close all documents without saving them:** File *Tab →* Close *.*

3.8 Arrange All

This will rearrange all actively opened documents opened. If the documents are minimized, they will not be **Arranged** on the screen.

1. *Open 2 or more documents.*

2. *View Ribbon Tab→Windows Group→* *Switch Windows→*
   (Choose each file to make sure they are maximized).

3. *View Ribbon Tab→Windows Group→* *Arrange all.*
4. *The opened documents will be arranged on the interface.*

3.9 Split

This will place a movable bar that **Splits** the screen into multiple windows.
Place your cursor in any position on the document.

View Ribbon Tab→ Windows Group→ *Split button.*
There are 2 ways to remove a **Split**:

1. *View Ribbon Tab→ Windows Group→* *button.*
2. *Double-click on the Split on the interface.*

Practice Exercise 34 - Split

This will **Split** the screen in the middle so you will be able to view both ends of the database.
1. *Open any document.*
2. **Split:** *Select in the middle of your document→ View Ribbon Tab→Windows Group→* *Split Button.*
3. *Scroll down to see the results.*
4. *Move the Split bar by using your mouse.*
5. *Remove Split: Double-click on the Split Bar or*

6. *View Ribbon Tab→ Windows Group→* *button.*

Student Project D - Working with Document Views

1. **File** *Tab*→ ☐ Open → ☐ Browse →*C:\Data\Worde365-1\Document Views Practice1.docx.*
2. **View the formatting marks:** *Home Ribbon Tab→Paragraph Group→¶ Show/Hide.*
3. **Hide the rulers:** *View Ribbon Tab→Show Group→* ☐ Ruler *(Make sure the ruler is on).*
4. **Switch to** ☐ **Draft View:** *View Ribbon Tab→Views Group→* ☐ *Draft View.*
5. **Display the horizontal ruler:** *View Ribbon Tab→Show Group→* ☑ Ruler.
6. **Change the magnification to 75%:** *View Ribbon Tab →Zoom Group→* 🔍*Zoom→* ◉*%75*
7. **Switch to Outline View:** *View Ribbon Tab→Views Group→* ☐*Outline View.*
8. **Return to Draft View:** *View Ribbon Tab→Views Group→* ☐*Draft View.*
9. **Return the magnification to 100%.** *View Ribbon Tab →Zoom Group →* ☐ 100%
10. **Switch to** ☐ **Print Layout View:** *View Ribbon Tab→Views Group→* ☐ *Print Layout View.*
11. **Switch to Read Mode View:** *View Ribbon Tab→Views Group→* ☐☐ *Read Mode View.*
12. **Open both the Document Views.docx and Document ViewsA.docx at the same time:** **File** *Tab* → ☐ Open → ☐ Browse →
13. *(Select both documents using the* **Ctrl** *key).*
14. **Switch documents:** *View Ribbon Tab→Windows Group→Switch Windows.*
15. **Compare the documents:** *Review Ribbon Tab→* ☐*Compare Group→* ☐*Compare Documents:*

Compare Documents		?	✕
Original document		**Revised document**	
Document Views.docx	☑ ☐	Document ViewsA.docx	☑ ☐
Label changes with		Label changes with	Author

16. **Scroll the documents simultaneously, and then scroll the Terms document independently.** *View Ribbon Tab→Windows Group→*
17. *Click* ☐ View Side by Side .
18. *Return to the full-screen view.*
19. *Hide the formatting marks.*
20. **Close all documents:** **File** *Tab →* Close .

Chapter 4 - Character Formatting

Character Formatting enhances the appearance of the text. Examples of **Character Formatting** include **Font Typeface**, and **Size**. A **Font Typeface** is defined as a group of characters sharing similar type attributes. **Font Size** refers to the height of a printed character on a page; the higher the number, the larger the character. **Font Style** refers to type enhancements, such as **Bold** and **Italic**. **Underlining** can also be used to format characters.

> **FONT TYPEFACE**
> Times New Roman
> Arial
> Courier
>
> **FONT SIZE**
> Times New Roman 8
> Times New Roman 12
> ## Times New Roman 18
>
> **UNDERLINE**
> Single underline
> Word only underline

The **Font Group** in the **Home Ribbon Tab** contains buttons to apply the most common character attributes. Using these buttons is the easiest method to apply those formats. You can also apply **Character Formatting** using the **Font Dialog Box**. The **Font Dialog Box** contains all the character attributes in one place. The **Font Dialog Box** provides the best method of applying several characters' attributes at the same time or applying formatting that is not available in the **Font Group**, such as **Double-Strikethrough**.

4.1 Changing An Existing Font

Microsoft Word includes many **Font** typefaces from which you can choose. They range from heavy bold typefaces to thin light ones. You can view a list of available **Font** typefaces and appearances from the **Font Group** on the **Home Ribbon Tab**.

You can mix **Fonts** within a document. If you have a document with headings and text in paragraphs beneath each heading, you can select one **Font** for the headings and another for the paragraphs. Varying the **Font** within a document improves the readability of the text and emphasizes key points.

Fonts can be applied to existing text, or you can select a **Font** prior to typing text. Thereafter, any text you type appears in the selected **Font** until you select a new **Font**.

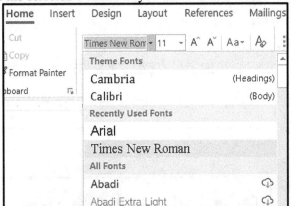

Practice Exercise 35 - Font Type

1. File → Open → Browse → *C:\Data\Word365-12\Formatting Character.docx.*
2. *Home Ribbon Tab→Font Group.*
3. *Click in the selection bar to the left of "Terms and Conditions" of Sale.*

> Terms and Conditions of Sale

4. *Click Font* ⌄.
5. *Scroll as necessary and click Tahoma.*
6. *Click anywhere in the document to deselect the text.*
7. *Click one line above the paragraph beginning "All shipments are FOB."*
8. *Select Arial from the Font list.*
9. *Type the word "Delivery."*

> Delivery
> All shipments are FOB Mike's Sporting Goods regional warehouse. Unless previous arrangements have been made, shipments will be made by the most economical method.

4.2 Modifying The Font Size

Font Size is measured in points. One point is approximately 1/72 of an inch. The larger the **Font Size**, the larger the text. Therefore, a word with a 36-point font size is approximately one-half inch in height.

Generally speaking, larger **Font Sizes** are used for headlines and headings and smaller **Font Size** is used for body text.

A **Font Size** can be applied to existing text, or you can select a **Font Size** prior to typing text. As you type, you can mix **Font Sizes**. For example, if you are creating a newsletter, you can use 22-point font for the headings and a 12-point font for the text. Varying the **Font Size** within a document improves the readability of the text and emphasizes key points.

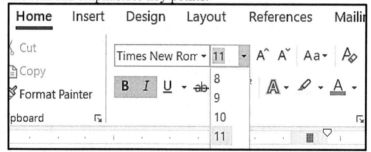

Practice Exercise 36 - Font Size

1. *Home Ribbon Tab→Font Group.*
2. *Click in the selection bar to the left of "Terms and Conditions of Sale."*

> Terms and Conditions of Sale

3. *Click Font Size* ⌄.
4. *Click 14.*

> Terms and Conditions of Sale

5. *Click in the line above the paragraph "Net payment is due in 45 days."*
6. *Select 14 from the Font Size list on the Font Group.*
7. *Type the word "Payment."*
8. *Change the font of the word "Payment" to Arial.*

> Payment
> Net payment is due in 45 days.

9. *Deselect the text.*

4.3 Using Bold And Italics

You can change the character formats of existing text, either to add emphasis or to enhance the appearance of the text. The most commonly used character formats are **Bold** and **Italic**.

You can tell which character formats have been applied to specific text by positioning the insertion point in the text. For example, if **Bold** formatting has been applied to the current text, the **Bold** button is activated when you position the insertion point in the text.

> **B** *I*

Practice Exercise 37 - Bold Italic

1. *Home Ribbon Tab→Font Group.*
2. *Click in the selection bar to the left of the "Minimum Order" heading.*

> Minimum Order
> Minimum order is $250.00

3. *Click* **B** *Bold.*
4. *Click* *I* *Italic.*
5. *Deselect the text.*

> *Minimum Order*
> Minimum order is $250.00 net.

6. *Scroll as necessary and click above the paragraph "Prior to returning."*
7. *Click the Bold and Italic buttons.*
8. *Type the word "Returns."*

> *Returns*
> Prior to returning n

9. *Click on the word Returns.*
10. *Click the* *I* *Italic button to remove the italic formatting.*

> **Returns**
> Prior to returning merchan

4.4 Underlining Text

There are several **Underline** types from which you can choose. If you just want to place a single line under the text, you can use the **Underline** button on the **Formatting** toolbar.

If you want to apply a different type of **Underline**, you can choose from several listed on the **Font** page in the **Font Dialog Box**. **Underline** styles include double, thick, thin, dotted, dashed, and wavy lines. All **Underline** styles place the **Underlines** under all text and spaces except the **Words only** style, which places a single **Underline** under words, but not under spaces in a document.

The **Font Dialog Box** contains a **Preview** box in which you can view how each of the **Underline** styles will affect your text before actually applying them.

Practice Exercise 38 - Underlining

1. ***Home Ribbon Tab→Font Group.***
2. ***Drag to select the text "whether verbal or written" in the first paragraph.***

> The following terms and conditions govern all transactions between Mike's Sporting Goods and Specialty Sports. Any change in terms and/or conditions, whether oral or written, must be approved by the management of Mike's Sporting Goods.

3. ***Click □ located in the lower right corner of the Font Group.***
4. ***Click Underline style ▼.***
5. ***Click Words only.***

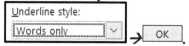

6. ***Deselect the text to view the underline style.***

> The following terms and conditions govern all transactions between Mike's Sporting Goods and Specialty Sports. Any change in terms and/or conditions, <u>whether</u> <u>oral</u> <u>or</u> <u>written</u>, must be approved by the management of Mike's Sporting Goods.

4.5 Highlighting Text

In **Microsoft Word**, you can **Highlight** important **Text**, just as you might use a **Highlighting Marker** to **Highlight Text** on paper.

Highlighting is more effective on the computer screen than on the printed page. Although you can **Highlight**

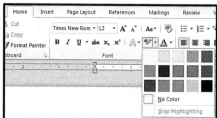

Text in a variety of colors, you should use a light **Highlight** color if you plan on printing the document.

If you have only one text selection to **Highlight**, you should select the text before clicking the **Highlight** button. This method applies the **Highlighting** to the selected text only and the **Highlight** button is not activated for subsequent **Highlighting**. If you want to **Highlight** multiple selections, you can first activate the **Highlight** button. With this method, the **Highlight** button remains activated; all text you select will be **Highlighted** until you click the **Highlight** button again to disable it.
You can also remove **Highlighting** from document text. When you remove **Highlighting**, the document text returns to normal.

Practice Exercise 39 - Highlight Text

1. ***Home Ribbon Tab→Font Group.***
2. ***Scroll as necessary to display the "Payment" and "Minimum Order" paragraphs at the top of the document.***
3. ***Click*** [✏] ***Text Highlight.***
4. ***Drag to select the text "Net payment is due in 45 days" under the Payment heading.***
5. ***Drag to select the text "Minimum order is $250.00" in the Minimum Order paragraph.***
6. ***Click*** [✏] ***Text Highlight.***

> Payment
> Net payment is due in 45 days.
>
> *Minimum Order*
> Minimum order is $250.00 net.

4.6 Format Painter

You can use the **Format Painter** button in the **Clipboard Group** on the **Home Ribbon Tab** to copy the character format of specific text and apply it to other text. This feature saves time when multiple formats have been applied to text and you want to format additional text with all the same formats. When the **Format Painter** is active, the mouse pointer changes into an I-beam with a paintbrush to its left.
Tip: Select some text, then **Double-click** on the **Format Painter**. It will remain active until it is clicked again (or press the [Esc] key). This will allow you to **Format Paint** multiple areas.

Practice Exercise 40 - Copying Character Formatting

1. ***Home Ribbon Tab→Font Group.***
2. ***Scroll as necessary and click on the word "Breakage" in the "Breakage and Loss" heading.***

> Breakage and Loss
> If goods become damaged en

3. ***Click*** [🖌] ***Format Painter.***
4. ***Click Prices.***

> Prices
> Subject to change, witho
> Mike's Sporting Goods

5. ***Click on the "Prices" heading, if necessary, and Double-click the*** [🖌] ***Format Painter button.***
6. ***Scroll up and click the "Returns" heading, the "Delivery" heading, and drag to select the "Minimum Order" heading.***

> **Delivery**
> All shipments are FOB Mike's Sportin
> been made, shipments will be made by
>
> **Payment**
> Net payment is due in 45 days.
>
> **Minimum Order**
> Minimum order is $250.00 net. Minim

7. *Click the Format Painter button again to disable the feature* 🖌.

4.7 Changing Character Case

You can use the **Change Case** menu to quickly change text **Case** in a document. For example, you can change a lowercase sentence to uppercase.

You can also toggle from uppercase to lowercase in the selected text. Toggling the case of selected text can save time if you have inadvertently typed text with the **Caps Lock** feature enabled.

In addition to the **lowercase** and **UPPERCASE** options, the **Change Case** menu includes a number of other **Change Case** options. The **Sentence case** option capitalizes the first letter in each selected sentence. The **Capitalize Each word** option capitalizes the first letter of each word. The **tOGGLE cASE** option reverses the **Case** for each letter.

Practice Exercise 41 - Change Case

1. *Display the paragraph under the "Cancellation" heading at the bottom of the document.*
2. *Press* Ctrl *key and click on the first sentence of the last paragraph.*

> Cancellation
> ORDER CANCELLATIONS MUST BE MADE PRIOR TO SHIPMENT OF MERCHANDISE. The following items may not be canceled: special orders, promotional items, personalized uniforms, and autographed memorabilia.

3. *Click* Aa▾ *Change Case.*
4. *Select the Sentence case.*

> Cancellation
> Order cancellations must be made prior to shipment of merchandise. The following items may not be canceled: special orders, promotional items, personalized uniforms, and autographed memorabilia.

5. *Deselect the text and review the document.*
6. **Close the file without saving it:** File *Tab* → Close.

Student Project E - Using Character Formatting

1. File *Tab* → Open → Browse →
   C:\Data\Word365-12\Formatting Character Practice1.docx.
2. *Change the font size of the title, "Mike's Sporting Goods," to 20 points.*
3. *Change the font type of the title, "Mike's Sporting Goods," to Arial.*
4. *Create a Double-Underline under the title "Mike's Sporting Goods."*
5. *Bold the "Corporate History" heading and change the font size to 14 points.*
6. *Italicize the names of both founders in the first paragraph.*
7. *Use the Font Dialog Box to change the case of the "Corporate History" heading to small caps.*
8. *Use the Format Painter to copy the formatting from the "Corporate History" heading to both the "Our Public Year"s and "Future Growth headings."*
9. *Correct the capitalization in the last sentence of the second paragraph.*

10. *Position the insertion point at the end of the second paragraph, after the word exciting. Change the font to Arial and bold. Add a space and type the following sentence: Mike's Sporting Goods is the Number One Sporting Goods Company on the Globe!*

11. *Highlight the text "six new international distributors" in the paragraph under "Future Growth", then remove the highlighting from the text.*

12. **Close the document:** File *Tab* → Close .

Mike's Sporting Goods

CORPORATE HISTORY

Mike's Sporting Goods was founded *by John Moore, Sr.* and his son *John Moore II* in downtown Philadelphia, PA in 1956. Excellent word-of-mouth and reasonable prices helped propel this business from that small location to a larger facility, also located in downtown Philadelphia, in 1962. In 1974, the senior Mr. Moore retired, leaving John Moore II as the sole owner.

OUR PUBLIC YEARS

In 1992, Mike's Sporting Goods became a publicly owned company. Since that time, Mike's Sporting Goods has become one of the nation's premier sporting good concerns and continues to offer a full line of top-quality athletic merchandise. Headquartered now in Rancho Cordova, California, we have branch offices throughout the US and abroad. Individuals can now buy direct from Mike's Sporting goods through our new Direct Distribution Program. Next year should be exciting **Mike's Sporting Goods is the**

Chapter 5 - Paragraph Formatting

Paragraph Formatting refers to the layout of the paragraph on the page and involves **Alignment, Spacing**, and **Indentation Options**. **Alignment** refers to the relative location of text to the margins. **Spacing** refers to the distance between lines above, below, or within a paragraph.

> **PARAGRAPH ALIGNMENT**
> This paragraph is aligned with the left margin.
> This paragraph is aligned with the right margin.
> This paragraph is centered between the margins.
> Every line of a justified paragraph (except the last line) is aligned to both the left and right margins. You will often find justified paragraphs used in books.
> **PARAGRAPH and LINE SPACING**
> Paragraph spacing refers to space above or below the paragraph. Line spacing
>
> refers to the spacing between each line of the paragraph.

5.1 Aligning Paragraphs

Paragraph Alignment refers to the position of each line of text in a **Paragraph** between the left and right margins.

The **Paragraph Group** on the **Home Ribbon Tab** contains four **Alignments buttons, Align Text Left, Center, Align Text Right, and Justify.**

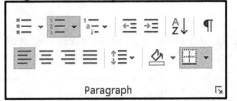

Left Alignment aligns text to the left margin and produces a ragged right margin.

Right Alignment aligns text to the right margin and produces a ragged left margin.

Center Alignment centers text between the left and the right margins and produces a ragged left and right margin.

Justified Alignment aligns text to both the left and right margins so that neither margin is ragged. When a paragraph is justified, **Microsoft Word** adds extra space between words to justify the text.

Practice Exercise 42 - Aligning Paragraphs

1. `File` → `Open` → `Browse` → *C:\Data\Word365-12\Formatting Paragraph.docx.*
2. *Home Ribbon Tab →Paragraph Group.*
3. *Click on the text "Mike's Sporting Goods" at the top of the page.*
4. *Click Right Align paragraph* ⬚.

Mike's Sporting Goods

5. *Click Left Align paragraph* ⬚.

Mike's Sporting Goods

6. *Click Center Align paragraph* ▤.

Mike's Sporting Goods

7. *Click in the first paragraph, "Thank you for choosing."*

8. *Click Justify Align paragraph* ▤.

Thank you for choosing Mike's Sporting Goods as your primary supplier of recreational equipment. Mike's is proud of its twenty-year history of supplying quality products and excellent customer service. We have grown with the sporting goods industry, and currently serve customers throughout the United States, Canada, and Mexico.

9. *Left aligns the "Dear Rob" paragraph.*

Dear Rob:

Thank you for choosing Mike's Sporting Goods as your primary supplier of recreational

10. *Right align the telephone and fax numbers located under the title.*

Tel. 610.555.8878
Fax 610.555.3434

11. *Select the last two paragraphs in the body of the letter and justify them.*

The enclosed packet includes Mike's new product catalog, highlights of the benefits of stocking your store with Mike's Sporting Goods products, details of the terms and conditions of all sales, and our advertising agreement.

An equipment and supply order form is also included. Your initial credit limit is $3,500. After six months, we will review your credit status and adjust the limit, as warranted. I look forward to receiving your first order and working with you to meet all of your equipment and supply needs.

12. *Click anywhere to deselect the paragraphs.*

5.2 Using Click And Type To Align Text

The **Click and Type** feature allows you to insert new text or graphics exactly where you point to a blank area of a document. If you are creating a special page such as a title page, the **Click and Type** feature allows you to create a title in the middle of the page without having to press the Enter key. You can simply **Double-click** where you want the title to appear.

When the **Click and Type** feature is active, the mouse pointer appears as an
I-beam with an alignment symbol attached. As you move the **I-beam** slowly across a blank line in a document from the left to the right margin, the **Alignment** symbol changes. This change occurs because **Microsoft Word** separates the blank areas of a line into **Alignment** zones. To enter text, point to the position on the page where you want to enter text, **Double-click** the mouse button, and type the text.

The **Click and Type** feature is only available in the ▤ **Print Layout** or ▤⊕**Web Layout Views**. Depending upon the location of the blank area in which you want to use the **Click and Type** feature, you may have to first click in a blank area of the document to activate it.

Practice Exercise 43 - Center Alignment Character

1. *Scroll to view the company name at the top of the letter.*

2. *Point to the blank area several lines under the word "P.S." and move the mouse pointer down in the center until a center alignment character appears with it.*

3. *Double-click the mouse button.*
4. *Type "1234 Leisure Drive, Media, PA 19107", all on one line.*
5. *Italicize the text 1234 Leisure Drive, Media, PA 19107.*

> P.S. If you have any questions, please feel free to call!
>
>
>
> 1234 Leisure Drive, Media, PA 19107

Test It: *Test out the* 🔲 *Right-Align and* 🔲 *Left-Align character. Double-click when you see a character and type some text.*

5.3 Modifying Paragraph Spacing

Paragraph Spacing refers to space above and below a **Paragraph**. You can vary **Paragraph Spacing** based on your individual needs.

You can adjust **Paragraph Spacing** on the **Indents and Spacing** page in the **Paragraph Dialog Box**. Any changes you make are previewed in the **Paragraph Dialog Box**.

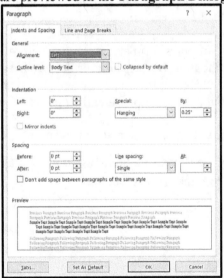

Practice Exercise 44 - Paragraph Spacing

1. *Scroll to view the first paragraph in the body of the letter.*
2. *Click on the "Thank you for choosing," paragraph.*
3. *Home Ribbon Tab→Paragraph Group.*
4. *Click* 🔲.
5. *Click the Indents and Spacing tab, if necessary.*
6. *Click Before* 🔲 *to 6 pt.*
7. *Click After* 🔲 *to 6 pt.*

Spacing		
Before:	6 pt	▲▼
After:	6 pt	▲▼

8. *Click* OK .

> Dear Rob:
>
> Thank you for choosing Mike's Sporting Goods as your primary supplier of recreational equipment. Mike's is proud of its twenty-year history of supplying quality products and excellent customer service. We have grown with the sporting goods industry, and currently serve customers throughout the United States, Canada, and Mexico.
>
> The enclosed packet includes Mike's new product catalog, highlights of the benefits of

9. *Click on "Mike's Sporting Goods" company name at the top of the letter and use the Paragraph Dialog Box to change the Before spacing to 12 points.*

5.4 Revealing Formatting

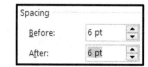 The **Reveal Formatting** task pane displays the attributes for the selected document text. Attributes are grouped under headings, the most common being **Font**, **Paragraph**, and **Section**.

The **Font** heading shows the name and point size of the font, as well as the language of the text. If other font attributes have been applied (for example, highlighting), they will also be listed here.

The **Paragraph** heading displays the alignment and indentation of the current paragraph. In addition, if other paragraph attributes have been added (such as spacing or tabs), they will also be displayed.

The **Section** heading displays attributes for margins, layout, and paper size.

You can expand and collapse the **Font**, **Paragraph**, or **Section** headings to view or hide the attributes. The underlined attributes under each heading are links to the corresponding dialog boxes; when you click a link, the corresponding dialog box opens, and you can make changes as desired.

You can also use the task pane to compare the differences in formatting between two text selections.

Tip: A quicker way to display the **Reveal Formatting Pane** is to press Shift F1 keys or add **Reveal Formatting** to the **Quick Access Toolbar**.

Chapter 5 - Paragraph Formatting

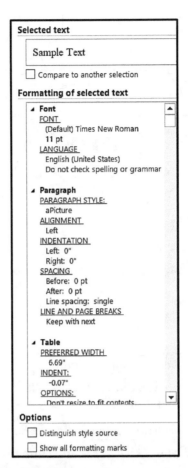

Practice Exercise 45 - Reveal Format

1. *Position the insertion point in the text Tel. 610.555-8878.*
2. *Home Ribbon Tab →Styles Group.*
3. *Click ⬛located in the lower right corner of the Styles Group*
4. *Click Style Inspector 🔍 located at the bottom of the gallery.*

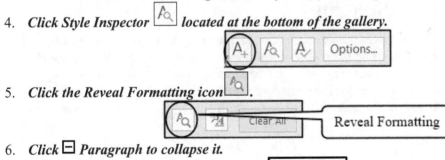

5. *Click the Reveal Formatting icon🔍.*
6. *Click ⊟ Paragraph to collapse it.*
7. *Click ⊞ Paragraph to expand it.*
8. *Click on the "Mike's Sporting Goods" title.*
9. *Click Paragraph / Spacing.*
10. *Change the Before spacing to 6 points and close the Paragraph Dialog Box.*

Page 51

11. *Click in the text 1234 Leisure Drive.*
12. *Click* ☑ *Compare to another selection.*
13. *Click on the text Mike's Sporting Goods at the top of the page.*

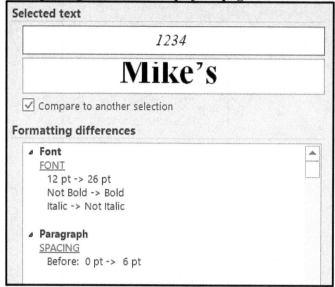

14. *Deselect the Compare to another selection option.*

☐ Compare to another selection

15. *Select all the text in the title Mike's Sporting Goods and click the*

◢ Font
FONT *Font link under the Font heading in the Reveal Formatting task pane.*

16. *Apply the effect of the Small caps* ☑ Small caps *and close the Font Dialog Box.*
    Tip: *Notice the new Effects link under the Font heading.*

EFFECTS
Small caps

17. *Leave the task pane open.*

5.5 Modifying Line Spacing

Line Spacing refers to the distance between each line in a paragraph. You can use the **Line Spacing** list in the **Paragraph Group** on the **Home Ribbon Tab** to adjust paragraph **Line Spacing**. The options on the **Line Spacing** list start with 1.0 (single spacing) and increment by .5, up to 3.0.

The **Line Spacing** list also includes the **Line Spacing Options** option, which opens the **Paragraph Dialog Box**. The **Line spacing** option in the **Paragraph Dialog Box** includes the additional options: **At least**,

✓	1.0
	1.15
	1.5
	2.0
	2.5
	3.0
	Line Spacing Options...
	Add Space <u>B</u>efore Paragraph
	Add Space <u>A</u>fter Paragraph

Exactly, and **Multiple**. After selecting one of these options, you can change the specific point size in the **At** box in the **Line Spacing** options.

Practice Exercise 46 - Reveal Format Line Spacing

1. *Home Ribbon Tab→Styles Group→Click* ⬚ *→Styles Inspector Icon* ⬚ *→Reveal Formatting Icon* ⬚.
2. *Scroll to view the first paragraph in the body of the letter.*
3. *Click on the paragraph "Thank you for choosing."*
4. *Click the Line Spacing button* ⬚ *arrow.*
5. *Click 1.5.*

> Thank you for choosing Mike's Sporting Goods as your primary supplier of recreational equipment. Mike's is proud of its twenty-year history of supplying quality products and excellent customer service. We have grown with the sporting goods industry, and currently serve customers throughout the United States, Canada, and Mexico.

6. *Select the three lines in the inside address, from Mr. Robert Campanellas to 44183.*
7. *Display the Line Spacing list and select the Line Spacing Options option.*
8. *Select the Exact option from the Line spacing list and change the At box to 14 pt.*

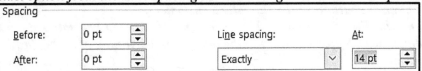

Spacing				
<u>B</u>efore:	0 pt ▲▼	Li<u>n</u>e spacing:		A<u>t</u>:
After:	0 pt ▲▼	Exactly ∨		14 pt ▲▼

9. *Close the Paragraph Dialog Box.*
   Tip: *Notice the Spacing attribute in the Reveal Formatting task pane.*

5.6 Format Painter

The **Format Painter** allows you to copy the paragraph formatting of specific text and apply it to one or more other paragraphs. This feature saves time when the formatted paragraph you copy contains multiple formatting attributes.

Practice Exercise 47 - Format Painter

1. *Scroll to view all three paragraphs in the body of the letter.*
2. *Click on the paragraph "Thank you for choosing."*

3. *Home Ribbon Tab→Clipboard Group→Format Painter icon* 🖌.
4. *Scroll as necessary and click on the second paragraph in the body of the letter.*
5. *Copy the paragraph formatting to the third paragraph in the body of the letter.*
6. *Click the Show/Hide button in the Paragraph Group to display all the formatting marks, if necessary.*
7. *Delete the Formatting Marks directly above and below the second paragraph.*

> ¶
>
> An·equipment·and·supply·order·form·is·also·included.·Your·initial·credit·limit·is·$3,500.·
>
> After·six·months,·we·will·review·your·credit·status·and·adjust·the·limit,·as·warranted.·I·look·
>
> forward·to·receiving·your·first·order·and·working·with·you·to·meet·all·of·your·equipment·
>
> and·supply·needs.¶

8. *Finally, hide the formatting marks and close the task pane.*
9. **Close the file without saving it:** File *Tab* → Close → Don't Save.

5.7 Alignment Guides

Use **Alignment Guides** to help you polish your digital presentations giving them a truly professional look and feel, including PDF content. **Exercise:**

Layout Ribbon Tab→Arrange Group→ 🗗 *Align→* ☑ *Alignment Guide* ✓ Use Alignment Guides →
Insert Ribbon Tab→Illustrations Group→ 🖼Picture*→(Insert a Picture).*

Select Picture→Format Ribbon Tab→Arrange Group→ 🖼Wrap Text*→*
🖼 *Tight→Move picture to the middle of the screen.*

The anchor will show how it is aligned ⚓. The green **Alignment Guides** will appear when you move the graphic to the middle or the end of the page.
Tip: In **Excel 2010** the **Layout Ribbon Tab** was called **Page Layout Ribbon**.

Student Project F - Paragraph Formatting

1. File *Tab→* 📂 Open → 📁 Browse →
   C:\Data\Word365-12\Formatting Paragraph Practice1.docx.
2. *Left align the paragraph To our valued customers:*
3. *Change the line spacing for the list from Special offers to Promotional items to 1.5 lines.*
4. *Change the paragraph spacing in the paragraph beginning Morning to 12 points before and 12 points after.*
5. *Display the Reveal Formatting task pane. Using the Spacing link to change the Before spacing of the Morning paragraph to 6 points.*
6. *Use the Format Painter to copy the Morning paragraph format to the Midday and Evening paragraphs.*
7. *Center the first paragraph on the second page, Directions to.*
8. *Display the rulers, if necessary, and then scroll to the end of the document. Use the Click and Type feature to place the insertion point at a position measuring 3 inches on both the horizontal and vertical rulers.*
9. *Close the Reveal Formatting task pane.*
10. **Close the document:** File *Tab* → Close → Don't Save.

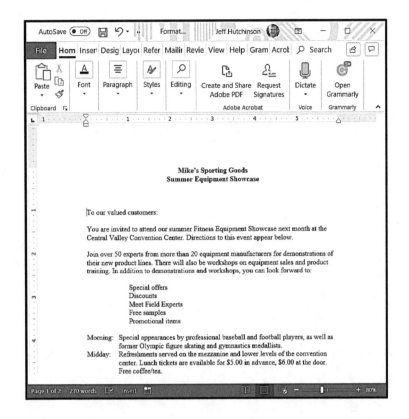

Chapter 6 - Indenting Paragraphs

Indenting a Paragraph refers to moving it away from the left, the right, or both margins. This feature has many uses, including calling attention to sections in a document or indicating a subordinate text. Additionally, the first line of each paragraph in many letters and documents is often indented from the left to improve readability.

6.1 Changing The Left Indent

The **Indent** buttons in the **Paragraph Group** on the **Home Ribbon Tab** move the paragraph to the next tab stop. By default, tab stops are set every half-inch (0.5 in or 1.27 cm). Therefore, you can use the **Increase Indent** button to indent a paragraph to the right in half-inch increments and the **Decrease Indent** button to decrease a paragraph indent in half-inch increments.

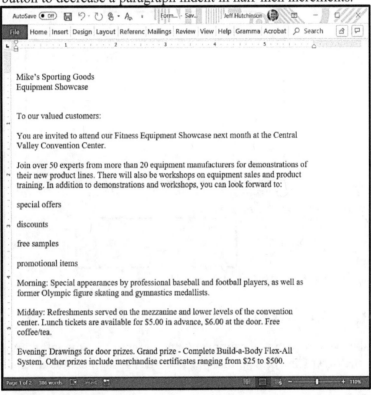

Practice Exercise 48 - Left Indent

1. **File** *Tab→* **Open** *→* **Browse** *→C:\Data\Word365-12\Formatting Indenting.docx.*
2. *Click on the special offers line.*
3. *Home Ribbon Tab→Paragraph Group →Click* ▤ *three times.*
4. *Select the three other paragraphs that make up the list (discounts, free samples, and promotional items) and the blank lines between them, and indent them one and a half inches, to line up under special offers.*

Join over 50 experts from more than 20 equipme
their new product lines. There will also be works
training. In addition to demonstrations and works

special offers

discounts

free samples

promotional items

5. *Select the entire list and use the Decrease Indent button to decrease the indent by one tab stop, to one inch.*

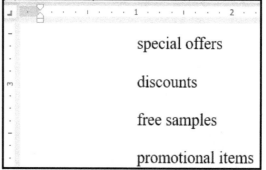

6. *Click on the special offers paragraph and open the*  *Paragraph Dialog Box.* **Tip***: Notice the Left indentation setting of 1 in or 2.54 cm.*

Indentation	
Left:	1"

Tip: you can also open the **Ruler** to measure 1".

6.2 Indenting The First Line

There are several ways in which you can indent a paragraph from the left margin. For example, you can **Indent** only the **First Line** of a paragraph. The **First Line** indent is often used to begin a paragraph of text. It is easy to create this type of indent using the horizontal ruler.

The **Indent Marker** on the left side of the horizontal ruler is composed of two **Indent Markers** and a **Box**. The top triangle is the **First Line Indent** marker and the bottom triangle is the **Hanging Indent** marker. The **First Line Indent** marker and the **Hanging Indent** marker move independently of each other; however, you can drag the **Left Indent** marker (the box) to move the **First Line Indent** and **Hanging Indent** markers simultaneously.

Indent Marker	Use
First Line Indent ▽	Indents only the first line of the selected paragraph from the left margin.
Hanging Indent △	Indents all lines of a paragraph other than the first line from the left margin.
Left Indent ▢	Moves both the **First Line Indent** marker and the **Hanging Indent** marker simultaneously.

> Morning: Special appearances by professional baseball and football players, as well as former Olympic figure skating and gymnastics medallists.
>
> Midday: Refreshments served on the mezzanine and lower levels of the convention center. Lunch tickets are available for $5.00 in advance, $6.00 at the door. Free coffee/tea.
>
> Evening: Drawings for door prizes. Grand prize - Complete Build-a-Body Flex-All System. Other prizes include merchandise certificates ranging from $25 to $500.
>
> The hours for the Equipment Showcase are 9:00 a.m. to 8:00 p.m. We look forward to seeing you at the convention center.

Practice Exercise 49 - First Line Indent

1. *View Ribbon Tab→Show Group→ ☑ Ruler (Make sure the ruler is on).*
2. *Scroll as necessary and drag to select the two paragraphs beginning Morning and Midday.*
3. *Drag ▽ to the first tab mark on the ruler.*
   A dotted line appears as you drag and the indent is applied to the first line of each selected paragraph when you release the mouse button.

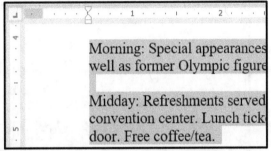

4. *Place the insertion point anywhere in the Morning or Midday paragraphs.*
5. *Select Format Painter: Home Ribbon Tab→Clipboard Group→ ✑ Format Painter.*
6. *Click in the Evening paragraph to apply the same indented formatting.*

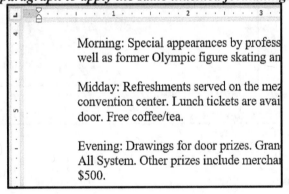

6.3 Creating A Hanging Indent

You can indent all the lines of a paragraph except the first line. This type of indent is known as a **Hanging Indent**. A **Hanging Indent** is often used for lists or bibliographic references.

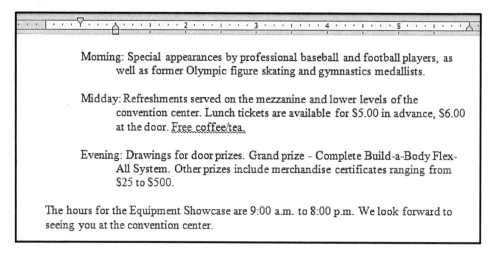

Practice Exercise 50 - Hanging Indent

1. **View Ribbon Tab→Show Group→ ☑ Ruler** *(Make sure the ruler is on).*
2. **Drag to select the three paragraphs beginning Morning, Midday, and Evening.**
3. **Drag △ to the second tab mark.**
4. **Drag ▽ back to the first tab mark on the ruler.**

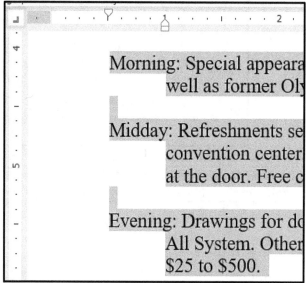

5. **Open the Paragraph Dialog Box and notice the Left and Hanging indentation settings.**
6. **Home Ribbon Tab→Paragraph Group→ Click ⌐ in the lower right corner.**

6.4 Creating A Right Indent

You can **Indent** a paragraph from the **Right** margin. You may want to do this, for example, to make a paragraph stand out on a page or to indicate a subordinate paragraph.

You can **Indent** selected text from the **Right** margin by dragging the **Right Margin** marker on the horizontal ruler. The **Right Margin** marker is identical to the **Hanging Indent** marker, except that it appears alone near the right end of the horizontal ruler.

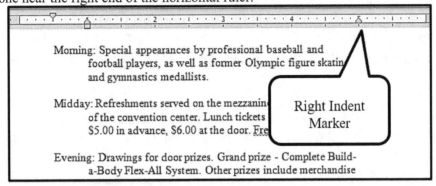

Practice Exercise 51 - Right Indent

1. *View Ribbon Tab→Show Group→☑ Ruler (Make sure the ruler is on).*
2. *Drag to select the three paragraphs beginning Morning, Midday, and Evening.*
3. *Drag Right Indent Marker △ to the second last tab mark.*

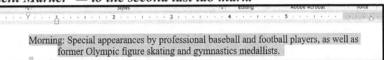

4. *Open the Paragraph Dialog Box and notice the Right indentation setting.*
5. *Home Ribbon Tab→Paragraph Group→Click ⬛ in the lower right corner.*

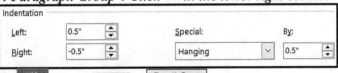

6. **Close the document:** File *Tab* → Close → Don't Save.

Student Project G - Indent

1. File *Tab*→ 📂 Open → 📁 Browse →
   C:\Data\Word365-12\Formatting Indenting Practice1.docx.
2. **Create a first-line indent of 0.5 inches (one-tab stop) in the paragraph beginning "Mike's Sporting Goods Manufacturers."**
3. *Select Paragraph→Home Ribbon tab→ Paragraph Group→⬛ Paragraph Settings→*

4. **Increase the indent of the list starting with the word "Equipment" and ending with the word "Memorabilia" three-tab stops to the right.**
5. *Select "Equipment" through "Memorabilia" bullets→Home Ribbon tab→ Paragraph Group→ ▸⬛ Increase Indent.*
6. **Create a hanging indent of 1.5 inches (three-tab stops) for the Equipment paragraph below the list.**
7. *Select Paragraph→Home Ribbon tab→ Paragraph Group→⬛ Paragraph Settings→*

Special:	By:
Hanging	1.5"

8. **Indent the second paragraph under "Equipment" three-tab stops to the right.** *Select Paragraph →Home Ribbon tab →Paragraph Group →*
9. ⊞ *Increase Indent→* ⊞ *Increase Indent→* ⊞ *Increase Indent.*
10. **Create a hanging indent of 1.5 inches (three tabs) for the Clothing, Supplies, and Memorabilia paragraphs.**
11. *Select all paragraphs→Home Ribbon tab→ Paragraph Group→* ⊡ *Paragraph Settings→*

Special:	By:
Hanging ⌄	1.5" ⭥

12. **On page 2, indent the paragraph under "Terms and Conditions of Sale" one-tab stop to the right. Then, create a right indent at the one-tab stop to the left for the same paragraph.**
13. *Select paragraphs→Home Ribbon tab→ Paragraph Group→* ⊞ *Increase Indent→Move the Right tab stop to 6.5 inches.*

> The following terms and conditions govern all transactions between Mike's Sporting Goods and Specialty Sports. Any change in terms and/or conditions, whether oral or written, must be approved by the management of Mike's Sporting Goods.

14. **Close the document:** File *Tab →* Close → Don't Save .

Results of student project above.

Page 1 Result

Mike's Sporting Goods - Your One Stop Sports and Leisure Source

Products Distributed by Mike's Sporting Goods

Mike's Sporting Goods manufactures the finest equipment, clothing and supplies available. For items not produced by Mike's Sporting Goods, we stock only first-quality merchandise supplied by leading Sporting Goods Manufacturers.

Our product lines are:

> **Equipment**
> **Clothing**
> **Supplies**
> **Memorabilia**

Equipment	We produce a full line of baseball, basketball, fishing, football, hockey, lacrosse, and soccer equipment. All equipment comes with a one year limited warranty. (See specific item warranty for details.)
	Mike's Sporting Goods also distributes tennis and racquetball equipment manufactured by Olympic Racquet Company, and skating equipment produced by National Skates, Inc. Because we order in large quantities, we are able to pass the savings along to you, our customer.
Clothing	We manufacture our own high quality clothing and uniforms endorsed by many professional athletes. Mike's Sporting Goods uses only the best material and fabric in creating our complete line of sportswear for baseball, basketball, football, hockey, lacrosse, tennis, soccer and softball players, as well as swimmers and cyclists.
Supplies	Our selection of game-related supplies (tape, mouth-guards, ice-packs, ointment, etc.) is almost unlimited. Once again, because we order in large quantities, we are able to pass the savings along to you, our customer.
Memorabilia	In addition to equipment, clothing and sports supplies, Mike's Sporting Goods stocks a tremendous selection of baseball cards, posters and pictures (some autographed) and commemorative programs.

Page 2 Result

Terms and Conditions of Sale

The following terms and conditions govern all transactions between Mike's Sporting Goods and Specialty Sports. Any change in terms and/or conditions, whether oral or written, must be approved by the management of Mike's Sporting Goods.

Delivery
All shipments are FOB Mike's Sporting Goods regional warehouse. Unless previous arrangements have been made, shipments will be made by the most economical method.

Chapter 7 - Document Formatting

Document Formatting refers to the layout of text on a page and involves **Margin, Paper Size**, and **Page Orientation Options. Margin** refers to the distance between the edge of the paper and the text. **Paper Size** refers to the physical size of the paper (for example, 8 ½ in. x 11 in.). **Orientation** refers to how the text will be printed on the page, either vertically or horizontally.

7.1 Inserting A Manual Page Break

When typed text exceeds the number of lines that will fit on a page, **Microsoft Word** inserts an automatic page break. There may be times, however, when you want to **Insert A Page Break Manually**. For example, you may want to keep a heading with the text below it. **Microsoft Word** provides this capability.

You can distinguish an automatic page break from a **Manual Page Break** by its appearance in the document. In ⊟ **Draft View**, an automatic page break appears as a dotted line. A **Manual Page Break**, on the other hand, displays the words **Page Break** in the middle of a dotted line.

If you add or remove the text or alter the page layout in any way, **Automatic Page Breaks** adjust accordingly; **Manual Page Breaks** do not.

To insert a **Manual Page Break**, position the insertion point where you want to begin a new page and press the Ctrl Enter keys combination.

Practice Exercise 52 - Manual Page Break

1. File → Open → Browse → *C:\Data\Word365-12\Formatting Document.docx.*
2. *View Ribbon Tab →Views Group → ⊟Draft View.*
3. *Turn on the Paragraph marks: Home Ribbon Tab →Paragraph Group →*

¶ *Paragraph Mark.*

4. *Scroll as necessary and click to the left of the text "Terms and Conditions of Sale" at the bottom of page 1.*

5. *Layout Ribbon Tab→Page Setup Group→* Breaks ▾ *Breaks gallery→Page Break option* .

6. **Tip:** *Observe the page break. This can be seen as long as you are showing the paragraph mark* ¶.

7. *View Ribbon Tab→Views Group→* *Print Layout button.*

7.2 Removing A Manual Page Break

Automatic Page Breaks cannot be deleted but the spaces above the **Automatic Page Break** will remove them. However, **Manual Page Breaks** are inserted by the user and can be **Removed**. A **Manual Page Break** is similar to any other typed character and can be removed by selecting the **Page Break** and pressing the Delete key. You can also use the Backspace key to delete a **Manual Page Break**.

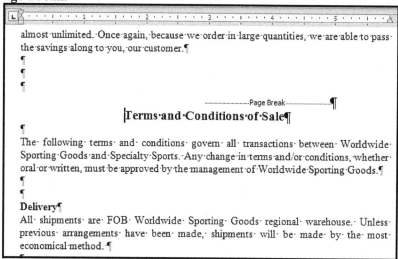

Practice Exercise 53 - Remove Page Break

1. *View Ribbon Tab→Views Group→* *Draft View.*

2. *Make sure your Paragraph mark is turned on:* ¶.

3. *Scroll to page 3.* **Tip:** *Notice that a manual page break appears above the Advertising Agreement title.*

4. *Click the manual page break above the Advertising Agreement title*

5. *Press* Delete *key.*

Tip: *Notice that an automatic page break now appears above the Advertising Agreement title.*

7.3 Changing the Page Orientation

Page Orientation refers to how the text will appear on the printed page. **Microsoft Word** includes two possible **Page Orientations**: **Portrait** and **Landscape**. Which orientation you use depends on the desired look of the document.

In **Portrait Orientation**, the shorter edges of the paper are at the top and bottom and the long edges are on the left and right. Letters and memos are ideally suited for **Portrait Orientation**.

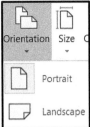

In **Landscape Orientation**, the long edges of the paper are at the top and bottom and the shorter edges are on the left and right. **Landscape Orientation** is most often used for graphics, charts, spreadsheets, and drawings.

When you change the **Page Orientation**, automatic page breaks are readjusted. You may then have to create manual page breaks to group-related information.

Practice Exercise 54 - Page Orientation

1. **Switch to ▤ Print Layout View.**
2. **View Ribbon Tab →Views Group → ▤Print Layout button.**
3. **Click the Orientation button ▤.**
4. **Click the Landscape option ▭.**
5. **Move to the top of the document. Switch to print layout to view the new page orientation.**
6. **Open the Page Setup Dialog Box and return the document to portrait orientation. Page Layout Ribbon Tab →Page Setup Group → Click ▣ located in the lower right corner of the Page Setup Group.**

7.4 Changing The Document Margins

Margins define the typing area on a page. They control the amount of blank space between the text and the top, bottom, left, and right edges of the paper. By default, **Margins** are measured in inches. For example, if all the **Margins** are set to .5 inches, there is a half-inch of blank space on all edges of the page. You can select different dimensions for the top, bottom, left, and right **Margins**, if desired.

You can modify **Margins** on the **Margins** tab in the **Page Setup Dialog Box**. You can use the **Margin** spin boxes to select the **Margin** width or you can type the desired width directly into the box.

The **Margins** tab offers several other options. The two **Gutter** options provide additional space at the top or side **Margin** to prevent text from being hidden when a document is bound.

The **Multiple pages** list provides several options for managing large documents, including **Mirror margins**, which set opposite **Margins** for facing pages in two-sided documents. The **2 pages per sheet** option split a single document page into two horizontal or vertical pages, each containing the same **Margin** settings. This option can be used to create a folded page handout, such as a flyer. If you wish to print a booklet with multiple pages, you can use the **Book fold** option.

Practice Exercise 55 - Reveal Formatting

1. **View Ribbon Tab→Views Group→** **Print Layout View.**
2. **Go to the top of the document.**
3. **Open the Reveal Formatting task pane from the Style Inspector in the Styles Dialog Box and expand the Section heading.**

   Home Ribbon Tab→Styles Group→Click **→Click the Styles Inspector Icon** **→Click** **Reveal Formatting Icon.**
4. **Click Layout Ribbon Tab→Page Setup Group.**

5. **Click** **dropdown arrow.**
6. **Click the Custom Margins tab.**
7. **Click Top** **to 1.3".**
8. **Click Bottom** **to 1.9".**
9. **Click Left** **to 2".**
10. **Click Right** **to .8".**
11. **Click** **.**
12. **Switch to print preview to view the changes in the document. View the pages in a 1 x 2 Pages arrangement.**

7.5 Changing The Paper Size

The default **Paper Size** in **Microsoft Word** is 8 1/2 x 11 inches. Although you will use this **Paper Size** for most memos and letters, it is not the only available **Paper Size**. Another popular **Paper Size** is legal (8 1/2 by 14 inches), which can be used under special circumstances, such as for legal documents. You can also create a custom **Paper Size**. When you change the **Paper Size**, the text and automatic page breaks readjust accordingly. Depending on how the document appears, you may have to revise your manual page breaks.

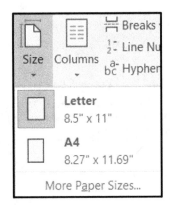

Practice Exercise 56 - Paper Size

1. *Layout Ribbon Tab→Page Setup Group.*
2. *Click* [icon] *Size dropdown arrow.*
3. *Click Legal.*
4. *Move to the top of the document, if necessary.*
5. **Switch to Print Preview to preview the changes:** File *Tab →Print.*
6. *Close Print Preview.*
7. **Close the document:** File *Tab→* Close *→* Don't Save .

Student Project H - Document Formatting

1. File *Tab→* Open *→* Browse *→*
   C:\Data\Word365-12\Formatting Document Practice1.docx.
2. *Switch to Print Preview and scroll through the document. Then close Print Preview.*
3. *Change the top and bottom margins to 1.5" each.*
4. *Change the left and right margins to 1" each.*
5. *Change the paper orientation to landscape.*
6. *Insert a page break before the text Directions to the Central Valley Convention Center.*
7. *Delete the page break. (Tip: Switch to* [icon] *Draft View or Home Ribbon Tab→Paragraph*
   Group→[icon]*Paragraph Mark in* [icon] *Print Layout View).*
8. *Change the paper size to Legal and the paper orientation to Portrait.*
9. *Switch to Print Preview to view the document. Then, close Print Preview.*
10. **Close the document:** File *Tab→* Close *→* Don't Save .

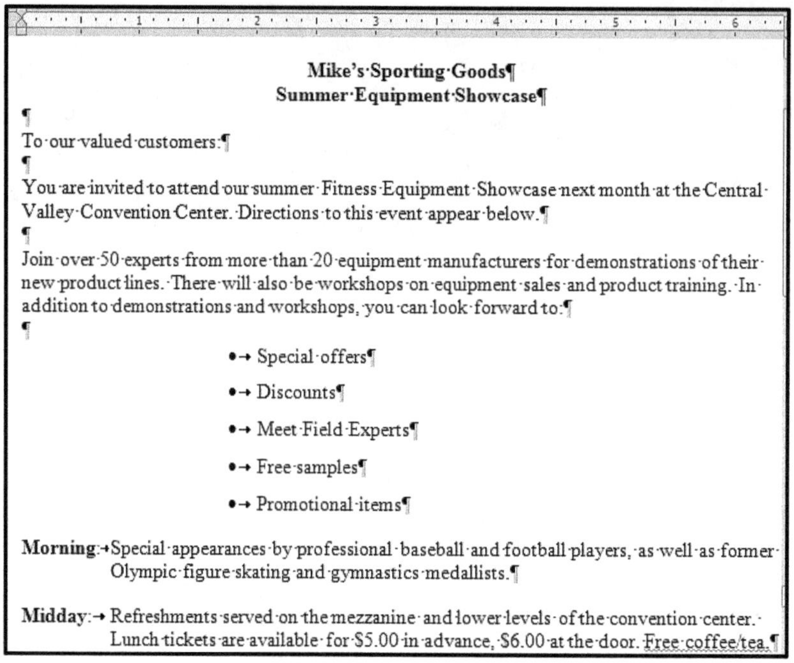

Mike's·Sporting·Goods¶
Summer·Equipment·Showcase¶

¶
To·our·valued·customers:¶
¶
You·are·invited·to·attend·our·summer·Fitness·Equipment·Showcase·next·month·at·the·Central·
Valley·Convention·Center.·Directions·to·this·event·appear·below.¶
¶
Join·over·50·experts·from·more·than·20·equipment·manufacturers·for·demonstrations·of·their·
new·product·lines.·There·will·also·be·workshops·on·equipment·sales·and·product·training.·In·
addition·to·demonstrations·and·workshops,·you·can·look·forward·to:¶
¶

- •→ Special·offers¶
- •→ Discounts¶
- •→ Meet·Field·Experts¶
- •→ Free·samples¶
- •→ Promotional·items¶

Morning:→Special·appearances·by·professional·baseball·and·football·players,·as·well·as·former·
Olympic·figure·skating·and·gymnastics·medallists.¶

Midday:→ Refreshments·served·on·the·mezzanine·and·lower·levels·of·the·convention·center.·
Lunch·tickets·are·available·for·$5.00·in·advance,·$6.00·at·the·door.·Free·coffee/tea.¶

Chapter 8 - Dates And Symbols

8.1 Inserting The Date And Time

Microsoft Word can automatically insert the **Current Date** and/or **Time** into a document. For example, if you are creating a legal document and the creation **Date** and **Time** are crucial and need to be seen whenever the document is opened or printed.

The **Update Automatically** option in the **Date** and **Time Dialog Box** inserts the date as a field that automatically displays the **Current Date** and/or **Time**

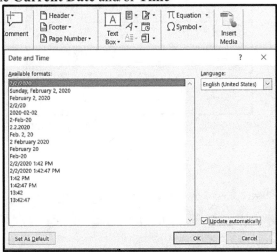

each time you open or print the document. If the **Update automatically** option is not selected, the **Date** and/or **Time** of insertion into the document appears.

Practice Exercise 57 - Insert Date And Time

1. **File** *Tab→* **Open** *→* **Browse** *→C:\Data\Word365-12\Date and Symbols.Docx.*
2. *Click on the third blank line below the Excel Sporting Goods address.*
3. *Insert Ribbon Tab →Text Group→Click* 🕐 *Date & Time.*
4. *Click Month Day, Year (third format from the top).*
5. *Click* ☑ Update automatically *Update automatically.*
6. *Click* OK *.*

Excel Sporting Goods
1234 Leisure Drive
Media, PA 19107
(610) 555-4321

February 4, 2020

8.2 Inserting Symbols

Microsoft Word provides many **Symbols** for use in documents. These symbols are associated with individual character sets. The available character sets are listed in the **Font** list in the **Symbol Dialog Box**.

The most commonly used character sets are **(normal text)**, **Symbol**, and **Wingdings**. The **(normal text)** character set includes characters such as a single quotation (') and the paragraph symbol (¶), in addition to the numbers, **Symbols**, and letters found on a standard keyboard.

This font set also includes a wide variety of special and foreign language characters, such as umlauts (ä) and tildes (ñ), organized by language subsets.

Practice Exercise 58 - Symbols

1. ***Click at the end of the text Excel Sporting Goods at the top of the page.***
2. ***Insert Ribbon Tab →Symbols Group →Click*** Ω Symbol ▾ ***Symbol →More Symbols.***
3. ***Click the Symbols tab, if necessary.***
4. ***Click the Font*** ▾ ***dropdown arrow.***
5. ***Scroll as necessary and click (normal text) at the top of the list.***
6. ***Click ® (seventh row, third column from the right).***
7. ***Click*** Insert ***→*** Close .

Excel Sporting Goods®
1234 Leisure Drive
Media, PA 19107
(610) 555-4321

8. ***Scroll to the list beginning with the text "The enclosed packet includes:" and insert the symbol of a hand pointing to the right before each item in the list. The hand symbol is located in the Wingdings character set. Then, close the Symbol Dialog Box***

The enclosed packet includes:

☞ Excel's new product catalog
☞ Highlights of the benefits of stocking your store with Excel Sporting Goods products
☞ Details of the terms and conditions of all sales
☞ Our advertising agreement

8.3 Inserting Special Characters

There may be times when you want to use **Special Characters** in a document. For example, you might want to insert a non-breaking hyphen (which prevents a hyphenated word such as **open-ended** from being separated by a line break), or you might want to insert a non-breaking space (which prevents two words from being separated by a line break). Special characters are inserted using the **Special Characters** page of the **Symbol Dialog Box**.

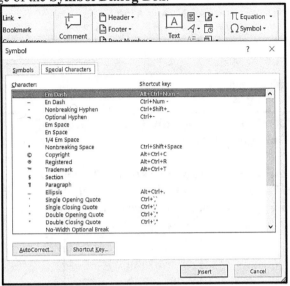

Practice Exercise 59 - Special Characters

1. *Scroll as necessary and click between the period and the letter C in the text Mr.Campanellas (last paragraph in the body of the letter, fourth sentence)*
2. *Insert Ribbon Tab →Symbols Group →Click Ω Symbol ▾ Symbol.*
3. *Click More Symbols.*
4. *Click the Special Characters tab.*
5. *Click Nonbreaking Space.*
6. *Click Insert →Close.*
7. *Type the word credit and a space before the word limit in the third sentence of the same paragraph.*

> An equipment and supply order form is also included. Your initial limit credit limit is $3500.
> After six months, we will review your credit status and adjust your limit, as warranted.
> Mr. Campanellas, I look forward to receiving your first order and working with you to meet all of your equipment and supply needs.

Tip: *Notice that the text Mr. Campanellas stays together because the space inserted between Mr. and Campanellas is a non-breaking space.*

8. *Display the formatting marks (Home Ribbon Tab →Paragraph Group →*

   ¶ Paragraph marker). **Tip**: *Notice the symbol that appears between Mr. and Campanellas to indicate the presence of a non-breaking space.*

> An·equipment·and·supply·order·form·is·also·included.·Your·initial·limit·credit·limit·is·$3500.·
> After·six·months,·we·will·review·your·credit·status·and·adjust·your·limit,·as·warranted.·
> Mr.°Campanellas,·I·look·forward·to·receiving·your·first·order·and·working·with·you·to·meet·all·of·your·equipment·and·supply·needs.¶

9. *Hide the formatting marks.*
10. **Close the document without saving it:** File *Tab →* Close *→* Don't Save.

Student Project I - Inserting Dates and Symbols

1. File *Tab →* 🗁 Open *→* 🗁 Browse *→C:\Data\Word365-12\Date and Symbols Practice1.Docx.*

2. **Insert the current date at the top of the document using the second format (Day, Date, Year). Set the date to update automatically.**
   Click on the top of the document →Insert Ribbon Tab →Text Group →
   Date & Time button →Sunday, August 22, 2013 → ☑ Update Automatically.

	Wednesday, February 5, 2020
Excel Sporting Goods Equipment Showcase	

3. **Scroll to the four-line list beginning with the text "special offers." Insert the checkmark symbol from the Wingdings character set (located at the end of the list) in front of each line in the list:**
   Click in front of the word special offers →Insert Ribbon Tab →
   Symbols Group →Symbol button →More Symbols →Font: Wingdings →
   Scroll to the bottom of the list and checkmark the symbol.

   > ✓ special offers
   > ✓ discounts
   > ✓ free samples
   > ✓ promotional items

4. **Scroll to the Build-a-Body Flex-All System text in the paragraph beginning Evening. Insert the Trademark (™) character after the word System.**
   Click on the word System →Insert Ribbon Tab → Symbols Group →
   Symbol button →More Symbols →Special Characters tab →
   Choose the Trademark symbol.

   > Evening: Drawings for door prizes. Grand prize - Complete Build-a-Body Flex-All System™. Other prizes include merchandise certificates ranging from $25 to $500.

5. **Close the document without saving it:** File *Tab →* Close *→* Don't Save .

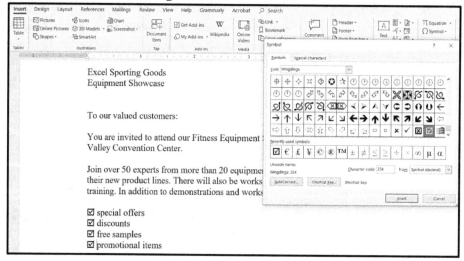

Chapter 9 - Graphics Images

9.1 Inserting Clip Art

(Word 2010 and Word 2007 Only Feature)
You can include **Clip Art** in a **Microsoft Word 2007 and 2010** document. A **Clip Art** picture can enhance a document by depicting an idea that may be difficult to describe or by making the document more visually appealing. **Microsoft Word 2007 and 2010** supply a collection of images with a wide range of subjects, known as clip art; more are available online if you have an Internet connection. You can use the **Clip Art** task pane to insert clip images. **Tip:** The **Clip Art** button has been changed to Online Pictures in **Word 2013+**.

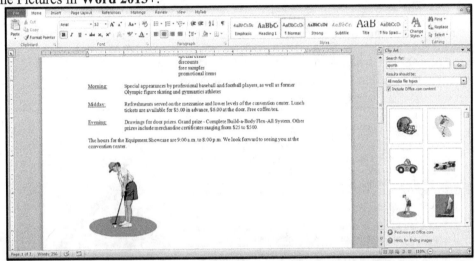

9.2 Online Pictures PowerPoint (2013/2016)

This inserts a picture from an online picture service.
This is only available in **Word 2013+**.
Tip: Clip Art is available in **Word 2007/2010,** but **Clip Art** is posted online for **Word 2013+.** Use the **Online Pictures** feature to find **Clip Art.**

Practice Exercise 60 - Online Pictures

Insert Ribbon Tab →Illustrations Group→Online Pictures.

9.3 Inserting A Picture

Here, you can insert a **Picture** from an existing graphic file into a **Microsoft Word** document. **Pictures** can include scanned images, photographs, and drawn objects saved as files. Before inserting a **Picture**, you can preview it to verify that it is the one you want.

Practice Exercise 61 - Picture

Insert a **picture** from a graphic file. Go to the second page of the document.
1.   Click at the beginning of the **Body Lean Exercise Bike** paragraph on page 2.

2.   ***Insert Ribbon Tab →Illustrations Group→ Picture →***

C:\Data\Word365-12\Graphics2.bmp → Insert .

3. **Make the following formatting changes:**

3a. ***Right-click on the "Bike" picture→Wrap Text*** Wrap Text ▾ →
Click Tight Tight .

3b. ***Right-click on the bike picture→Wrap Text*** Wrap Text ▾ →
More Layout Options→ Position Tab: ◉ ***Alignment: Right.***

Position	Text Wrapping	Size

Horizontal

◉ Alignment | Right ▾ | relative to | Column ▾ |

3c. **Change the Height of the image to 2 inches.**

Select Image→Format Ribbon Tab→Size Group→ ⬍🔲 Height: 2" .

Tip: Notice that the width of the image reduces accordingly
so that the original aspect is preserved.

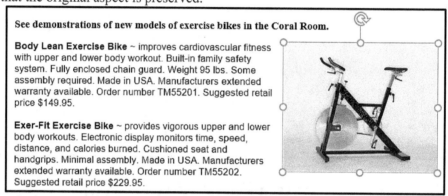

See demonstrations of new models of exercise bikes in the Coral Room.

Body Lean Exercise Bike ~ improves cardiovascular fitness with upper and lower body workout. Built-in family safety system. Fully enclosed chain guard. Weight 95 lbs. Some assembly required. Made in USA. Manufacturers extended warranty available. Order number TM55201. Suggested retail price $149.95.

Exer-Fit Exercise Bike ~ provides vigorous upper and lower body workouts. Electronic display monitors time, speed, distance, and calories burned. Cushioned seat and handgrips. Minimal assembly. Made in USA. Manufacturers extended warranty available. Order number TM55202. Suggested retail price $229.95.

4. ***Deselect the image by clicking anywhere in the document.***

5. **Close the document:** File *Tab→* Close *→* Don't Save .

9.4 Shapes

Shapes are a gallery of drawing objects.
To add the Shape:
    Click the object with the left mouse and let go→Draw the shape on the Microsoft Word screen.

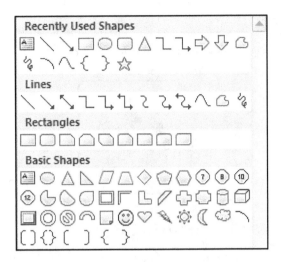

9.5 Icons

These are small shape icons used to enhance a document.

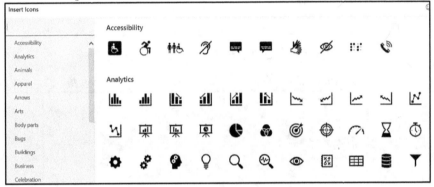

9.6 3D Models

This will insert 3D objects. There are several **3D** categories displayed.

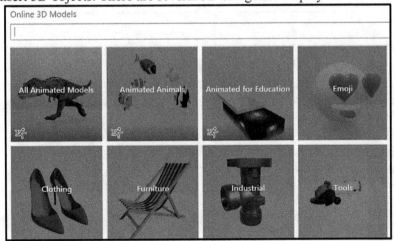

Practice Exercise 62 - 3D Models

1. **File** *Tab→* **Open** → **Browse** → *C:\Data\Word365-12\Graphics1.Docx.*
2. *Place the cursor on the bottom of page 1→ Insert Ribbon Tab →Illustrations Group→*
   3D Models→From Online Sources→ Building→Castel (or any desired object).

9.7 Creating SmartArt Graphics

Microsoft Word provides a number of predefined graphics called **SmartArt**. These range from graphical lists and process diagrams to more complex graphics, such as **Venn** diagrams and organization charts. Using **SmartArt** enables you to include complex graphical elements into your document with ease.

Practice Exercise 63 - Smart Art

1. **File** *Tab→* **Open** → **Browse** →*C:\Data\Word365-12\Graphics5.Docx.*
2. *Click on the document below THE SALES FUNNEL.*
3. *Insert Ribbon Tab →Illustrations Group→ SmartArt →Click the Process category.*

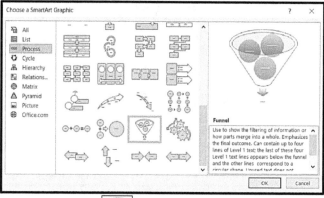

4. *Scroll down as necessary and click Funnel→ OK .*
5. *Enter Text*
   You may find that a text pane opens automatically on insertion of the SmartArt. In this case, you can type the text directly into the text pane items. However, you can also edit the text directly in the shapes:
   Click on [Text] in the first (topmost) shape, and type "Suspects."
   Click on [Text] in the second shape, and type "Suspects."
   Click on [Text] in the third shape, and type "Prospects."
   Click on [Text] in the fourth bullet and type "Customers."

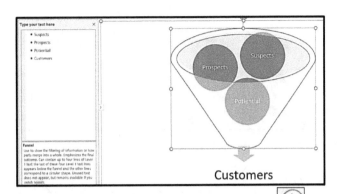

6. ***Change the colors of a SmartArt graphic. →Design Ribbon Tab →*** 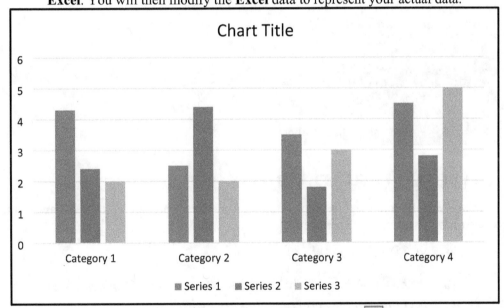 ***Change Colors.***
7. ***Point at the individual thumbnails to view the color schemes.***

8. ***Scroll as necessary and click*** ***Gradient Loop - Accent 6.***
9. ***Click anywhere in the document away from the SmartArt graphic.***

10. **Close the document:** `File` *Tab →* `Close` *→* `Don't Save`.

9.8 Create A Chart

When you Create a **Chart**, the system creates a standard layout and then opens the numeric data in **Excel**. You will then modify the **Excel** data to represent your actual data.

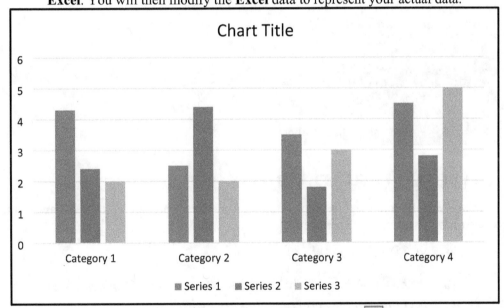

Edit Chart Data - *Click on chart →Design Ribbon Tab →* *Edit Data button.*

Practice Exercise 64 - Charts

1. ***Insert Ribbon Tab →Chart →Column***

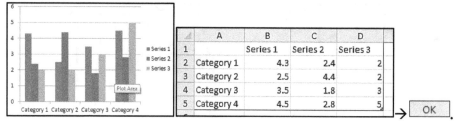

	A	B	C	D
1		Series 1	Series 2	Series 3
2	Category 1	4.3	2.4	2
3	Category 2	2.5	4.4	2
4	Category 3	3.5	1.8	3
5	Category 4	4.5	2.8	5

Word Chart   **Excel Data:**

2. Modify the Excel data   *3. Exit out of Excel to see the results.*

	A	B	C	D
1		Sample1	Sample2	Sample3
2	Test1	4.3	2.4	2
3	Test2	2.5	4.4	2
4	Test3	3.5	1.8	3
5	Test4	4.5	2.8	5

9.9 ScreenShot

This is a feature to capture an image from the window behind the Screenshot Button. ***Insert Ribbon Tab→Illustrations Group→Screenshot Button→Screen clipping→Draw a box around the area to be clipped→The clipped image will appear in Word.***

Example: *Cut an Icon from the desktop:*

9.10 Creating WordArt Objects

You can use **WordArt** to create a graphic text object. These can be used to add emphasis to company logos, text advertisements, and newsletters.

Practice Exercise 65 - Word Art

1. **File** *Tab→* Open *→* Browse *→C:\Data\Word365-12\Graphics3.Docx.*
2. *Click at the beginning of the paragraph You are invited.*
3. *Insert Ribbon Tab →Text Group→* WordArt *→Click WordArt* *(first row, fifth column).*
4. *Type "Winter Preview."*

5. *Apply the following formats to the WordArt text:*
   Select Arial (or similar font) from the Font list.
   Select 24 from the Size list.
   Bold the text.

6. [OK] .

9.11 Creating Watermarks

A **Watermark** is a graphic or text that appears behind the text or objects on a page. **Watermarks** are commonly used to identify the status of a document (**DRAFT** or **CONFIDENTIAL**, for example). When you add a **Watermark** to a page, you can apply it to all pages of the document or just to the current section. **Tip:** The **Watermark** feature was moved to the **Design Ribbon Tab** in **Microsoft Word**.

Tip: Excel 2010: *Page Layout Ribbon Tab →Watermark* [Watermark ▾].

Practice Exercise 66 - Watermarks

Create a watermark. If necessary, switch to [▤] Print Layout View.

1. *Design Ribbon Tab →Click [] Watermark →Click [] Custom Watermark →* [⦿ Picture watermark]
   → [Select Picture...] *→From a File:* [Browse]

2. **Open the file in:** *C:\Data\Word365-12\Graphics4.bmp →* [Insert] *→* [OK] .

> To all Northeast Regional Sales Reps:
>
> **Winter Preview**
>
> You are invited to attend our Winter Sports Equipment Preview on September 14 in Boston, Massachusetts.
>
> Join over 50 experts from more than 20 manufacturers for demonstrations of their new product lines. There will also be seminars on equipment sales and product training. In addition to demonstrations and seminars, you can also look forward to:
>
> - Special offers
> - Discounts
> - Free Samples
> - Promotional Items
>
> The Winter Preview will take place from 9:00 a.m. to 8:00 p.m. We look forward to seeing you there.
>
> Directions and a schedule of events are enclosed.

3. **Switch to** ⬚ **Print Layout View and view two pages to see the document.** `File`
    Tab→Print→Select the - in the Zoom Slider located in the lower right corner.
    Tip: *Notice that the watermark appears on each page. The default formatting is Washout so that the background image does not obscure the text.*

4. *Open the Custom Watermark Dialog Box and select the Text watermark option. Enter the text* ***Excel Sporting Goods****, change the text color to any dark green option, and position the text diagonally. Select the Semitransparent option, if necessary. Select* `OK` *. View the document in the* ⬚ *Print Layout View.* **Tip:** *Note that the Text watermark has replaced the Picture watermark; Microsoft Word will only allow one watermark in a document or section.*

5. **Close the document:** `File` *Tab →* `Close` *→* `Don't Save` .

9.12 Word Wrap

(Word 2013+ Feature)
You can now place graphic images anywhere in the text similar to the **Desktop Publishing** functionality by using the Word Wrap feature.
Tip: It is called **Live Layout**.

Practice Exercise 67 - Word Wrap

1. *Type a sentence or two.*
2. *Insert a graphic image: Insert Ribbon Tab → Illustrations Group → Pictures → (Choose a picture from C:\Data\Word365-12 folder.*
3. *Select the picture →Format Ribbon Tab →Arrange Group → Wrap Text → Tight → (Move picture around to position it).*

9.13 Embed Video

(Word 3013+ Feature)

A new icon, called **Online Video,** will allow you to add **Videos.**

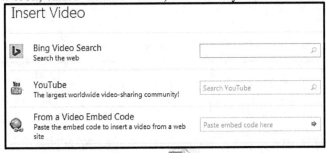

Excel 2010: *Insert Ribbon Tab →Media Group →   Insert Media →Bing Video Search →Choose a video.* **Tip:** Your computer may need to install **Adobe Flash player.**

Student Project J - Graphics

1. **File** *Tab→* **Open** *→* **Browse** *→C:\Data\Word365-12\Graphics Practice1.Docx.*

2. **Make sure you are in** Print Layout View, **and display the horizontal ruler, if necessary.** *View Ribbon Tab → Views Group → Print Layout View.*

3. **Go to the top of the document, if necessary, and insert the graphic file from the student data folder.** *Click on the top of the document→Insert Ribbon Tab→Illustrations Group→* 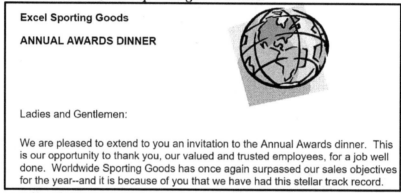 *Pictures button→ C:\Data\Word365-12\Graphics Practice1.Bmp.*

4. **Format the picture with a tight text-wrapping style and horizontally align it to the right, relative to the margin. Then, change the height to 3 inches.**

   4a. *Right-click on the graphics image→ Wrap Text→ Tight text-wrapping.*

   4b. *Right-click on the graphics image→ Wrap Text→ More Layout Options→X Alignment: right relative to: Margin→* OK .

   4c. *Format Ribbon Tab→Size Group→Height: 3 inches.*

Excel Sporting Goods

ANNUAL AWARDS DINNER

Ladies and Gentlemen:

We are pleased to extend to you an invitation to the Annual Awards dinner. This is our opportunity to thank you, our valued and trusted employees, for a job well done. Worldwide Sporting Goods has once again surpassed our sales objectives for the year--and it is because of you that we have had this stellar track record.

5. *Scroll down to view the paragraph beginning with the text Thanks to you, on page 1. Use the* **Arrow** *keys to scroll down to the beginning of the words "Thanks to you."*

6. *Change the text-wrapping style to the square and the horizontal alignment to left, relative to the margin. Then, change the height to 1.2 inches.*

   6a. *Right-click on the clip art image→ Wrap Text→Square text-wrapping.*

   6b. *Right-click on the graphics image→ Wrap Text→ More layout options→ Position Tab→ Alignment: left relative to: Margin.*

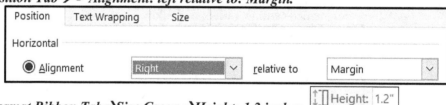

   6c. *Format Ribbon Tab→Size Group→Height: 1.2 inches.*

Student Project J - Continued

1. **Create a text watermark.** *Type "Thank You" as the text, set the color to red. Make the watermark semi-transparent and have it appear diagonally on the page. Set the size to 36. Click in the text (not in a graphic image)→Design Ribbon Tab→Page Background Group→* Watermark button→ Custom Watermark→X Text watermark→Text: Thank You→Color: Red→Layout: Diagonal→X Semitransparent.

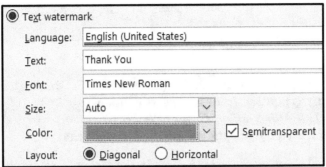

2. *Click in the blank line at the top of page 2. Create a WordArt object, selecting the style in the third row and fourth column.*

   Click in the blank area on the top of page 2→Insert Ribbon Tab→Text Group→ A *WordArt button→Choose the third-row fourth column.*

3. *Type three separate lines as follows: type "Seminars", press* Enter *key, type "and", press* Enter *key, and type "Demonstrations."*

   Type: Seminars
   *   and*
   *   Demonstrations*

4. *Change the font size to 20 and bold the text. Then, select* OK *to insert the WordArt object.*

   Size: 20→Bold button→ OK .

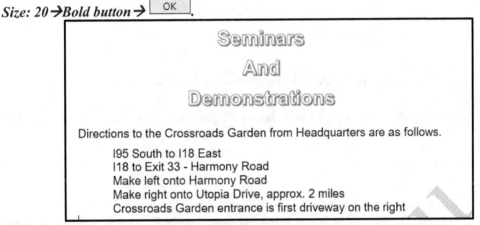

5. *Change the WordArt: Select the WordArt image→Format Ribbon Tab→ WordArt Styles→* A

   Text Effects→ A *3-D Rotation→* *Off Axis 1: Right.*

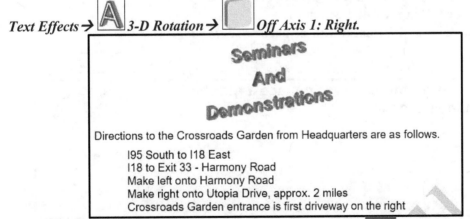

6. *View both pages of the document in the Print Layout View or* File *Tab→Print.*

7. *Close the document without saving it.* File *Tab →* Close *→* Don't Save .

Student Project K - Using SmartArt.

1. **Create a new, blank document.** File *Tab →* New *→* ☐ *Blank Document.*
2. **Select the SmartArt button from the Insert Ribbon Tab:**
   Insert Ribbon Tab →Illustrations Group →SmartArt button.
3. **Select the Segmented Cycle option from the Cycle category:**
   Cycle → *Segmented Cycle (located in the second row and third column) →* OK .
4. *Type Products, Services, and Support in the text fields.*
   Type "Products", "Services", and "Support" in each segment.
5. *Change the colors to Gradient Loop - Accent 4.*
   Select the SmartArt →Design Ribbon Tab →SmartArt styles Group →
   Change colors button → *Gradient Loop - Accent 4.*
6. *Apply the Flat Scene style to the SmartArt graphic.*
   Select the SmartArt →Design Ribbon Tab →Smart Art Styles gallery →
   Flat Scene style (3D group, sixth column).
7. **Close the document without saving it:** File *Tab →* Close *→* Don't Save .

Student Project L - Add picture To A Table

1. **Create a new blank document.** File *Tab →* New *→* ☐*Blank Document.*
2. **Create a new 2 column by 3-row table.** *Insert Ribbon Tab →Tables Group →* *Table*
   2x3 Table
   icon →
3. **Place a clipart image in the 2nd column in the 1st row:** Insert Ribbon *Tab →Illustration Group →* *Pictures → C:\Data\Word365-12\Graphics Practice1.bmp*
4. **Enter some text in the row 1 column 1.**
5. **Select the table and format it with no borders:** *Select the Table →*
   Design Ribbon Tab →Borders Group → *Borders button →* No Border .

This is a different way to place a graphic image inside text.

Chapter 10 - Setting Tabs

When you need to create a document in which the text appears at fixed locations across the page, you can use tabs to space the text. **Tabs** can serve many functions in a document. For example, you can use a combination of tabs to create a table for an office telephone list.

Tab Stops appear on the horizontal ruler. **Microsoft Word** allows you to **Set Left**, **Center**, **Right**, and **Decimal Tab Stops** in any combination. **Tab Stops** are a component of paragraph formatting and, therefore, apply to every line in a paragraph. Each paragraph, however, can have a different combination of **Tab Stops**.

Each type of **Tab Stop** positions texts differently. Text and numbers are aligned flush-left to a **Left-Aligned Tab Stop**, centered under a **Center Tab Stop**, and aligned flush-right to a **Right-Aligned Tab Stop**. Finally, the first decimal point or period occurring in the text or number is aligned with a **Decimal Tab Stop**. (If there is no period or decimal in the text or number, it is aligned flush-right to the decimal tab.) **Decimal Tabs** are most useful when you need to enter a list of numbers and you want the decimal points of the numbers to be aligned. By default, left-aligned tabs are set at half-inch intervals across the page.

The following illustration represents how text appears with the various tab settings:

LEFT	CENTER	RIGHT	DECIMAL
JoAnne Morgan	Vice President	Active Wear	170.90
Francis Orr	Manager	Diving	250.30
Robert Maxwell	Associate	Shoes	79.00
Betty Fields	Supervisor	Racquet Sports	98.70

10.1 Setting Tab Stops

Tab Stops can be positioned anywhere on a line, and you can set a combination of **Left-Aligned, Center, Right-Aligned, Decimal**, and **Bar Tabs** for each paragraph.

You can create **Tab Stops** by clicking the **Tab Selector** button on the left side of the horizontal ruler until the desired tab character appears and then clicking the desired location on the horizontal ruler.

You can also use the **Tabs Dialog Box** to enter a specific tab type and location.

You can have as many **Tab Stops** as desired in a document.

The following five types of tabs are available:

Tab Character	Tab Type
⌊	**Left**
⊥	**Center**
⌋	**Right**
⊥.	**Decimal**
▮	**Bar**

Tab Stops only apply to the current paragraph or selected text. After creating **Tab Stops**, you should make sure that you start typing the **Tabbed** text on a line formatted with the desired **Tabs**. In addition, each time you press the **Enter** key, you create another paragraph formatted with the same **Tab Stops**.

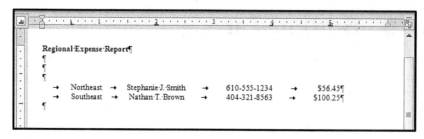

Practice Exercise 68 - Stop Tabs

1. **File** *Tab→* **Open** *→* **Browse** *→C:\Data\Word365-12\TabsA.docx.*
2. *View Ribbon Tab→Show Group→* ☑ **Ruler** *(Make sure the ruler is on).*
3. *Home Ribbon Tab→Paragraph Group→¶ Paragraph Mark (Show/Hide button).*
4. *Press* **Ctrl** **End** *keys to move to the bottom of the document.*
5. *Click to* └ *Left tab, if necessary.*
6. *Click at 0.5 inches on the horizontal ruler.*
7. *Click to* ┴ *Center tab.*
8. *Click at 2 inches on the horizontal ruler.*
9. *Click to* ┘ *Right tab.*
10. *Click at 4 inches on the horizontal ruler.*
11. *Click to* ┷ *Center decimal tab.*
12. *Click at 5 inches on the horizontal ruler.*

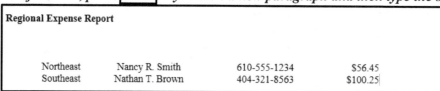

13. *Press* **Tab** *key to move to the first tab stop and type the word "Northeast."*
14. *Press* **Tab** *key to move to the next tab stop and continue entering text as shown in the chart below.*
15. *At the end of the line, press* **Enter** *key to start a new paragraph and then type the second line.*

Regional Expense Report			
Northeast	Nancy R. Smith	610-555-1234	$56.45
Southeast	Nathan T. Brown	404-321-8563	$100.25

16. *Open the Reveal Formatting task pane.*
    Tip: *Notice the tab settings under the Paragraph section.*
17. *Close the Reveal Formatting task pane.*
18. **Close the document:** **File** *Tab →* **Close** *→* **Don't Save**.

10.2 Deleting And Moving Tab Stops

You can **Delete Tab Stops.** For example, you may want to **Delete Tab Stops** if you are removing data from a telephone list. Although you can use the **Tabs Dialog Box** to **Delete Tab Stops**, it is much easier to just drag them off the horizontal ruler.

After you have removed a **Tab Stop**, any text positioned at that **Tab Stop Moves** to the next defined **Tab Stop** or the first default **Tab Stop** after the last defined **Tab Stop**.

Tab Stops can also be moved to other positions on the ruler to accommodate the text in your columns or to align a column under a column heading. **Moving** a **Tab Stop** moves the text aligned to that **Tab Stop** to the new position.

If you wish to move a whole column of tabbed text, select all the tabbed text before moving any tabs.
If **Tab Stops** are set differently for certain paragraphs in your tabbed text (such as the title), some tabs may appear dimmed on the ruler when you select all the tabbed text. You can drag a dimmed **Tab Stop** to **Delete** or **Move** it.

Regional Expense Report

Region	Sales Rep.	Phone	Expenses
Northeast	Stephanie J. Smith	610-555-1234	$56.45
Southeast	Nathan T. Brown	404-321-8563	$100.25
Central	Thomas A. Stevenson	312-888-3265	$68.99
Northwest	George W. Adams	206-664-5874	$8.88
Southwest	Frances L. Wallace	213-564-6972	$45.90
Can. & Mex.	Henry D. Norris	713-567-9134	$33.25

Practice Exercise 69 - Adjusting Tabs

1.   **File** *Tab→* ☐ Open *→* ☐ Browse *→C:\Data\Word365-12\TabsB.docx.*

2.   *If necessary, display the horizontal ruler in* ☐ *Print Layout View and display the formatting marks. Also, it may be easier to work with the tab stops if you zoom to the Text width.*

3.   *Triple-click Region.*

Region	Sales Rep.	Phone	Expenses

4.   *Drag the left tab at 5 inches off the ruler. Select and drag it down.*

Region	Sales Rep.	Phone	Expenses

5.   *Drag to select all the text below the heading row from Northeast to Can. & Mex.*

Northeast	Stephanie J. Smith	610-555-1234	$56.45
Southeast	Nathan T. Brown	404-321-8563	$100.25
Central	Thomas A. Stevenson	312-888-3265	$68.99
Northwest	George W. Adams	206-664-5874	$8.88
Southwest	Frances L. Wallace	213-564-6972	$45.90
Can. & Mex.	Henry D. Norris	713-567-9134	$33.25

6.   *Drag the decimal-aligned tab at 5 inches to 5.5 inches.*

Northeast	Stephanie J. Smith	610-555-1234	$56.45
Southeast	Nathan T. Brown	404-321-8563	$100.25
Central	Thomas A. Stevenson	312-888-3265	$68.99
Northwest	George W. Adams	206-664-5874	$8.88
Southwest	Frances L. Wallace	213-564-6972	$45.90
Can. & Mex.	Henry D. Norris	713-567-9134	$33.25

7.   *With the tabbed text still selected, move the Right-Aligned tab from 4 inches to 4.5 inches, and then move the centered tab from 2 inches to 2.5.*

Northeast	Stephanie J. Smith	610-555-1234	$56.45
Southeast	Nathan T. Brown	404-321-8563	$100.25
Central	Thomas A. Stevenson	312-888-3265	$68.99
Northwest	George W. Adams	206-664-5874	$8.88
Southwest	Frances L. Wallace	213-564-6972	$45.90
Can. & Mex.	Henry D. Norris	713-567-9134	$33.25

8. *Hold* Alt *key and click and hold the right tab at 4.5 inches and drag it to 4.41", relative to the left margin.*

Northeast	Stephanie J. Smith	610-555-1234	$56.45
Southeast	Nathan T. Brown	404-321-8563	$100.25
Central	Thomas A. Stevenson	312-888-3265	$68.99
Northwest	George W. Adams	206-664-5874	$8.88
Southwest	Frances L. Wallace	213-564-6972	$45.90
Can. & Mex.	Henry D. Norris	713-567-9134	$33.25

10.3 Clearing All Tabs

After typing all of your tabbed text, you may want to be able to return to the default tabs in order to enter more tabbed or paragraph text. You can return to the default tab set by placing the insertion point below the tabbed text and then **Clearing** the existing tabs. **Clearing Tabs** remove them from the current or selected paragraph(s).

You can choose to **Clear** a specific **Tab**, or you can **Clear All** Tabs simultaneously. A quick way of **Clearing Tabs** is to use the **Tabs Dialog Box**.

Practice Exercise 70 - Clear Tabs

1. *If necessary, display the horizontal ruler in* ▤ *Print Layout View and display the formatting marks. Also, it may be easier to work with the tab stops if you zoom to the Text width.*

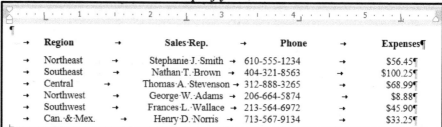

→	**Region**	→	**Sales Rep.**	→	**Phone**	→	**Expenses¶**
→	Northeast	→	Stephanie J. Smith →	610-555-1234		→	$56.45¶
→	Southeast	→	Nathan T. Brown →	404-321-8563		→	$100.25¶
→	Central	→	Thomas A. Stevenson →	312-888-3265		→	$68.99¶
→	Northwest	→	George W. Adams →	206-664-5874		→	$8.88¶
→	Southwest	→	Frances L. Wallace →	213-564-6972		→	$45.90¶
→	Can. & Mex.	→	Henry D. Norris →	713-567-9134		→	$33.25¶

2. *Press* Ctrl End *keys to move to the end of the document.*
3. *Press* Enter *key.*
4. *Click* ▣ *in the Paragraph Group.*
5. [Tabs...] → [Clear All] → [OK] .

10.4 Creating A Leader Tab

You can use the **Tabs Dialog Box** to apply a **Leader** to a tab. A **Leader** is a dotted, dashed or solid line that appears in the space between the last character to the left and the first character of the text aligned to the **Tab Stop** to which the **Leader** has been applied.

Leader characters can have many uses. For instance, they can visually connect text on a line, such as a chapter heading aligned to the left margin and its page number aligned to the right in a table of contents.

If you add or remove text to the left or right of a **Leader Tab**, the length of the **Leader** changes accordingly to accommodate the text.

Practice Exercise 71 - Leader Tabs

1. *If necessary, display the horizontal ruler in* ⊟ *Print Layout View and display the formatting marks. Also, it may be easier to work with the tab stops if you zoom to the Text width.*
2. *Position the insertion point at the end of the document and press* Enter *key to add a blank line below the existing text.*
3. *Click* ⊡ *in the Paragraph Group.*
4. *Click* [Tabs...].
5. *Type "6" in the Tab stop position box.*
6. *Click* [⦿ Right] *Under Alignment.*
7. *Click* [⦿ 2 ......] *Under Leader.*

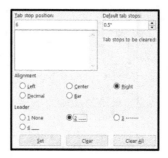

8. *Click* Set → OK .
9. *Type "For further information, call Dee" and then press* **Tab** *key.*
   Tip: Notice the leader that appears after the text.
10. *Type 555-5645.*
    Tip: Notice that the leader adjusts to accommodate the new text.

	Region		**Sales Rep.**		**Phone**		**Expenses¶**
	Northeast		Stephanie J. Smith	→	610-555-1234		$56.45¶
	Southeast		Nathan T. Brown	→	404-321-8563		$100.25¶
	Central		Thomas A. Stevenson	→	312-888-3265		$68.99¶
	Northwest		George W. Adams	→	206-664-5874		$8.88¶
	Southwest		Frances L. Wallace	→	213-564-6972		$45.90¶
	Can. & Mex.		Henry D. Norris	→	713-567-9134		$33.25¶

For further information, call Dee...555-5645¶

11. **Close the document:** File *Tab* → Close → Don't Save .

Student Project M - Setting Tabs

1. *Create a new document.*
2. *Set left-aligned tabs at 0.75 and 1.75 inches on the horizontal ruler.*
3. *Set a Right-Aligned tab at 3.5 and 6.25 inches.*
4. *Set a decimal tab at 5.25 inches.*

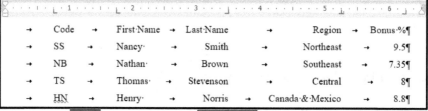

5. *Start the Code column at the left margin. Enter the text as shown in the following graphic:*

	Code		First Name	Last Name		Region		Bonus %¶
	SS		Nancy	Smith		Northeast		9.5¶
	NB		Nathan	Brown		Southeast		7.35¶
	TS		Thomas	Stevenson		Central		8¶
	HN		Henry	Norris		Canada & Mexico		8.8¶

6. **Close the document:** File *Tab* → Close → Don't Save .

Chapter 11 - Numbers And Bullets

11.1 Typing A Numbered Or Bulleted List

There may be times when you need to include a **Numbered** or **Bulleted List** in a document. **Numbered Lists** are often sequential items or items listed in order of importance. For example, you may want to number specific steps on a list or add letters to an outline detailing the hierarchy of a corporation. When you want to emphasize items in a list in no particular order, you can use a **Bulleted List**.

One way to create a **Numbered List** is to use the **AutoFormat** feature, which applies numbers or bullets as you type. Whenever you type a **1** (Arabic or Roman) or an **A** (uppercase or lowercase) and a period (**.**), dash (**-**), or parenthesis (**)**) followed by space or tab indent and then text, **Microsoft Word** assumes you want to sequentially list the items. Whenever you type an asterisk (*****) followed by a space or a tab indent and then type text, **Microsoft Word** assumes you want to create a **Bulleted List**. Thereafter, each time you press the Enter key, the next applicable number or letter in the sequence appears in a **Numbered List** or another bullet appears in a **Bulleted List**.

After typing the first line of **Numbered** or bulleted text and pressing the Enter key, the **AutoCorrect Options** button displays. At this point, you can accept the **AutoFormat** and continue typing your list, or you can use the **AutoCorrect Options** list to undo the previous automatic list formatting or to end the list on the current line.

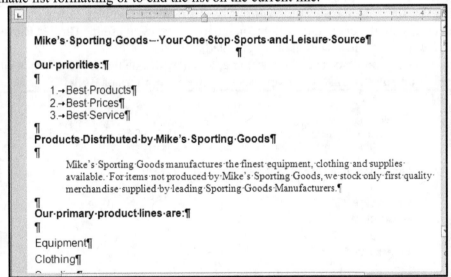

Tip: To turn off the **Autoformat Bullet** feature: *File Tab →Options →Proofing →*

Practice Exercise 72 - Bullet List Number List

1. **File** *Tab →* Open *→* Browse *→C:\Data\Word365-12\Bullets.docx.*
2. *Display the formatting marks, if necessary.*
3. *Click on the second line below the text Our priorities:*
4. *Type "1" (including the period).*

5. *Press* Spacebar *key.*
6. *Type "Best Products".*
7. *Press* Enter *key.*
8. *Type "Best Prices" and press* Enter *key and then type "Best Service".*

> Our·priorities:¶
>   1.→Best·Products¶
>   2.→Best·Prices¶
>   3.→Best·Service¶

9. *Go to the end of the document, type an asterisk (*), press* Spacebar *key, type "special orders" and press* Enter *key.*
10. *Enter the text "personalized uniforms" and "autographed memorabilia" as the next two items in the Bulleted List.*
11. *Press* Enter *key twice to disable the bullets.*

> **Cancellation**:·Order·cancellations·must·be·made·prior·to·shipment·of·merchandise.·The·
> following·items·may·not·be·canceled:¶
> ¶
>   •→ Special·Orders¶
>   •→ Personalized·Uniforms¶
>   •→ Autographed·Memorabilia¶
> ¶

11.2 Adding Numbers Or Bullets To Text

Microsoft Word can generate a **Numbered** or **Bulleted List** from existing text. When you use the **Numbering Button** in the **Paragraph Group**, **Microsoft Word** numbers each paragraph of the selected text sequentially, beginning with the number 1. When you use the **Bullets Button**, **Microsoft Word** adds a bullet to each paragraph of the selected text.

These buttons are a great time-saver. For example, you may decide that a previously created, unnumbered or **unBulleted List** would appear better with **Numbers** or **Bullets**.

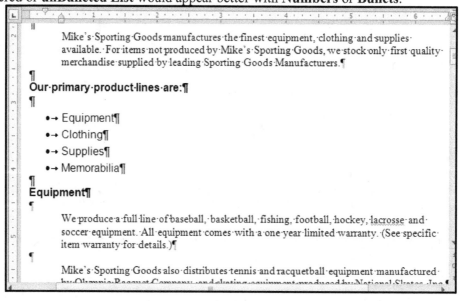

Practice Exercise 73 - Add Bullets To Text

1. **Display Format Marks:** *Home Ribbon Tab →Paragraph Group →*
   ¶ *Paragraph Mark (Show/Hide button).*
2. *Scroll as necessary to page 2 and drag to select the text from the highest quality products to well-trained, knowledgeable sales staff.*

3. *Click* ⊞ *Numbering List.*

```
1.→ highest·quality·products¶
2.→ superior·selection¶
3.→ competitive·pricing¶
4.→ outstanding·service¶
5.→ friendly·customer·support¶
6.→ stock·control¶
7.→ cooperative·advertising·agreements¶
8.→ semi-annual·promotions¶
9.→ well-trained,·knowledgeable·sales·staff¶
```

4. *Scroll to page 1 and select the four items under the Our primary product lines are: heading and use the left-hand part of the Bullets button in the Paragraph Group to create a Bulleted List.*

```
•→ Equipment¶
•→ Clothing¶
•→ Supplies¶
•→ Memorabilia¶
```

5. *Deselect the Bulleted List.*

11.3 Deleting A Numbered Or Bulleted Item

Items can be deleted from a **Numbered** or **Bulleted** list. If an item in a **Numbered** list is deleted, **Microsoft Word** automatically renumbers the remaining items as needed. It is often helpful to display the formatting marks to assist you in this task.

The selection bar (the blank area to the left of a paragraph) provides a quick method of selecting a list item.

Practice Exercise 74 - Deleting Bullets

1. *Go to the Numbered list on page 2.*
2. *Click to the left of 4. outstanding service.*
3. *Press* Delete *key several times*

```
1.→ highest·quality·products¶
2.→ superior·selection¶
3.→ competitive·pricing¶
4.→ friendly·customer·support¶
5.→ stock·control¶
6.→ cooperative·advertising·agreements¶
7.→ semi-annual·promotions¶
8.→ well-trained,·knowledgeable·sales·staff¶
```

4. *Delete the Supplies Bulleted item on page 1.*

```
•→ Equipment¶
•→ Clothing¶
•→ Memorabilia¶
```

11.4 Adding A Numbered Or Bulleted Item

You can **Add** an item to a **Numbered** or **Bulleted List**. If you add an item to a **Numbered List**, **Microsoft Word** automatically renumbers the existing items as needed.

Practice Exercise 75 - Adding Bullets

1. *Go to the Numbered list on page 2.*
2. *Click to the right of 2. superior selection.*
3. *Press* Enter *key.*
4. *Type the text "extended product warranties" after the new number.*

> 1.→ highest·quality·products¶
> 2.→ superior·selection¶
> 3.→ extended·product·warranties¶
> 4.→ competitive·pricing¶
> 5.→ friendly·customer·support¶
> 6.→ stock·control¶
> 7.→ cooperative·advertising·agreements¶
> 8.→ semi-annual·promotions¶
> 9.→ well-trained,·knowledgeable·sales·staff¶

5. *Scroll to page 1 and add a new bulleted item, Team Supplies, after the Equipment bullet.*

> ● → Equipment¶
> ● → Team·Supplies¶
> ● → Clothing¶
> ● → Memorabilia¶

11.5 Removing Numbers Or Bullets From Text

If you decide that **Numbers** or **Bullets** are no longer appropriate, you can **Remove** them from the text. You can use the **Numbering** or **Bullets Buttons** in the **Paragraph Group** to **Remove Numbers** or **Bullets** from a List.

Practice Exercise 76 - Removing Bullets

1. *Go to the top of page 1.*
2. *Drag to select the Numbered list beginning with 1. Best Products*

> **Our·priorities:**¶
> 1.→ Best·Products¶
> 2.→ Best·Prices¶
> 3.→ Best·Service¶

3. *Click* [icon] *Numbering.*
4. *The paragraphs remain indented, so you may wish to reformat them to match the surrounding text.*

> Our·priorities:¶
> 1.→ Best·Products¶
> 2.→ Best·Prices¶
> 3.→ Best·Service¶

5. *Move to the end of the document and select the Bulleted List that begins with the text special orders.*
6. *Click the* [icon] *Bullets button to remove the bullets from the list.*

> ¶
> Special·Orders¶
> Personalized·Uniforms¶
> Autographed·Memorabilia¶
> ¶

7. *Click the* [icon] *Decrease Indent button to move the list to the left margin.*

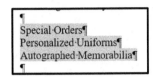

11.6 Format As You Type

This feature automatically formats lists as bullets. Sometimes, you may not want this action and it can be turned off.

File Tab→Options→Proofing→Autocorrect button→Format As You Type Tab.

Apply as you type	
☐ Automatic bulleted lists	☐ Automatic numbered lists

Student Project N - Numbers And Bullets

1. **File** *Tab→* ☐ Open → ☐ Browse *→C:\Data\Word365-12\Bullets Practice1.docx.*
2. *Insert bullets in front of the four items, beginning with the text Special offers.*
3. *In the same Bulleted List, insert a new bulleted item, Meet field experts, after the Discounts item.*
4. *Format the bullets as small, open circles.*
5. *Delete the Discounts item.*
6. *Position the insertion point two lines below the text Also available will be:*
7. *Click the Bullets button and type the following two lines of bulleted text: "Prizes awarded every hour" and "Seminars".*
8. *End the Bulleted List.*
9. *Format the bullets of this second list as round-filled circles.*
10. *Go to page 2 and number the directions.*
11. *Add the following new item after item 2: Take I40 West to Exit 20 for Rte 327 West.*
12. *Remove the numbers from the directions.*
13. **Close the document: File** *Tab→* Close → Don't Save .

Mike's Sporting Goods
Summer Equipment Showcase

To our valued customers:

You are invited to attend our Summer Fitness Equipment Showcase next month at the Central Valley Convention Center.

Join over 50 experts from more than 20 equipment manufacturers for demonstrations of their new product lines. There will also be workshops on equipment sales and product training. In addition to demonstrations and workshops, you can look forward to:

o Special offers
o Meet field experts
o Free samples
o Promotional items

Also available will be:
- Prizes awarded every hour
- Seminars

Morning: Special appearances by professional baseball and football players, as well as former Olympic figure skating and gymnastics medalists.

Chapter 12 - Spelling And Grammar

In order to help you check your **Microsoft Word** documents for errors in **Spelling and Grammar**, **Microsoft Word** includes a **Spelling and Grammar** feature. This feature works in two ways. One way is to automatically check **Spelling and Grammar** as you enter text. This method is enabled by default. Another way to check **Spelling and Grammar** in a document is to invoke the **Spelling and Grammar** checker after the document has been created. Both methods find the same errors.

A red, wavy underline appears under a word if it is misspelled or not in the dictionary. A green, wavy underline appears if a grammar rule is violated. If there is a wavy blue line that would indicate contextual spelling which means the word does not fit in the sentence or out of context. A purple, dotted underline, called a smart tag indicator, appears under certain types of data, such as a person's name. Pointing to the smart tag indicator displays the **Smart Tag Actions** button, which provides a list of actions you can take regarding the data.

12.1 Checking Spelling/Grammar As You Type

This feature examines the words in a document and compares them to the words found in the main dictionary. When a word is found that is not in the main dictionary, a single red, wavy line appears beneath the word.

As you type, the **Mark grammar errors as you type** feature examines your document and compares it to a specified grammatical style. When the **Grammar Checker** finds a word or phrase that appears grammatically incorrect, a green, wavy line appears beneath the text. The green, wavy lines only appear after you end a sentence with punctuation and begin typing another sentence or after you press the Enter key to end a paragraph.

You have two choices when **Microsoft Word** identifies text as incorrect. You can ignore the wavy line and continue typing, or you can **Right-click** the identified text and select one of the suggestions or commands on the shortcut menu.

The shortcut menu for correcting errors may include suggestions for a replacement. You can select replacement text, ignore the word or phrase if it is correct, or add the word to your custom dictionary. Ignored words are ignored for all documents, but only in the current **Microsoft Word** session; words added to the custom dictionary are permanent.

You can quickly move to the next spelling or grammatical error by clicking the **Proofing Status** icon on the status bar. This icon, which resembles an open book, displays a red cross when additional errors are present in a document, or a blue tick when there are no errors. The **Proofing Status** icon, however, is only visible if the **Spelling and Grammar** options have been enabled.

> You are cordially invited to view our new Exerfit products which appears in our fall Exerfit catalog.

Practice Exercise 77 - Format As You Type

1. **File** *Tab* → **New** → **Blank document.**
2. **On the first line of the document, type the following sentence, including the misspelling of the word cordially:**
   You are cordialy viewing our new Exerfit products which appear in our fall Exerfit catalog.
3. *Press Enter key after typing the text.*
4. *Right-click cordially.*
5. *Click cordially.*
   Tip: If it is not flagged as misspelled, try *Right-click → Smart Lookup.*

6. *Click* 🔲 *on the status bar.*
7. *Select Ignore All to accept the spelling of Exerfit.*
   Tip: *Notice that the second occurrence of the word no longer contains a red, wavy line.*
8. *Use the* 🔲 *Proofing Status button (located in the status bar as a book icon) to find the next error and select the appropriate replacement suggestion.* **Tip:** Notice that the grammatical error will only be found once the focus reaches the end of the sentence.
9. **Close the document:** File *Tab* → Close → Don't Save .

12.2 Adding To The Custom Dictionary

If you **Spell Check** documents that correctly contain words that do not appear in the main dictionary, you can add frequently used words to a custom dictionary.

A **Custom Dictionary** is a dictionary to which you can add words, and which is kept separate from **Microsoft Word's** main dictionary. **Microsoft Word** supplies a default custom dictionary named **CUSTOM.DIC**, but you can create as many **Custom** Dictionaries as you want. A **Custom Dictionary** can contain any word that is not in the main dictionary. For example, you might want to create a scientific dictionary containing scientific terms you use regularly or a product dictionary containing proper spellings for the products your company manufactures.

You can set the **Spell Checker** to ignore words in uppercase or that contain numbers; you can set it to ignore the Internet and file addresses and not to flag repeated words.

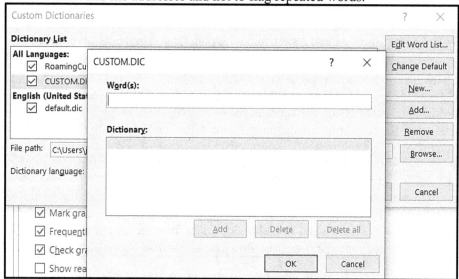

Practice Exercise 78 - Custom Dictionary

1.  $\rightarrow$ C:\Data\Word365-12\SpellingAll.docx.
2. *Type in the word "Delan."*

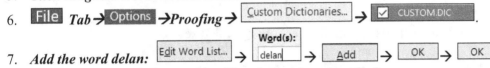

3. **File** *Tab* $\rightarrow$ Options *button* Options.
4. *Click Proofing in the left column.*
5. *Click ☑ Ignore words in UPPERCASE to deselect it.*
6. **File** *Tab* $\rightarrow$ Options $\rightarrow$ *Proofing* $\rightarrow$ Custom Dictionaries... $\rightarrow$ ☑ CUSTOM.DIC.
7. *Add the word delan:* 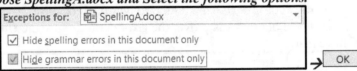.
8. *Now when you type the word it will no longer be misspelled.*

12.3 Setting Exceptions For A Document

Unless you have disabled **Check spelling as you type**, while you are working on a document the **Spelling and Grammar** checker operates in the background searching for mistakes. However, it is useful sometimes to hide the wavy underlining that marks spelling or grammar errors.

You can choose to hide spelling and grammatical errors in specific documents that are open, or in all new documents you create.

Practice Exercise 79 - Exceptions

1. **File** *Tab* $\rightarrow$ Open $\rightarrow$ Browse $\rightarrow$ C:\Data\Word365-12\SpellingAll.docx.
2. *You should now have two documents open. Make sure you are in the document C:\Data\Word365-12\SpellingA.docx. If necessary, press* Enter *key at the top of the document to display the red and green wavy underlines.*
3. **File** *Tab* $\rightarrow$ Options *button* $\rightarrow$ *Proofing.*
4. *Choose SpellingA.docx and Select the following options.*

Exceptions for:	☑ SpellingA.docx	▼
☑ Hide spelling errors in this document only		
☑ Hide grammar errors in this document only	$\rightarrow$ OK	

5. *View the effect of these changes in SpellingA.docx. Spell (red underline) and Grammar (green underline) checking is not active but Contextual spelling (blue underline) is not turned off.*

12.4 Running The Spelling Checker

You can invoke the spelling checker to **Spell-Check** a document. The spelling check proceeds from the insertion point downward. You do not need to spell-check the entire document; you can check a word, sentence, paragraph, or any selected text within a document.

A word identified as misspelled appears in the **Spelling and Grammar Dialog Box**, highlighted in red, with possible correct spellings listed in the **Suggestions** list box. There are several alternatives available when a word is identified as incorrect. You can select the correct spelling of the word in the **Suggestions** list box and use the **Change** or **Change All** buttons to change just the current occurrence or all occurrences of the misspelled word. However, if the list of possible alternative spellings in the **Suggestions** list box does not contain the correct spelling, you can type the correct spelling directly into the **Spelling and Grammar Dialog Box**. If the word is correct, you can use the **Ignore Once** or **Ignore All** buttons to disregard just the current occurrence or all occurrences of the word. Another alternative for a correctly spelled word (such as a company name or technical term) is to use the **Add to Dictionary** button to add the word to the custom dictionary.

In addition to searching for misspelled words, the spelling checker also identifies repeated words (such as **the the**). If you make a mistake during a spell-check, you can use the **Undo** button in the **Spelling and Grammar Dialog Box** to reverse the previous change.

Tip: The keyboard command to start **Spell Checking** is the **F7** key.

12.5 Running The Grammar Checker

You can invoke the **Grammar Checker** to check a document for grammatical errors. If the **Grammar Checker** finds improper grammar usage or a sentence that does not meet the selected style options, the **Spelling and Grammar Dialog Box** opens.

You do not need to **Grammar Check** an entire document; you can check a sentence, paragraph, or any selected text within a document. By default, **Microsoft Word** checks the spelling at the same time.

When text is identified with a grammatical error, the phrase or sentence containing the identified text appears in the **Spelling and Grammar Dialog Box**, with the identified text in green. Possible corrections appear in the **Suggestions** list box. After selecting a correction, you can use the **Change** button to correct the error.

If you are unsure why the **Grammar Checker** has identified the text, you can select the **Explain** button, which opens **Microsoft Word Help** with an explanation of the grammatical rule that was violated. After viewing the rule, you can correct the identified text by selecting a suggestion or by typing a correction either in the **Spelling and Grammar Dialog Box** or directly in the document itself.

If you want to keep the identified text as it is written, you can select the **Ignore Once** button to ignore just this one occurrence of the rule, the **Ignore Rule** button to ignore all occurrences of the rule in the document, or the **Next Sentence** button to skip over the error. You can use the **Undo** button to reverse any changes you have made.

File	Home	Insert	Design	Layout	References	Mailings	Review	View	Help	Grammarly	Acrobat

Tip: The keyboard command to start **Spell Checking** is the **F7** key.

12.6 Using Contextual Spelling

Contextual Grammar Errors enable **Microsoft Word** to suggest alternatives to words that may be inappropriately spelled for their context. For example, if you type "Meet me their at noon", **Microsoft Word** will apply a wavy blue underline to "their." This indicates that **Microsoft Word** has an alternative that may be **contextually** more appropriate, in this case, "there."

For this feature to be active, both the **Use Contextual Grammar Errors** and "Check Spelling as you type" options must be enabled, and the **Hide** spelling errors option must be disabled. These options are in the **Proofing** section of the **Word Options Dialog Box** which is accessed via the **Office** menu.

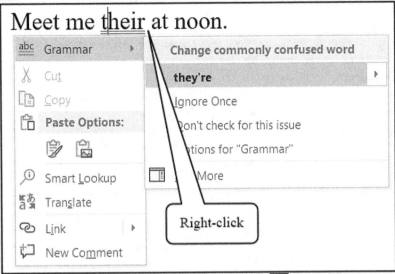

Tip: The keyboard command to begin **Spell Checking** is the F7 key.

Practice Exercise 80 - Spell, Grammar, And Context checking

1. *Make sure C:\Data\Word365-12\SpellingAll.docx is open.*
2. *Run the spelling checker to check a document for errors.*
3. *Review Ribbon Tab→Proofing Group.*
4. *Click* **abc ✓** *Spelling and Grammar.*
5. *Click govern.*
6. *Click Change.*
7. *Click Ignore All to ignore all occurrences of SportsWorld.*
8. *Double-click wrtn.*
9. *Type "written".*
10. *Click Change.*
11. *Click Delete to delete the second instance of by.*
12. *Click Add to Dictionary to add Decaton to the custom dictionary.*
13. *Click* OK .
14. *Continue checking spelling errors.*

Student Project O - Checking Spelling And Grammar

*Close the file C:\Data\Word365-12\SpellingAll.docx if it is open and reopen
C:\Data\Word365-12\SpellingAll.docx. Then, run the spell checker again.*
1. *The following are some suggestions to practice and verify.*
2. *Open the Proofing options in the Word Options Dialog Box (available in the Options menu).*
3. *Change the writing style to Grammar Only.*
4. *In the Grammar Settings Dialog Box, change the following grammar settings: under Require, always check for commas before the last list item, and check for required punctuation inside quotes; under Grammar, do not check for fragments and run-ons.*
5. *Click the Recheck Document button in Proofing to reset previously checked words in the current document.*
6. *Close the Word Options Dialog Box.*

7. *Start the Spelling and Grammar checker.*
8. *Replace the incorrect spelling of Employeees with Employees.*
9. *Ignore the spelling of Jaglom.*
10. *Capitalize Wednesday.*
11. *Pattison is spelled correctly. Ignore all occurrences of this word.*
12. *Delete the second occurrence of the word at.*
13. *Replace the grammatically incorrect an with a.*
14. *Correct the typographical error ofsteak with of steak.*
15. *Replace the incorrect spelling of salmonn with salmon.*
16. *Use Explain for information about the suggestion. Change the text by adding the comma.*
17. *Change the text by placing the punctuation inside the quotation marks.*
18. *Close the Spelling and Grammar checker.*
19. **Close the document:** File *Tab* → Close → Don't Save .

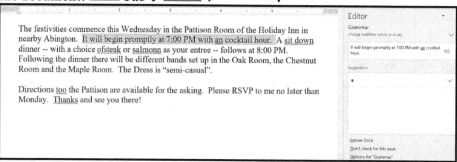

Chapter 13 - Printing

Setting up the printer to print a document is a necessary step in this process.

13.1 Previewing A Document

Before printing, you can **Preview A Document** to see how the content appears on each page. The **Print** feature displays the pages as they will appear when printed. The default view in print displays the full page, making the content difficult to read; however, you can increase the magnification of the document by using the zoom slider located in the lower right corner. This option makes the text easier to read.

If your document contains multiple pages, you can view several pages at one time. The page images are reduced as necessary to fit in the document window. The pages displayed initially depend on the zoom slider position. If the magnification is zoomed out you will see multiple pages displayed on the screen.

This feature has much different than in **Word 2007**. In all older version's it used the print preview feature which also let you zoom in and out but in a separate **Print Preview Screen.**

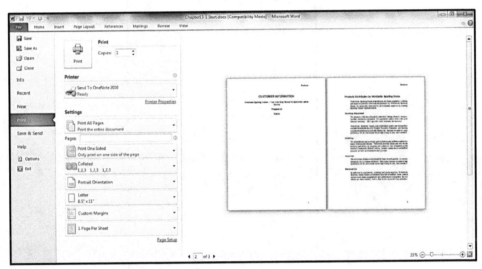

Practice Exercise 81 - Preview A Document

1. **File** *Tab* → **Open** → **Browse** → *C:\Data\Word365-12\PrintingA.docx.*
2. *Press* **Ctrl** **Home** *keys.*
3. **File** *Tab.*
4. *Point to* **Print** ▸.
   Tip: *In Word 2007 you must click Print Preview and use the mouse to magnify the image.*
5. *Use the Zoom Slider in the lower right corner to magnify the image.*
6. *Press* **PgDn** *or* **PgUp** *key to move through the document.*
7. *Click the Home Ribbon Tab to continue editing the document.*
8. ☒ *Close Print Preview*

Tip: *In Word 2007/2010, you must close the Print Preview screen* .

13.2 Printing Options

When **Printing** a document, you can choose different options to print. The following will outline those options.

Print Copies - You can specify the number of copies you wish to **Print**.

Printer - Specify the printer you wish to print to.

Printer Properties - You can change the characteristics of the printed page. For example, a color printer will allow color-related options and a Black/White Laser printer will only allow you to change the grayscale of the printed output.

Settings/Print all pages - Will print the entire document.

Settings/Page - Will allow you to print the specified page, you can also specify a page range to print. Individual pages are separated by a comma (,) and page ranges by a dash (-). The page range **4,6,8-10** prints page 4, page 6, and pages 8, 9, and 10.

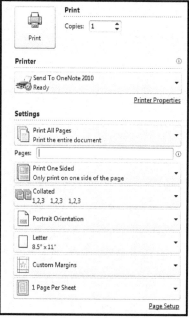

Settings/Print One-Sided - You can print both sides of the paper if your printer supports that feature.

Settings/Collated - If you are printing multiple copies you can print to keep all the Page 1 together or keep the entire document together printed multiple times.

Settings/Portrait - You can change the orientation from Portrait to Landscape.

Settings/Letter - You can change the different paper types depending on the size of the paper used.

Settings/Custom Margin - This will allow you to change the margin if the document does not fit on the printed paper properly.

Settings/1 page per sheet - You can force multiple pages on a single sheet to save paper and reduce the document size. The default is 1 Page per sheet.

Page Setup - This is the same dialog box used in **Word 2007** and provides many of the options listed above but from a dialog box popup.

Practice Exercise 82 - Print Options

1. **File** *Tab →Print.*
2. *Orientation →Landscape.*

3. *Review the changes in the Print Preview on the right side of the screen.*
4. *Custom Margins →Narrow Margins.*
5. *Review the changes in the Print Preview on the right side of the screen.*
6. *If you press the print button on the top it will print the document. Do not press the print button at this time unless you want a hard paper copy of the exercise.*
7. **Close the document:** `File` *Tab →* `Close` → `Don't Save` .

13.3 Printing Envelopes And Labels

Microsoft Word makes it simple to address and **Print Envelopes And Labels**. The procedures for creating envelopes and labels are similar, and both are completed in the **Envelopes And Labels Dialog Box**. The primary difference is that you have fewer options when creating labels. With envelopes, you have separate delivery and return address boxes; with labels, you have a single address entry box. Envelopes can also be added to the current document; labels can only be created in a new document.

Envelopes and labels are available in a multitude of sizes. **Envelope And Label** sizes supported by **Microsoft Word** are listed first by printer type, then by label product, and then by product number. These options are listed in the **Envelope Options And Label Options Dialog Boxes**. If the available sizes do not meet your particular needs, you can create an envelope or label it in a custom size, for which you define the width and height.

How you feed an envelope into the printer is specific to the printer. **Microsoft Word** selects a feed method based upon the selected envelope size and printer. If necessary, however, you can select a different method in order to print the envelope properly.

If a document is open, **Microsoft Word** tries to find the delivery address. If it does not find a delivery address, you must enter it yourself.

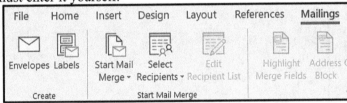

Practice Exercise 83 - Print Envelops

1. `File` *Tab→* `Open` → `Browse` *→C:\Data\Word365-12\PrintingB.docx.*
2. *Mailings Ribbon Tab →Create Group.*
3. *Click Envelops* ✉.
4. *Click the Envelopes tab, if necessary.*
5. *Click in the Return address box.*
6. *Type the return address as follows:*
   Mike's Sporting Goods
   1234 Leisure Drive
   Media, PA 19107
7. *Click Options.*
8. *Click the Envelope Options tab, if necessary.*
9. *Click Envelope size* ▾.
10. *Click Size 10 (4 1/8 x 9 1/2 in)*
11. *Click* `OK` .
12. *Click Add to Document.*

13. *Click No.*
14. **Close the document:** File *Tab* → Close → Don't Save .

Student Project P - Printing

1. File *Tab* → Open → 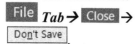 Browse → *C:\Data\Word365-12\PrintingC Practice1.docx.*
2. *Preview the document, changing to the Two Pages layout by zooming in using the Zoom Slider.*
3. *Magnify the top of page 2.*

4. *Close the Print layout by clicking on the* ← *icon.*
5. *Print two copies of the second page of the document.*
6. *Address a standard size 10 envelope to the following address:*
   Ms. Nancy Smith
   Northeast Region
   P.O. Box 5567
   Hartford, CT 095547
7. *Enter your name and home address as the return address.*
8. *Add the envelope to the document. Do not save the return address as the default.*
9. **Close the document:**
   File *Tab* → Close →
   Don't Save .

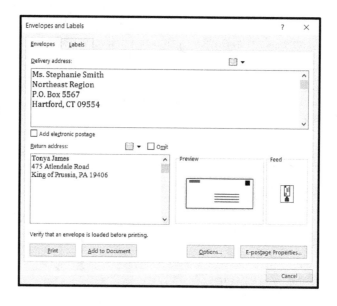

Chapter 14 - Secure Documents

Some Microsoft Word documents need to be secured in order to prevent access to information. Here, we will discuss several ways to secure a document.

Practice Exercise 84 - Open Salary Review

*File Tab → **Open** → Browse → C:\Data\Word365-12\Salary Review.Docx.*

*File Tab → **Save As** → C:\Data\Word365-12\My Salary Review.Docx.*

14.1 Password To Open

This will prevent someone from opening the file by requiring a **Password**.

Practice Exercise 85 - Open Password

Continue from the previous practice exercise.

1. **Set the open password:** *File Tab → **Save As** → Browse → Tools → General Options →*
   Password to Open: xxx → **OK** → **Confirm Password:** xxx → **OK** → **Save**.
2. **Close the file:** *File Tab → **Close**.*
3. **Open it to see the Password Dialog Box:**
   *File Tab → **Open** → Browse → C:\Data\Word365-12\My Salary Review.Docx.*

4. **Remove previous settings:** *File Tab → **Save As** → Browse → Tools →*
   *General Options → Password to Open: (Remove Password) → **OK** → **Save***

14.2 Protect Document

This is another way to set an open password. It accomplishes the same as "**Password To Open.**"

Practice Exercise 86 - Protect Document

Continue from the previous practice exercise.

1. *File Tab→Info→* [🔒] *Protect Document→* [🔒] *Encrypt with Password.*
2. *File Tab→* `Save As` *→ C:\Data\Word365-12\My Salary Review.Docx→* `Save`.
3. *File Tab→* `Close` *→File Tab→* `📂 Open` *→ Browse→*
   C:\Data\Word365-12\My Salary Review.Docx.

14.3 Password To Modify

This will require a **Password** to **Modify** the document. If you do not know the **Password**, you can open the file in read-only mode. At this point, you can make changes to the file but you cannot save the file to the original file name.

> General Options
>
> File encryption options for this document
>
> Password to open: [   ]
>
> File sharing options for this document
>
> Password to modify: [•••]
>
> ☐ Read-only recommended

Practice Exercise 87 - Modify Password

Continue from the previous practice exercise.
1. Set **Password** to **Modify**.

   File Tab→ `Save As` *→Browse→ Tools →General Options→ (Remove previous settings)*
   →Password to Modify: xxx→ `OK` *→* `Save`.

> Password   ?   ×
>
> 'My Salary Review.docx' is reserved by
>
> Enter password to modify, or open read only.
>
> Password: [•••]
>
> [Read Only]   [OK]   [Cancel]

2. **Test it: Close the file then, open it to see the Password Dialog Box:** *File Tab→* `Close`.
3. *File Tab→* `📂 Open` *→ Browse→*
   C:\Data\Word365-12\My Salary Review.Docx→ Password: xxx→ `OK`.

14.4 Read-Only Recommended

You don't have to set the **Password** to use this feature. It will give you the following prompt:

> Microsoft Word   ×
>
> ? The author would like you to open this as read-only, unless you need to make changes. Open as read-only?
>
> [Yes]   [No]   [Cancel]

Practice Exercise 88 - Read-Only

Continue from the previous practice exercise.
1. *File Tab→* `Save As` *→Browse→Tools →*
   General Options →(Remove previous settings)→
   ☑ *Read-only recommended→* `OK` *→* `Save`.

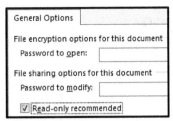

2. **Close the file and then open it to see the Prompt:**

2a. *File Tab →* Close.

2b. *File Tab →* Open *→ Browse →C:\Data\Word365-12\My Salary Review.Docx.*

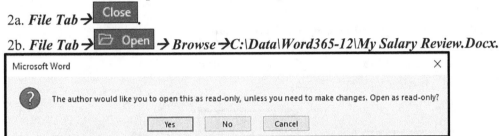

If you choose **Yes**, you will be able to modify the file, but you will not be able to save it to the same file name. If you choose **No**, you will be able to modify the file and save it to the original file.

3. **Remove Read-Only:** *File Tab →* Save As *→Browse →Tools →*
General Options → ☐ Read-only recommended *→* OK *→* Save.

14.5 Mark As Final

This will **Mark** the file **As Final**. When opened, you will receive the following message:

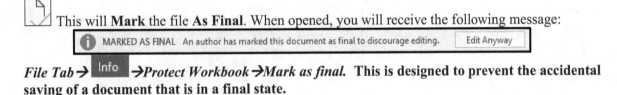

File Tab → Info *→Protect Workbook →Mark as final.* **This is designed to prevent the accidental saving of a document that is in a final state.**

Practice Exercise 89 - Mark As Final

Continue from the previous practice exercise.

1. *File Tab →* Protect Document *→Mark as final →* OK.
2. **The following menu appears when you Mark a document as Final:**

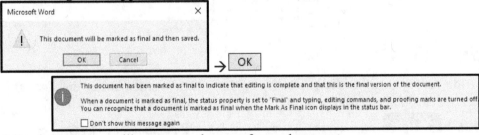

The following message will appear on the top of your document:

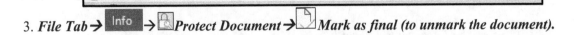

3. *File Tab →* Info *→ Protect Document →Mark as final (to unmark the document).*

14.6 Editing Restriction

This Sets Formatting **and** Editing Restrictions.

1. *File Tab→* Open *→Browse→ C:\Data\Word365-12\Highlights.Docx→* Open .
2. *File Tab→* Info *→*Protect document*→*
   Restrict Editing:
   ✓*Allow only this type of editing in the document.*
   Exceptions: *No Changes (Read-Only)*
   Start Enforcement: *Yes, Start enforcing protection*
3. **Click on the button:** Yes, Start Enforcing Protection
4. **Enter Password:**

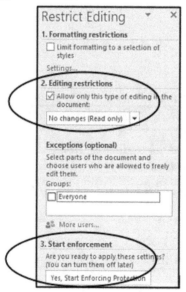

Test It: *Test by deleting text.*

14.7 Hiding Text

This will **Hide Text** that can be used to identify the document, describe information, or define a source location for a graphic image.

1. *File Tab→* Open *→Browse→C:\Data\Word365-12\Stockholder Insert.Docx→* Open .
2. *Select Heading "To Our Stockholders."*
3. *Home Ribbon Tab→Font Group→ Font Dialog Box →Font Tab→Effects→ ✓ Hidden→* OK .
4. **Test it:** *Select the Paragraph and set it to hidden.*
5. *File Print to see if it is Hidden.*
6. **Unhide:** *Select Text near the Hidden area→Home Ribbon Tab→*

7. *Font Group→Font Dialog Box* ▣*→Font Tab→ Effects→* ☐̲Hidden̲*→* ⟨ OK ⟩.

14.8 Document Properties

This will show the **Properties** of the **Document**.
File Tab→Info →Properties→Advanced Properties.

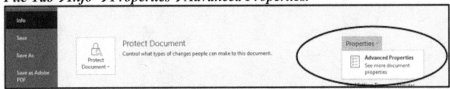

14.9 Document Inspector

This will remove personal information from the hidden locations of a file.

File Tab →Info → *Check for Issues →* *Inspect Document→* ⟨Reinspect⟩.

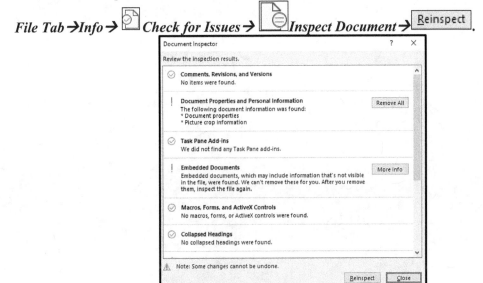

Chapter 15 - Tables

Tables can be used to organize your information to better understand the data entered.

15.1 Creating A Table

It is often useful to place information from your documents into a **Table** format. For example, an employee phone list is usually easier to read on a **Table**.

You can navigate a **Table** using the mouse or the keyboard. Using the mouse, just click on the desired cell. Using the keyboard, press the **Tab** key or **Arrow** keys. If there is text in the next cell and you press the **Tab** key, the text will be selected. If there is text in an adjacent cell and you use **Arrow** keys to access it, the text will not be selected. If you press the **Tab** key when the insertion point is in the last cell of the **Table**, **Microsoft Word** inserts a new row below the current row.

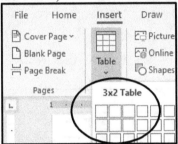

Practice Exercise 90 - Create Table

1. *Create a new, blank document.*
2. *Click Insert Ribbon Tab →Tables Group →Click Table Button.*
3. *Drag to create a 3x3 Table.*
4. *Click in the cell you want to select.*
5. *Press* **Tab** *key to move to the next cell.*
6. *Press* **Shift** **Tab** *keys to move to the previous cell.*
7. *Press* **Down Arrow** *key ↓ to move down one cell.*
8. *Press* **Right Arrow** *key → to move right one cell.*
9. *Press* **Left Arrow** *key ← to move left one cell.*
10. *Press* **Up Arrow** *key ↑ to move up one cell.*

15.2 Entering Text Into A Table

When creating a **Table**, the insertion point appears in the first cell of the **Table** by default. This makes it possible to immediately begin typing text into the **Table**.

Practice Exercise 91 - Entering Text In Table

Continue from the previous practice exercise.
1. *Click in the top-left cell, if necessary →Type Regional Office*
2. *Type the following text into the Table. To move from cell to cell, press* **Tab** *key or use the mouse.*

Regional Office
Office Manager
Phone Number
Northeast
Nancy J. Smith
610-555-1234
Southeast
Nathan T. Brown
404-321-8563

3. *Press* `Ctrl` `Home` *keys →Press* `Enter` *key (this will insert a blank line above the Table)*
4. *Type the heading text Regional Office Phone List and press* `Enter` *key. Then bold, center, and italicize the heading text.*
5. *Click outside of the Table, on the left side Row 1.*
    Note: Look for the white arrow ⇗ on the left.

6. *The row should be selected.*
7. *Press Bold and Center formatting.*

Regional Office Phone List		
Regional Office	**Office Manager**	**Phone Number**
Northeast	Nancy J. Smith	610-555-1234
Southeast	Nathan T. Brown	404-321-8563

15.3 Using Table Styles

Microsoft Word's built-in **Table Styles** provide many combinations of shading and borders to make the **Table** easier to view as well as to add a more finished, professional look. As soon as an existing **Table** is selected or the insertion point is positioned within an existing **Table**, the **Table Tools Design** and **Layout** tabs are added to the **Ribbon**.

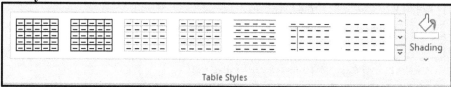

Practice Exercise 92 - Table Styles

Continue from the previous practice exercise.
1. *Click anywhere in the Table →Click Table Design Ribbon Tab.*
2. *Hover the pointer over any Table Style Button in the Table Styles Group.*
3. *Click the Down Arrow* ⊽ *to see more tab styles.*
4. *Choose the desired style.*

Regional Office Phone List		
Regional Office	Office Manager	Phone Number
Northeast	Nancy J. Smith	610-555-1234
Southeast	Nathan T. Brown	404-321-8563

5. *Click on the Table again and open the Table Styles gallery. Apply the Plain Tables Table Grid to the Table (located on the top of the Styles gallery). Notice that all Table formatting has been removed.*

Regional Office Phone List		
Regional Office	**Office Manager**	**Phone Number**
Northeast	Nancy J. Smith	610-555-1234
Southeast	Nathan T. Brown	404-321-8563

15.4 Convert To Text

You can easily convert an existing **Table** to **Text**. You don't need to select a **Table** in order to use the command.

Practice Exercise 93 - Convert To Text

This will apply another conversion option is to convert the table to text.
Continue from the previous practice exercise.
1. ***Click anywhere in the Table.***
2. ***Layout Ribbon Tab(located on the right side of the ribbon)*** ➔
   Data Group ➔ Convert to Text ➔*Click* ⊙Tabs, *if necessary* ➔ OK .

Regional Office Phone List		
Regional Office	**Office Manager**	**Phone Number**
Northeast	Nancy J. Smith	610-555-1234
Southeast	Nathan T. Brown	404-321-8563

15.5 Converting Existing Text Into A Table

You can easily create a **Table** from the existing text in a document. The **Convert Text to Table Dialog Box** allows you to select the number of columns you want on the **Table**.

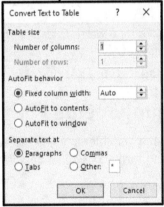

Practice Exercise 94 - Convert Text To Table

Continue from the previous practice exercise.
1. ***Select the Table, if necessary.***

Regional Office Phone List		
Regional Office	**Office Manager**	**Phone Number**
Northeast	Nancy J. Smith	610-555-1234
Southeast	Nathan T. Brown	404-321-8563

2. ***Insert Ribbon Tab*** ➔***Tables Group*** ➔***Table dropdown button*** ➔ Convert Text to Table...
   ➔ ***Choose the defaults*** ➔ OK .

15.6 Inserting Quick Tables

In addition to **Microsoft Word's** built-in **Table** styles, **Microsoft Word** also provides several **Quick Tables**. These are ready-formatted **Table** types for particular styles of **Tables**, including calendar month, matrix, and tabular list.

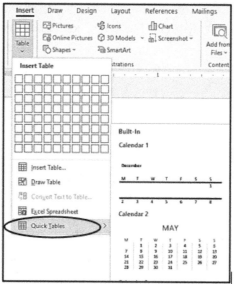

Practice Exercise 95 - Quick Tables

This will insert a **Quick Table.** If necessary, create a new, blank document.
1. ***Open a new blank document.***

2. ***Click Insert Ribbon Tab → Click Table Button*** **→ *Point to* Quick Tables → Scroll as necessary and click the Matrix Quick Table.***

3. **Close the document without saving it:** *File Tab →* Close *→* Don't Save.

15.7 Selecting Table Components

You can **Select** a single **Table** cell, row, or column using the mouse. You might want to **Select** a single cell, row, or column in order to format or edit its contents.

Practice Exercise 96 - Table Components

1. ***File Tab →*** Open ***→ Browse → C:\Data\Word365-12\Table Selecting.Docx.***
2. ***Select a Table cell, row, and column.***
3. ***Display the Table gridlines, if necessary:*** *Layout Ribbon Tab → Table Group →* ***View Gridlines.***
4. ***Click to the left of the text 125 lbs. (third row, second column).***

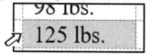

5. ***Click to the left of the Exer-Fit Stepper row.***

Life-Fit 1000 Stepper		
Exer-Fit Stepper	85 lbs.	TM55305

6. *Click above the Product column and look for the black down arrow ( ).*

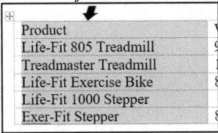

7. *Click anywhere in the middle of the Table.*
8. *Layout Ribbon Tab→Tables Group→View Gridlines.*
9. *Click anywhere in the document to deselect the cells.*

15.8 Inserting Rows And Columns Into A Table

You can **Insert A Row** above or below the current row or a column to the left or right of the current column. You can also add multiple rows or columns by first selecting the same number of rows or columns you want to add and then **Inserting the Rows or Columns.**

Practice Exercise 97 - Insert Below Insert Left

1. *Click on the Product cell→Click Layout Ribbon Tab→Rows & Columns Group→Click Insert Below   .*
2. *Click anywhere in the document.*
3. *Click on the Product cell. → Click Insert Left   .*

	Product		Weight	Order Number
	Life-Fit 805 Treadmill		98 lbs.	TM55805
	Treadmaster Treadmill		125 lbs.	TM55101
	Life-Fit Exercise Bike		89 lbs.	TM55205
	Life-Fit 1000 Stepper			
	Exer-Fit Stepper		85 lbs.	TM55305

4. *Click anywhere in the document.*
5. *Click on the Product cell and insert a row above the first row.*
6. *Click anywhere in the document to deselect the new row.*
7. *Press the keyboard* $\boxed{\text{Ctrl}}$ $\boxed{\text{Z}}$ *keys several times to test out the concept again.*

15.9 Merging Cells

You can **Merge** two or more adjacent cells into a single cell. You may want to **Merge Cells**, for example, to create a **Table** heading by spanning text in one cell across the entire **Table**.

Practice Exercise 98 - Merge Cells

This will select all the cells in the first column.

1. *Click Layout Ribbon Tab → Merge Group → Click Merge Cells*
2. *Type Equipment Catalog in the merged cell.*
3.
4. *Type Excel Sporting Goods in the cell above the Product cell. Then select the Excel Sporting Goods cell and the two blank cells to the right and merge the cells.*

5. *Bold the text Equipment Catalog and Excel Sporting Goods.*
6. *Center Excel Sporting Goods.*

Equipment Catalog	Excel Sporting Goods		
	Product	Weight	Order Number
	Life-Fit 805 Treadmill	98 lbs.	TM55805
	Treadmaster Treadmill	125 lbs.	TM55101
	Life-Fit Exercise Bike	89 lbs.	TM55205
	Life-Fit 1000 Stepper		
	Exer-Fit Stepper	85 lbs.	TM55305

15.10 Rotating Text In A Table

You can **Rotate** text in **Table** cells. This option allows you to create special effects. For example, you can change the orientation of long labels so that they fit within the **Table**.

Practice Exercise 99 - Rotating Text

This will **Rotate** text in a **Table**.
1. *Click on the Equipment Catalog cell.*
2. *Click Layout Ribbon Tab →Alignment Group →.*

3. Click Text Direction ⊡ twice.

Equipment Catalog	Excel Sporting Goods		
	Product	Weight	Order Number
	Life-Fit 805 Treadmill	98 lbs.	TM55805
	Treadmaster Treadmill	125 lbs.	TM55101
	Life-Fit Exercise Bike	89 lbs.	TM55205
	Life-Fit 1000 Stepper		
	Exer-Fit Stepper	85 lbs.	TM55305

15.11 Changing Column Width And Row Height

You can quickly adjust the **Width** of any **Table Column** by dragging its column border to the desired width. You can adjust as many columns in a **Table** as desired, although adjusting the width of any one column (except the last) does not affect the overall width of the **Table**. If you hold the **Alt** key as you drag a column or row border, the exact column or row measurement appears on the corresponding ruler. You can also change **Column Width** by dragging the **Table** column markers on the horizontal ruler.

Practice Exercise 100 - Change Widths

This will change the column width and row height. If necessary, switch to **Print Layout View**, and display the horizontal and vertical rulers.
1. *Drag the column border to the right of the text Equipment Catalog to the 1-1/2 inch mark on the horizontal ruler.*
2. *Drag the row border below the text Excel Sporting Goods down to the 3/4 inch mark on the vertical ruler.*
3. *Hold* **Alt** *key and click the column border to the right of the Equipment Catalog column. Continue holding* **Alt** *key and drag the column border until a column measurement of 1" appears on the horizontal ruler. Note: Watch the horizontal border.*

Equipment Catalog	Excel Sporting Goods		
	Product	Weight	Order Number
	Life-Fit 805 Treadmill	98 lbs.	TM55805
	Treadmaster Treadmill	125 lbs.	TM55101
	Life-Fit Exercise Bike	89 lbs.	TM55205
	Life-Fit 1000 Stepper		
	Exer-Fit Stepper	85 lbs.	TM55305

15.12 Distributing Rows And Columns Evenly

Although you can individually size each cell, row, and column in a **Table**, you may decide that a **Table** would look better if all the rows or columns were the same size.

Practice Exercise 101 - Distribute

1.   *Select by dragging from the Product cell to the TM55305 cell*
2.   *Click Layout Ribbon Tab →Alignment Group→Click Distribute Columns*
3.   *Click anywhere in the document to deselect the cells.*

Equipment Catalog	Excel Sporting Goods		
	Product	Weight	Order Number
	Life-Fit 805 Treadmill	98 lbs.	TM55805
	Treadmaster Treadmill	125 lbs.	TM55101
	Life-Fit Exercise Bike	89 lbs.	TM55205
	Life-Fit 1000 Stepper		
	Exer-Fit Stepper	85 lbs.	TM55305

15.13 Splitting Cells

You can **Split Cells** to break a single cell or group of cells into a larger number of cells. **Splitting Cells** is the opposite of merging cells. Instead of creating a single cell from multiple cells, you are creating multiple cells from a single cell.

Practice Exercise 102 - Splitting Cells

1.   *Drag to select the Life-Fit 1000 Stepper cell and the blank cell to its right.*
2.   *Click Layout Ribbon Tab →Alignment Group→Click Split Cells*
3.   *Click the Number of columns* ▲▼ *to 3. → Click* OK .
4.   *Click anywhere in the document to deselect the split cells. Notice that the new cells are sized consistently with the existing columns of cells.*
5.   *Type 99 lbs. in the blank cell in the Weight column and TM55545 in the blank cell in the Order Number column.*

Excel Sporting Goods		
Product	Weight	Order Number
Life-Fit 805 Treadmill	98 lbs.	TM55805
Treadmaster Treadmill	125 lbs.	TM55101
Life-Fit Exercise Bike	89 lbs.	TM55205
Life-Fit 1000 Stepper	99 lbs.	TM55545
Exer-Fit Stepper	85 lbs.	TM55305

(Equipment Catalog — vertical label)

15.14 Deleting Columns And Rows

You can **Delete** any **Rows** and/or **Columns** you no longer need in a **Table**. **Deleting** a **Column** or **Row** deletes not only the column or row but also all the contents of it.

Practice Exercise 103 - Delete Columns/Rows

1. *Click on the Equipment Catalog cell.*

2. *Click Layout Ribbon Tab → Rows & Columns Group → Click Delete* *→ Click Delete Columns.*

Excel Sporting Goods		
Product	Weight	Order Number
Life-Fit 805 Treadmill	98 lbs.	TM55805
Treadmaster Treadmill	125 lbs.	TM55101
Life-Fit Exercise Bike	89 lbs.	TM55205
Life-Fit 1000 Stepper	99 lbs.	TM55545
Exer-Fit Stepper	85 lbs.	TM55305

3. *Select the blank row below the Product cell and use the shortcut menu to delete the blank row.*

15.15 Setting Table Properties

When you create a **Table**, **Microsoft Word** sets certain defaults for the **Table** and the **Table** cells. You can customize the **Table** by changing **Table** settings to override these defaults. The options available in the **Table Properties Dialog Box** is listed in the following **Tables**:

Table Options

Preferred Width - Sets the **Width** of the entire **Table** to a specific measurement in inches or a percentage of the page width.

Alignment Controls the **Alignment** of the **Table** on the page; can be used to center, right, or left align a **Table**.

Indent From Left - Controls the Indent of the **Table** from the left margin; available only when the **Left Alignment** option is selected.

Text Wrapping - Controls the placement of text around a **Table**; when the **Around** option is selected, you can use the **Positioning Button** to specify the exact **Table** position, the distance between the text and the **Table**, and **Table** movement options.

Borders And Shading - Opens the **Borders** and **Shading Dialog Box**, in which you can change **Border** options and apply or modify **Shading**.

Options - Opens the **Table Options Dialog Box**, which allows you to set the default margins between text and cell borders for all cells in the **Table**, set the default spacing between cells, and set the **Table** to resize automatically to fit its contents.

Row Options

Specify Height - Sets the **Height** of the selected row to a specific or minimum height in inches; use the **Previous Row** and **Next Row Buttons** to select adjacent rows.

Allow Row To Break Across Pages - Allows a **Row** to be **Split Across** a **Page Break**; to prevent rows from breaking, deselect this option.

Repeat Header Row at the Top of Each Page - Sets the top row or rows in a **Table** as a header that **Repeats** at the top of the **Table** on each page; header rows make long **Tables** spanning multiple pages easier to read.

Column Options

Preferred Width - Sets the **Width** of the selected column(s) to a specific measurement in inches or a percentage of the **Table** width; use the **Previous Column** and **Next Column Buttons** to select adjacent columns.

Cell Options

Preferred Width - Sets the **Width** of the selected cell to a specific measurement in inches or a percent of the **Table** width.

Vertical Alignment - Controls the **Alignment** of text within a cell; use this option to align text to the top, center, or bottom of a cell.

Options - Opens the **Cell Options Dialog Box**, which allows you to set the margins within a cell, have text wrap within a cell, or allows **Microsoft Word** to size text to fit within a cell.

Practice Exercise 104 - Properties

1. ***Click on the Excel Sporting Goods cell→Click Layout Ribbon Tab →Tables Group→Click Properties***
2. ***Click the Table tab, if necessary→ Click Preferred width, if necessary.***
3. ***Enter 6 in the Preferred width spin box and Inches in the Measure box, if necessary. Select the Center option under Alignment → Click OK.***
4. ***Display the Reveal Formatting task pane Shift F1 keys. Click in the Table and expand the Table and Cell sections in the task pane, if necessary.***

5. *Select rows 2 to 8 (from the Product row to the end of the Table) →Properties Display the Row page in the Table Properties Dialog Box and set the row height to .5.*
6. *Switch to Print (File Tab→Print) and view the changes.*
7. *Close by selecting Home Ribbon Tab.*

15.16 Creating A Table Heading

You can **Create** a **Table Heading** that appears on multiple pages. For example, if your **Table** extends to two or more pages, you might want to have your column headings repeat at the top of each page.

Practice Exercise 105 - Table Headings

1. *File Tab→* Open *→ Browse → C:\Data\Word365-12\Table Heading.Docx.*
2. *Create a Table heading. If necessary, switch to Print Layout View. Print View and review page 2 and notice the there are no headers on the top row.*
3. *Select the top two rows of the Table.*
4. *Click Layout Ribbon Tab → Data Group →Click Repeat Header Rows* ⊞.
5. *Switch to Print View and select the Two Pages View. Notice that the Table heading appears on each page. (File Tab →Print →Choose the - in the zoom slider in the lower right corner)*
6. *Close the document without saving it: File Tab →* Close *→* Don't Save.

15.17 Sorting A Table Alphabetically

Tables are frequently used to list items that need to be **Sorted**. You can use the **Sort** feature to organize information in a **Table**. The **Sort** feature can sort by text, dates, and numbers. The column can be **Sorted** in ascending order (A to Z) or in descending order (Z to A). You can **Sort** on up to three columns and you can specify in what order the **Sort** should be performed. If you create column headings in the first row of the **Table**, you can specify the column heading rather than the column number when you **Sort** the **Table**.

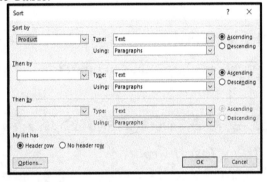

Practice Exercise 106 - Sorting

1. *File Tab →* Open *→ Browse → C:\Data\Word365-12\Table Sort.Docx.*
2. *Click anywhere in the Table, if necessary.*
3. *Click Layout Ribbon Tab →Data Group →.*
4. *Click Sort* A Z↓ *→Click* ○ *Header row, if necessary.*
5. *Click Sort by* ▾ *→Click Product.*
6. *Click Type* ▾ *→Click Text →Click* ○ *Ascending, if necessary.*
7. *Click* OK.
8. *Click anywhere in the document to deselect the Table. Notice that the items in the Table are sorted alphabetically by the Product column.*
9. *Click anywhere in the Table.*
10. *Click Layout Ribbon Tab →Data Group →Click Sort* A Z↓ *→Click* ○ *Header row, if necessary.*
11. *Click Sort by* ▾ *→Click Retail Price →Click* ○ *Ascending, if necessary.*

12. *Click the first Then by* ⌄ →*Click Release Date→Click* ◯ *Descending.*
13. *Click the second Then by* ⌄ →*Click Product→Click* ◯ *Ascending, if necessary.*
14. *Click* OK .
15. **Close the document without saving it:** *File Tab→* Close →Don't Save .

15.18 Border Painter

This will allow you to **Paint** the **Border** from an existing border.

Practice Exercise 107 - Border Painter

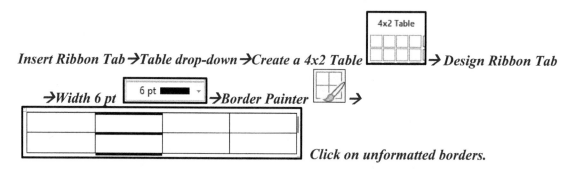

Insert Ribbon Tab →Table drop-down →Create a 4x2 Table → *Design Ribbon Tab*

→*Width 6 pt* 6 pt ▬ →*Border Painter* →

Click on unformatted borders.

15.19 Table Insert Control

When you move the cursor to the left of the **Table**, an **Insert Control** will appear.

Click on the **Plus Sign** to insert a new row.

Practice Exercise 108 - Table Insert Control

Insert Ribbon Tab →Table drop-down →Create a 4x2 Table →
Move the cursor to the front of the Table to see the + bubble appear.

Student Project Q - Working with Tables

1. *If necessary, create a new, blank document.*
2. **Show the paragraph marks:**
   Home Ribbon Tab→Paragraph Group→ ¶ *Show Paragraph Marks.*
3. **Use the Table Button in the Tables Group to insert the Quick Table Tabular List:**
   Insert Ribbon Tab →Table Button→ ▦*Quick Tables →Tabular List.*
4. **Overwrite the existing entries with the following text, using either the mouse or the keyboard to move from cell to cell:**
   Double click in the first box (top row left column →Delete the word Item→
   Type: Representative→ Tab *key→Continue typing the data in the example.*
5. **Delete the six rows that are not needed:**
   Select the column with the word Notebook→Select to the end of the Table→
   Layout Ribbon Tab → Rows & Columns Group→ ▦*Delete Button→*

⊟ˣ *Delete Rows.*

Representative	Clothing Line
Nancy J. Smith	Gymnastics
Nathan T. Brown	Martial Arts

6. **Insert two blank lines above the Table and type the title:**

   6a. *Click in front of the R in Representative →Press the* Enter *key →*
   Press the Enter *key →Type: Presentation Assignments.*

   6b. *Select Presentation Assignments →Home Ribbon Tab → Choose* **B** *Bold*
   and ≡ *Center the title.*

   6c. *Select the Table →Home Ribbon Tab →* ≡ *Center the Table.*

Presentation Assignments

Representative	Clothing Line
Nancy J. Smith	Gymnastics
Nathan T. Brown	Martial Arts

7. **Choose the desired Table Styles to reformat the Table:** *Click inside the Table →Design Ribbon Tab →Table Styles Group →Click the down arrow to the lower right of the Table Styles →Choose the desired Table style.*

Presentation Assignments

Representative	Clothing Line
Nancy J. Smith	Gymnastics
Nathan T. Brown	Martial Arts

8. **Use the Table Styles gallery to remove all Table formatting:** *Click inside the Table →Design Ribbon Tab →Table Styles Group →Click the* ▾ *down arrow to the lower right of the Table Style Group →Select* 🗑 *Clear.*

Representative	Clothing Line
Nancy J. Smith	Gymnastics
Nathan T. Brown	Martial Arts

9. **Use the View Gridlines Button in the Table Group to show Table gridlines.** *Click inside the Table →Layout Ribbon Tab →Table Group →*
   Click ⊞ *View Gridlines.*

10. *The following is an example of the result:*

Presentation Assignments

Representative	Clothing Line
Nancy J. Smith	Gymnastics
Nathan T. Brown	Martial Arts

11. **Close the document without saving it:** *File Tab →* Close *→* Don't Save .

Student Project R - Convert a Table

1. *File Tab →* 📂 Open *→ Browse →C:\Data\Word365-12\Table Convert Practice2.Docx.*
2. *Select the contents of the entire document.*
   Select the text by dragging using the mouse.

3. **Convert the selected text into a table:**
    Select the Text→Insert Ribbon Tab→Table→Convert Text To Table.
4. *Use two columns and eight rows. Leave the default behavior to Auto.*
    Separate the text at: ☑ *Tab*
    Number of columns: 2→Number of rows: 8→
    ☑ *Fixed column width: Auto→Separate text at:* ☑ *Tabs.*

5. *Deselect the text to view the Table.*
    Click outside the Table.
6. *Hide the formatting marks and close all documents without saving them.*

    Home Ribbon Tab→Paragraph Group→Show/Hide formatting marks ¶ .
7. *The following is an example of the result:*

Name	Phone Extensions
Adams, George W.	301
Adams, Stephen	656
Adelson, Troy	395
Anderson, Pamela	543
Bates, Norman	911
Boomer, Steve	789
Brown, Nathan T.	654

8. **Close the document without saving it:** *File Tab →* Close *→* Don't Save .

Student Project S - Editing a Table

1. *File Tab→* **Open** *→Browse→C:\Data\Word365-12\Table Edit Practice3.Docx.*
2. **If necessary, switch to Print Layout View:**
   View Ribbon Tab→Views Group→Print Layout View.
3. **Zoom to 75%:**
   View Ribbon Tab→ Zoom Button→ ● 75% checkbox→ **OK**
4. *Rotate the Excel Sporting Goods text so that it is vertical and oriented from bottom to top.*

   Select Excel Sporting Goods →Layout Ribbon Tab→Alignment Group→ Text Direction

   Button→ Text direction Button.
5. **Split it into 1 column and 42 rows:**

   Select the Excel Sporting Goods column→Layout Ribbon Tab→Merge Group→ Split

   Cells Button→Column: 1, Rows:42→ **OK** *.*

6. **Delete the Excel Sporting Goods column:**

   Select the "Excel Sporting Goods" column→Rows & Columns Group→ Delete Button→

   Delete Columns option.
7. **Make the Table 6 inches wide and centered:**

   Click inside the Table→Layout Ribbon Tab→Table Group→ Properties Button→Preferred

   width: 6 inches →Click the Alignment: Center Button→ **OK** *.*

8. *Change the width of the Name column to 4.7 inches and the Phone Extensions column to 1*
   inch. (Note: Try holding the Alt *key and dragging the border between the columns.)*
   Select the entire name column→click the line between the Name column and the Phone
   Extensions column→hold the Alt *key down→drag using the mouse.*

Corporate Phone List	
Eastern Region	
Name	Phone Extensions
Adams, George W.	301
Adams, Stephen	656

9. *Add a row above the Corporate Phone List row and type Excel Sporting Goods into it.*

Select top row→Layout Ribbon Tab→ Rows & Columns Group→ ⬛ *Insert Above Button→Type: Excel Sporting Goods.*

Excel Sporting Goods
Corporate Phone List

10. *Delete the Eastern Region row.*

Select the Eastern Region row→Layout Ribbon Tab→ Rows & Columns Group→ ⬛ *Delete Button→* ⬛ *Delete Rows Button.*

11. **Center the merged top 2 rows both horizontally and vertically:**

Select the top 2 rows→Layout Ribbon Tab→Merge Group→ ⬛ *Merge cells Button.*

Excel Sporting Goods Corporate Phone List	
Name	Phone Extensions

12. *Drag to decrease the merged cell's row height to approximately 0.7 inches. (Hint: hold the* [Alt] *key down while dragging the row up)*

Select the top row→click the line below the selected text box→hold the [Alt] *key down→drag using the mouse.*

Excel Sporting Goods Corporate Phone List	
Name	Phone Extensions

13. *Distribute the columns evenly across the page.*

Select the two columns→Layout Ribbon Tab→Cell Size Group→ ⬛ *Distribute Columns Button.*

Excel Sporting Goods Corporate Phone List	
Name	Phone Extensions
Adams, George W.	301

14. *Convert the entire Table to text, using tabs as separators.*

Select the Table→Layout Ribbon Tab→Data Group→ ⬛ *Convert to text Button→* ⦿ *Tabs→* [OK].

Excel Sporting Goods
Corporate Phone List
Name   Phone Extensions
Adams, George W.   301
Adams, Stephen   656
Adelson, Troy   395
Anderson, Pamela   543

15. *Close the document without saving it: File Tab→* [Close] *→* [Don't Save].

Student Project T - Sorting Table Data

1. *File Tab→ ⌷ Open → Browse→C:\Data\Word365-12\Table Sort Practice4.Docx.*
2. *Sort the Table only by the Presenter column in ascending order. Hint: You may need to select (none) in the first Then by the list.*

   Select in the Table→Layout Ribbon Tab →Data Group →⬚Sort Button→Sort by:

   Presenter→Type: Text→Using: Paragraphs → ☑ Ascending→ OK .

Sort by			
Presenter ▼	Type:	Text ▼	◉ Ascending
	Using:	Paragraphs ▼	○ Descending

3. *Click anywhere in the document to deselect the Table.*
   Click outside the Table.
4. *Next, sort the Table first by the Event column, then by the Location column, and finally, by the Presenter column, all in ascending order.*

   Select in the Table→Layout Ribbon Tab →Data Group →⬚Sort Button→Sort by:

   Event→Then by: Location→ OK .

Sort by			
Event ▼	Type:	Text ▼	◉ Ascending
	Using:	Paragraphs ▼	○ Descending
Then by			
Location ▼	Type:	Text ▼	◉ Ascending
	Using:	Paragraphs ▼	○ Descending

5. *Sort the Table by Start Time and then, by End Time only.*

   Select in the Table→Layout Ribbon Tab →Data Group → ⬚ Sort Button→Sort by: Start Time →Then by: End Time → OK .

Sort by			
Start Time ▼	Type:	Date ▼	◉ Ascending
	Using:	Paragraphs ▼	○ Descending
Then by			
End Time ▼	Type:	Date ▼	◉ Ascending
	Using:	Paragraphs ▼	○ Descending

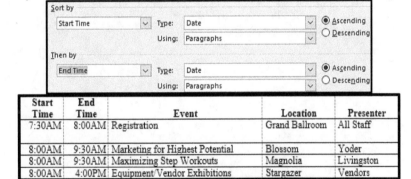

Start Time	End Time	Event	Location	Presenter
7:30AM	8:00AM	Registration	Grand Ballroom	All Staff
8:00AM	9:30AM	Marketing for Highest Potential	Blossom	Yoder
8:00AM	9:30AM	Maximizing Step Workouts	Magnolia	Livingston
8:00AM	4:00PM	Equipment/Vendor Exhibitions	Stargazer	Vendors

6. **Close the document without saving it:** *File Tab→ Close → Don't Save .*

Chapter 16 - Borders And Shading

16.1 Adding Borders And Shading To Text

You can use the **Borders and Shading Dialog Box** to add borders or shading to text and paragraphs. You can also remove borders and shading from text and paragraphs.

> ### *Excel Sporting Goods*
> *1234 Leisure Drive*
> *Media, MA 19107*
> *(610) 555-4321*

Practice Exercise 109 - Border Shading

1.   *File Tab→* 📁 *Open →Browse→C:\Data\Word365-12\Borders and Shading.Docx*
2.   *Click on the text Excel Sporting Goods, if necessary.*
3.   *Click Home Ribbon Tab →Paragraph Group →* ⊞▾ *Borders dropdown →Click* 📄 *Borders and Shading → Borders tab.*
4.   *Scroll as necessary and click the double line with the thick top line and thin bottom line (ninth style from the top).*
5.   *Click Color* ▾ *→Click Dark Blue (Standard Colors, ninth column).*
6.   *Click Width* ▾ *→Click 2 ¼ pt .*
7.   *Click Shading →Click Fill* ▾ .
8.   *Click Tan, Background 2 (first row, third column).*

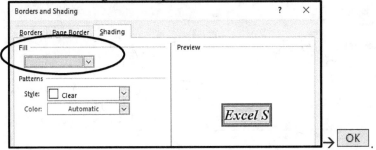

9.   *The result follows:*

> ### *Excel Sporting Goods*
> *1234 Leisure Drive*
> *Media, MA 19107*
> *(610) 555-4321*

16.2 Adding A Border To A Page

Page Borders can enhance the appearance of a document such as an invitation. The **Options Button** on the **Page Border** page provides selections for modifying the border placement on the page. Borders can be placed at specific distances from the edge of the page or the text.

Practice Exercise 110 - Page Border

This will add a page border to a document.

1. ***Click Design Ribbon Tab→Page Background Group→***

   Click Page Borders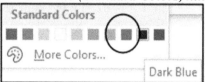
   (in previous versions the Page Borders was in the Home Ribbon Tab).
2. ***Click Shadow***
3. ***Scroll to the bottom of the Style list and select***
   3a. ***The thick gray gradient line (third style from the bottom).***
   3b. ***From the Color list, select Dark Blue (Standard Colors, ninth column).***

   3c. ***From the Width list, select 3 pt, if necessary.***
4. ***Click Apply to*** ⊡ ***→Click This section - First page only.***

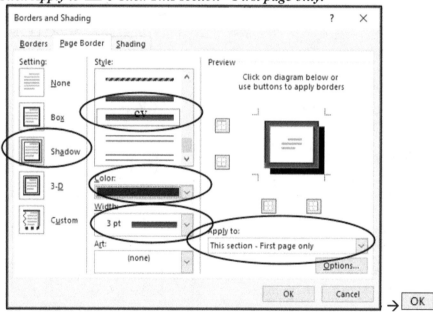

16.3 Adding A Border To A Table

Even though you can use the **Quick Table** feature to apply a combination of formats, shading, and borders to a **Table**, you can add your border style to a **Table** as well. Similar to adding borders to text, you can select a border style from the **Line Style**, **Line Weight,** and **Pen Color Buttons** in the **Draw Borders Group** on the **Table Tools Design** tab. In addition, you can apply diagonal borders to **Tables** in which the cells are divided diagonally.

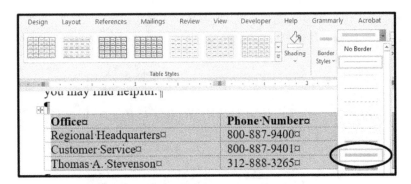

Practice Exercise 111 - Adding Border

1. **Scroll as necessary to view the Table at the bottom of the page.**
2. **Drag to select the entire Table.**
3. **Click Design Ribbon Tab(Right side)→Borders Group→**

    Click the Line Styles [_____ ⌄]
4. **Scroll as necessary and click the thin line style.**
5. **Click Borders** [▾] **→ Borders Group→ Click Outside Borders.**
6. **Display the Reveal Formatting task pane** Shift F1 **keys.**
7. **Select the entire Table.**
8. **Click the Borders link under the Cell section.**

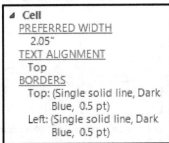

9. **Select the All setting on the Borders page.**

10. **Close the Borders and Shading Dialog Box.**
11. **Click anywhere in the document to deselect the Table and view the changes.**
12. **Close the Reveal Formatting task pane.**
13. **Close the document without saving it:** *File Tab→* Close *→* Don't Save .

Student Project U - Applying Borders And Shading

1. *File Tab→* Open *→Browse→*
    C:\Data\Word365-12\Borders and Shading Practice1.Docx.
2. **Place a 1½ point, red border under the title Equipment Showcase.**
    2a. Select the text "Equipment Showcase".

    2b. Home Ribbon Tab→Paragraph Group→ [⊞ ▾] **Border down arrow (Located in the lower right corner of the Paragraph Ribbon Group)→ Border down arrow →Borders and Shading (Located at the bottom of the list).**

2c. *Color:Red→Width: 1 ½ point→Apply to: Paragraph →*
Click on the bottom of the displayed box.

2d. OK

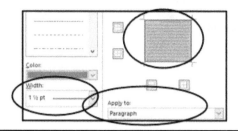

3. *Place a 1½ point, dark blue border at the Table located at the bottom of the page.*
3a. *Select the Table on page 1*

3b. *Home Ribbon Tab →Paragraph Group → Border down*
arrow → Borders and Shading

3c. *Color:Dark Blue→Width: 1 ½ point→Apply to:Table →*
Click the Box (Located on the left side of the dialog box).

3d. OK .

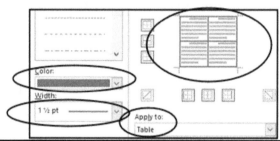

4. *Shade the first row of the Table with White, Background 1, Darker 25% (first column, fourth row), and add a 1½ point, dark blue border to the bottom edge of the row.*
4a. *Select the first row of the Table on page 1*

4b. *Home Ribbon Tab →Paragraph Group → Border down*
arrow → Borders and Shading→Shading tab →

4c. *Choose the White, Background 1, Darker 25%.*

4d. OK .

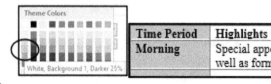

5. **Remove the shading:**
5a. *Select Excel Sporting Goods and Equipment Showcase titles.*

5b. *Home Ribbon Tab →Paragraph Group → Shading Button*

(Located next to the Borders Button)

5c. *Choose No Color* No Color

5d. OK .

Excel Sporting Goods
Equipment Showcase

6. *Remove the border under the title Equipment Showcase.*
   6a. *Select the text "Equipment Showcase"*

   6b. *Home Ribbon Tab→Paragraph Group→ Border down arrow →Choose* No Border *No Border option.*

Excel Sporting Goods
Equipment Showcase

7. *Apply a 3-D page border. Select the triple-line style with the thick line in the center (eleventh style from the top of the list).*

   7a. *Home Ribbon Tab→Paragraph Group→ Border down arrow →Borders and Shading*

   7b. *Choose Page Border tab→* 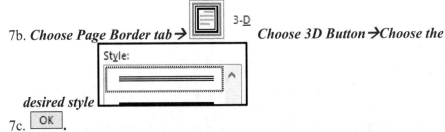 *Choose 3D Button→Choose the desired style*

   7c. OK .

8. *Switch to Print View to see the borders in the document. (File Tab→Print.)*

9. **Close the document without saving it:** *File Tab→* Close *→* Don't Save .

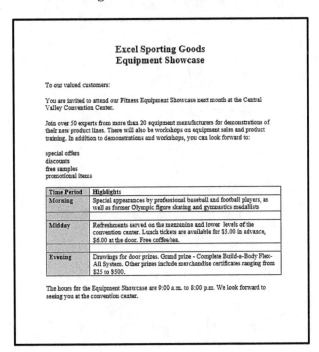

Chapter 17 - Newsletter-Style Columns

17.1 Creating Newsletter-style Columns

Some documents, such as brochures and **Newsletters**, look better in **Newsletter-Style Columns**. In this format, the text flows down one column to the bottom of the page and then wraps to the top of the next column to the right. If you want to apply columns to only part of the text in a document, you must first select the text. When you apply columns to text, **Microsoft Word** switches to **Print Layout View** (*View Ribbon Tab→Print Layout View*); you can only view **Newsletter-Style Columns** in **Print Layout View** or **Print View**. In ▤ **Draft View**, text formatted as columns appears as one single, narrow column. When you are working with columns, it is a good idea to display the ruler.

Practice Exercise 112 - Set 3 Columns

1. ***File Tab→*** 🗁 Open ***→ Browse→ C:\Data\Word365-12\Newsletter.Docx.***
2. ***Click Layout Ribbon Tab→ Page Setup Group→Click Columns*** ▤ ***→Click*** ▦ Three
3. ***Scroll to view page 2. Then, return to the top of the document.***
Tip: Notice that the header is not affected by the column format.

17.2 Navigating Columns

The quickest way to navigate **Newsletter-Style Columns** is to use the mouse; you simply click on the desired location to move the insertion point.

Practice Exercise 113 - Navigate Columns

This will navigate columns using the mouse. If necessary, display the **Rulers**, and switch to **Print Layout View**. Continue from the previous practice exercise.
1. ***Scroll as necessary to view the bottom of the middle column on page 1.***
2. ***Click at the end of the last line in the middle column.***
3. ***Press the Right Arrow key. Notice that the insertion point moves to the top of the next column.***
4. ***Press the Left Arrow key until the insertion point moves back to the last line in the middle column.***
5. ***Press Ctrl Home Keys to go to the top of the document.***

17.3 Changing The Number Of Columns

Once a document has been formatted for **Columns,** you may decide that its appearance could be improved if you used more or fewer **Columns.** You can increase or decrease the number of **Columns** as desired.

Practice Exercise 114 - Number Of Columns

This will change the number of columns. If necessary, display the **Rulers,** and switch to **Print Layout View.** Continue from the previous practice exercise.

Click Layout Ribbon Tab → Page Setup Group → Click Columns  ***→ Click*** .

17.4 Changing Column Width And Spacing

When **Columns** are created using the **Columns Button, Microsoft Word** creates columns of equal width. The column width and the space between columns are automatically calculated based on the width of the page and the margin size. When you create columns from the **Columns Dialog Box,** however, you can select from several column widths and spacing options. In addition, you can change the width and spacing of existing columns. You can drag the ruler to change column width and spacing. You can resize columns equally by selecting the **Equal column width** option in the **Columns Dialog Box**. To change the width of individual columns, however, you must deselect the **Equal column width** option.

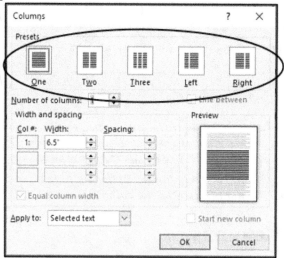

Practice Exercise 115 - Column Width And Spacing

This will change **Column Width** and **Spacing.** If necessary, display the **Rulers,** and switch to **Print Layout View.** Continue from the previous practice exercise.

1. ***Click Layout Ribbon Tab → Page Setup Group.***
2. ***Click Columns*** .
3. ***Click More Columns.***
4. ***Click*** ☑ ***Equal column width to deselect it, if necessary.***
5. ***Click column 1 Width*** ***to 2.5.***
6. ***Click column 1 Spacing*** ***to 1.***
7. ***Click*** OK .

17.5 Adding A Vertical Line Between Columns

You can add a **Vertical Line Between Columns**. **Vertical Lines** can make the text easier to read and enhance the appearance of the document. Vertical lines only appear in **Print View** or **Print Layout View** on the screen. They also appear in the printed document.

Practice Exercise 116 - Vertical Lines

This will add a **Vertical Line Between Columns**. If necessary, display the **Rulers**, and switch to **Print Layout View**.
Continue from the previous practice exercise.

1. *Click Layout Ribbon Tab → Page Setup Group.*
2. *Click Columns*
3. *Click More Columns.*
4. *Click* ☐ *Line between.*
5. *Click Apply to* ▾
6. *Click the Whole document, if necessary.*
7. *Click* OK
8. *Switch to Print View (File Tab → Print). Zoom in to see the vertical line, if necessary. Notice that the vertical line does not appear on the second page because that page contains only a single column of text.*
9. **Close document without saving it:** *File Tab →* Close.

Student Project V - Using Newsletter Style Columns

1. *File Tab →* ☐ Open *→ Browse → C:\Data\Word365-12\Newsletter Practice1.Docx.*
2. **Display the rulers:** *View Ribbon Tab → Show Group → ☑ Ruler.*
3. **If necessary, switch to Print Layout View:** *View Ribbon Tab →*

   Views Group → ☐ *Print Layout Button.*
4. **Select the text under the first title and format the text into 3 Columns:**

   Select the text under the first title → Layout Ribbon Tab → Page Setup Group → ☐ *Columns*

   Button → Choose [Three] *Three Columns.*

Product Boosts Sales by Two Million

Record sales of the new line of sportswear have boosted first quarter revenues to the tune of 2 million dollars.

It is expected that by the year 2004, one out of every 3 people in the United States and Canada will participate in recreational sports. By the year 2010, it is estimated that one out of every 2 people will participate in at least one recreational

sport per week. As the population growths, it is estimated that by the year 2020 that 1.5 out of every 2 people will participate in recreational sport per week.

On the drawing boards are expanded lines of children and infant sportswear, portable at-home fitness centers and more. The best is yet to come!

Sportswear with figurines depicting various occupational motifs will be available in June. A line designed for corporate sports team.

Research indicates that the upsurge in purchasing sportswear stems from a trend towards health fitness and safety.

5. **Select the text under the second title and format the text into 2 Columns:** *Select the text under the second title→Layout Ribbon Tab→Page Setup Group→ Columns Button→Choose Two Columns.*

HALVA Goes Retail

A turning point in the history of HALVA International came on January 18th at the Grand Opening of the first HALVA retail outlet in over 50 years as a mail-order house for racquet sports.

Attending the opening were city officials, the Governor of New

York, and the Prime Minister of Atlantis. Our own illustrious President was there for the occasion, and warmly greeted all in attendance. We were very pleased and honored to have such distinguish notable people at the grand opening. We could not have hoped for a finer guest list.

6. *Change the spacing between columns and add a vertical line:*

   Select the column text→Layout Ribbon Tab→Page Setup Group→ Columns Button→ More Columns→☑ Line between→Spacing: 0.7).

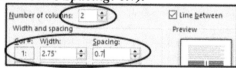

7. *Change the 3 columns to 2 columns:*

   Select the 3-column text→Layout Ribbon Tab →Page Setup Group→ Columns Button→ Two Columns)

8. *Review the ▱ Continuous section break between columns and titles.*

   Tip: You don't see the columns or graphics, but you can see where the column starts and stops.

View Ribbon Tab →Views Group →📄*Draft Button.*

towards health fitness and safety.

⸱⸱⸱Section Break (Continuous)⸱⸱⸱⸱⸱⸱⸱⸱⸱⸱⸱⸱⸱

HALVA Goes Retail

⸱⸱Section Break (Continuous)⸱⸱⸱⸱⸱⸱⸱⸱⸱⸱⸱⸱⸱

A turning point in the history of

9. **Switch to Print Layout to view the Columns:**

    View Ribbon Tab →Views Group →📄*Print Layout Button.*

10. **Close the document without saving it:** *File Tab →* Close *→* Do*n*'t Save .

Chapter 18 - Section Breaks

18.1 Inserting a Next Page Break

A **Section** is a portion of a document and can include as little as one paragraph or the entire document. Usually, you create a **Section** in order to format it differently from the rest of the document. If you want to change the margins, page layout, page orientation, column formats, page numbering, or headers and footers within part of a document, you can do that within a new **Section**.

In **Print Layout View**, a **Section Break** is only visible when you show the formatting marks ¶.

In **Draft View**, a **Section Break** is always visible. It appears as a double-dotted line in the document and is identified by the words **Section Break**, followed by the type of break-in parentheses. The following is an example of **Section Break**:

You can create a **Section** that starts from a new page by inserting a **Next Page Section Break**. For instance, you may need to print one page of a document in landscape orientation and the rest of the document in portrait orientation. To perform this task, you can create one or more **Next Page** sections and adjust the page layouts for each **Section** as desired.

Practice Exercise 117 - Inserting a Next Page Break

Insert a **Next Page** section break. If necessary, show the formatting markings.

1. *File Tab → Open → Browse → C:\Data\Word365-12\Page Sections1.Docx.*
2. *Scroll as necessary and click to the left of the text Directions and Information.*

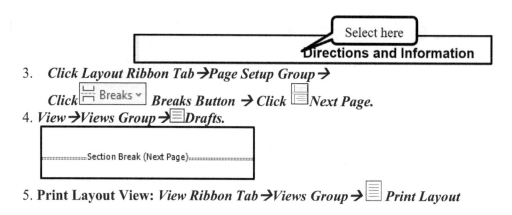

3. ***Click Layout Ribbon Tab→Page Setup Group→***
Click Breaks Button → Click Next Page.
4. ***View→Views Group→Drafts.***

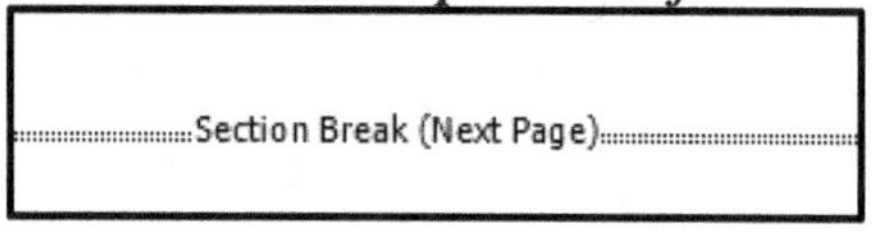

5. **Print Layout View:** ***View Ribbon Tab→Views Group→ Print Layout***

18.2 Formatting A Section

After you have created a **New Section**, you can set different margins, page layouts, page orientations, column formats, page numbering, headers, and footers for each **Section** in the document. **Section Formatting** is stored in the **Section Break** mark found at the end of each **Section**.

Practice Exercise 118 - Vertical Alignment

Continue from the previous practice exercise.

1. ***Press*** **Ctrl** **Home** ***keys.***
2. ***Click Layout Ribbon Tab →Page Setup Group→Click Page Setup→ Layout Tab.***
3. ***Click the Vertical alignment and select Center.***

4. ***Select the View Ribbon Tab, and select the Multiple Pages Button in the Zoom Group so that you can view both pages of the document. Notice the different page formatting in each section. Then, select the 100% Button in the Zoom Group to return to the regular view.***
5. ***Close document without saving it.***

18.3 Inserting A Continuous Break

To create a **New Section** on the same page as the previous **Section**, you must insert a **Continuous Section Break**. You would use this type of break to create multiple layouts on the same page. For instance, you might insert a **Continuous Section Break** to add newspaper-style columns to one part of a page.

Practice Exercise 119 - Continuous Break

1. ***File Tab→*** Open ***→Browse→C:\Data\Word365-12\Page Sections2.Docx.***
2. ***Click in the blank line above the table.***
3. ***Click Layout Ribbon Tab→Page Setup Group→***
Click Breaks Button→ Click Continuous.
4. **Position the insertion point in the section containing the table (but not in the table itself) and use the Page Setup Dialog Box to change the left margin of the section to 0.5 inches (or 1.25cm):** ***Place cursor above Table→Layout Ribbon Tab→Page Setup Group→Margin→Custom Margin→*****Left:** ***.5→*** OK.

Tip: Notice that the left margin of the section containing the table is different than the rest of the document. The paragraphs of text below the table are also included in the section formatting.

5. **Click in the blank line below the table and add another** ⬛**Continuous section break between the table and the following paragraph of text. Change the left margin of the section below the table to 1.25 inch (or 3.17cm):** *Place cursor Below Table→Layout Ribbon Tab→Page Setup Group→Margin→Custom Margin→Left: 1.25→* OK .

6. *Select the View Ribbon Tab, and select the* ▤ *One Page Button in the Zoom Group so that you can view the whole page. Notice the different margins in each section of the document.*

7. *Then, select the* 🔲 *100% Button in the Zoom Group to return to the regular view.*

Join over 50 experts from more than 20 equipment manufacturers for demonstrations of their new product lines. There will also be workshops on equipment sales and product training. In addition to demonstrations and workshops, you can look forward to: special offers, discounts, free samples, promotional items and more.

Product specialists will be available for the following items in our product line.

Product	Weight (lbs)	Release Date	Order Number	Retail Price	Features
Life-Fit 805 Treadmill	97	Jan. 1, 1994	TM55805	149.95	Manual incline Fold-away design
Life-Fit 820 Deluxe Treadmill	105	Jun 30, 1994	TM55820	299.95	Child-proof safety system Adjustable incline
Body Lean Exercise Bike	95	Oct 1, 1993	TM55201	149.95	Enclosed chain guard
Exer-Fit Exercise Bike	98	Apr 1, 1994	TM55202	229.95	Cushioned seat/handgrips Electronic display features
Treadmaster Rower	105	Jan 1, 1995	TM55301	169.95	Adjustable shocks Electronic display features
Body Lean Folding Stepper	65	Jun 1 1994	TM55302	99.95	Slip-resistant pedals Adjustable tension control

The hours for the Equipment Showcase are 9:00 a.m. to 8:00 p.m. We look forward to seeing you at the convention center.

18.4 Inserting An Odd/Even Page Break

🔲 You can create an ⬛**Even Page Section** break to begin a **New Section** on the next **Even-Numbered** page or an ⬛**Odd Page Section Break** to begin a **New section** on the next **Odd-Numbered** page. For instance, you might want to begin the first page of each chapter on an **Odd-Numbered** page.

If necessary, **Microsoft Word** prints a blank page to force the **Section** to the next even-numbered or **Odd-Numbered** page.

Practice Exercise 120 - Odd/Even Page

1. *Insert an* ⬛*Odd Page or* ⬛*Even Page section break. Move to the top of the document. Notice that the status bar (lower left corner) displays the page number as Page:1 of 1.*

2. *Click on the blank line below the Equipment Showcase title.*

3. *Click Layout Ribbon Tab→ Page Setup Group→Click* ⬛ *Breaks Button → Click* ⬛*Odd Page.*

4. *Notice that the status bar now displays the page number as Page: 3 of 3. Microsoft Word has inserted a blank page (page 2) in order to force the New Section to start on an Odd-Numbered page.*

Test it: View the three pages using the **Print View**. *File Tab→Print→Use the dash "-" in the zoom slider located in the lower right corner.*

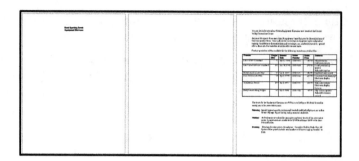

18.5 Modifying And Removing A Section Break

When you remove a **Section Break**, you also remove the formatting associated with that **Section**. The **Section Break** mark stores the formatting for the section above it, just as the paragraph mark stores the formatting of the paragraph preceding it.

When you **Remove A Section Break**, the text above the deleted **Section Break** assumes the section formatting of the text below the deleted **Section Break**.

Practice Exercise 121 - Remove A Section Break

1. *Modify and Remove a section break. Display the formatting marks and make sure you are in Print Layout View. Move to the top of the document.*
2. *View Ribbon Tab →Views Group →☷Draft →Double click on the section break to modify it→* `OK` .
3. *Click on the Section Break → Press the* `Delete` *key.*
4. *View Ribbon Tab →Views Group →☷Print Layout*
5. **Close the document without saving it:** *File Tab →* `Close` *→* `Don't Save` .

Student Project W - Using Section Breaks

1. *File Tab →* `Open` *→ Browse →C:\Data\Word365-12\Page Sections Practice1.Docx.*
2. **Create a Section Break to place the table title, the table, and the graph on a separate, Odd-Numbered page of the document:**
   2a. *Click above the title Southeastern Region Annual Sale (Located just above the table in the middle of the page) → Layout Ribbon Tab →Page Setup Group →☐ Breaks Button →* ☐*Odd Page break.*
   2b. *Click above the chart→ Layout Ribbon Tab →Page Setup Group →☐Breaks Button →☐Odd Page Break.*
3. **Change the Orientation of page 2 containing the table to the landscape:**
   3a. *Click anywhere in the table area →Layout Ribbon Tab →Page Setup Group →☐ Orientation Button →☐Landscape.*
4. **To view the whole document:**
   4a. *View Ribbon Tab →Zoom Group →⊞ Multiple Pages Button.*

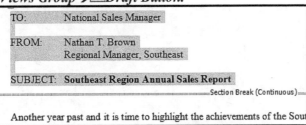

4b. *View Ribbon Tab→Zoom Group→* 100% *Button.*

5. **Insert a** Continuous **Section Break after the Subject:**
   5a. *Click under the subject on page 1→Layout Ribbon Tab→*

   Page Setup Group→ Breaks Button→Continuous Page Break.

6. **Apply the layout to the selected text only:**
   Select the TO, FROM, and SUBJECT paragraphs→Layout Ribbon Tab→Page Setup Group→

   Margin→Custom Margin (option on the bottom)→Left: 2".

   Tip: The rest of the page is not affected because of the Continuous Page Break.

7. **View the whole document to see the Sections:**
   View Ribbon Tab→Zoom Group→One Page Button.

TO:	National Sales Manager
FROM:	Nathan T. Brown
	Regional Manager, Southeast
SUBJECT:	**Southeast Region Annual Sales Report**

Another year past and it is time to highlight the achievements of the Southeast Regional Sales Representatives. Sales of Scuba gear peaked in the fourth quarter of the year and golf sales during the third quarter were the highest of all the regions.

8. **View the Break Markers:**
   View Ribbon Tab→Views Group→Draft Button.

TO:	National Sales Manager
FROM:	Nathan T. Brown
	Regional Manager, Southeast
SUBJECT:	**Southeast Region Annual Sales Report**

....Section Break (Continuous)........

Another year past and it is time to highlight the achievements of the Sout

9. **Close the document without saving it:** *File Tab→* Close *→* Don't Save .

Chapter 19 - Headers & Footers

19.1 Creating Headers/Footers

You can create your **Headers** and **Footers** for a document, but **Microsoft Word** also provides predesigned **Headers** and **Footers** which can be applied easily to your document. These are listed and displayed under the **Built-In** sections of the **Header** and **Footer Dialog Box**. If you create your **Header** or **Footer**, you can save it for future use in the **Header** and **Footer** galleries.

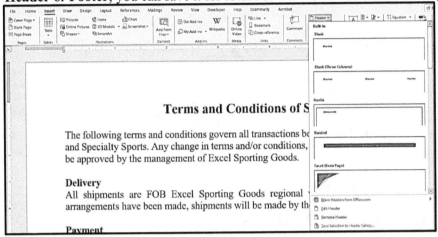

Practice Exercise 122 - Headers/Footers

Create **Headers/Footers** using the **Galleries**.

1. *File Tab→* Open *→Browse→ C:\Data\Word365-12\Headers and Footers1.Docx.*
2. *Click the Insert Ribbon Tab →Headers & Footers Group→Click* Header.
3. *Scroll as necessary and click the desired header style with a title.*
4. *Leave the header text as it is; it is using the Title field specified in document properties.*

5. *Click the Insert Ribbon Tab → Headers & Footers Group→Click* Footer.
6. *Scroll as necessary and click the desired header style with a title.*

19.2 Inserting Page Numbers Using The Gallery

If you want a document to contain **Page Numbers**, **Microsoft Word** can automatically number each page and will then keep the numbering updated as you edit the document. You can insert a **Page Number** into the **Header** or the **Footer**, or the left or right margins of the document.

Practice Exercise 123 - Insert Page Numbers

This will insert **Page Numbers** using the gallery. Open a new, blank document, if necessary. Make sure you are in **Print Layout View**. Continue from the previous practice exercise.

1. ***Click Insert Ribbon Tab→ Headers & Footers Group.***

2. ***Click*** 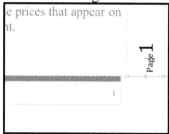 ***Page Number.***
3. ***Point to Page Margins.***
4. ***Click Vertical, Right.***

5. ***Click Close Header and Footer Close*** .

Tip: This will place a page number in the lower right corner.

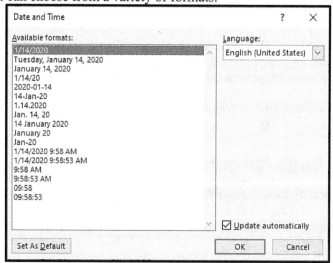

19.3 Inserting The Current Date

Microsoft Word can automatically add the **Current Date** in the **Header** or **Footer** of a document. This task is accomplished using the **Date & Time Button** available in the **Header & Footer Tools** tab. **Microsoft Word** inserts the date as a field, which then updates automatically to show the **Current Date**. You can choose from a variety of formats.

Practice Exercise 124 - Current Date

This will insert the **Current Date** into the **Header** or **Footer** of a document.

1. ***Open a new, Blank document.***

2. ***Click Insert Ribbon Tab → Headers & Footers Group→Click Header →Click Edit Header→Press*** Tab ***key twice.***
3. ***Header&Footer Ribbon Tab→Insert Group.***

4. *Click* ⬚ *Date & Time →Click the third option in the list→Click* OK .
5. *Select the* ⬚ *Go to Footer Button →Press* Tab *key twice.*
6. **Close the Header & Footer Tools Tab. Close the document without saving it.**

19.4 Creating A First Page Header/Footer

In many documents, the **First Page** has a different **Header** and **Footer** than the rest of the document. If you have a title page on which you do not want to display the **Header** or **Footer**, you can choose to have a **Different First Page Header or Footer.**

You can use the **Previous Section** and **Next Section Buttons** on the **Header & Footer** toolbar to navigate between the different **Headers** and **Footers**.

Practice Exercise 125 - Different First Page

1. *File Tab →* 📂 Open *→ Browse →C:\Data\Word365-12\Headers and Footers2.Docx.*
2. *Click Insert Ribbon Tab → Header&Footer Group →Click* ⬚ *Header →Click* ⬚ *Edit Header.*
3. *Header&Footer Ribbon Tab →Options Group →Click* ☑ *Different First Page.*
4. *Header&Footer Ribbon Tab →Insert Group →Select the* ⬚ *Date & Time Button on the Insert Ribbon Tab. Select your preferred date format and select* OK .
5. *Header&Footer Ribbon Tab →Navigation Group →* ⬚ Next *Click Next Section .*
6. *Header&Footer Ribbon Tab → Header & Footer Group →*
    Select the ⬚ *Page Number Button →* ⬚ *Top of Page option →*
    Select Accent Bar 1 from the gallery.
7. *Close the Header & Footer Tools tab.*
8. **View the first two pages in the Print View:** *File Tab →Print →Select the - in the Zoom Slider to zoom to two pages.* **Tip:** that the **Headers** are different from the first and the subsequent pages. Return to a **One-Page View.**

19.5 Alternating Odd And Even Headers/Footers

Documents that are printed on both sides and bound in book form contain facing pages. You can create different **Header and Footer** content for **Odd and Even Numbered Pages.** For example, you can alternate your page numbers by left-aligning the page number for ⬚ **Even Page Footers** and right-aligning the page number for **Odd Page Footers.** You can also create **Odd** and **Even Headers** and **Footers** that contain different text. You can use the **Previous Section** and **Next Section Buttons** on the **Header & Footer** toolbar to navigate between the different **Headers** and **Footers.**

Page |2

Even Page Header | You are invited to attend our Fitness Equipment Showcase next month at the Central Valley Convention Center.

Join over 50 experts from more than 20 equipment manufacturers for demonstrations of their new product lines. There will also be workshops on equipment sales and product training. In addition to demonstrations and workshops, you can look forward to: special offers, discounts, free samples, promotional items and more.

Practice Exercise 126 - Odd/Even Pages

Continue from the previous practice exercise.

1. *Click Insert Ribbon Tab → Header&Footer Group →Click ⬜ Header →Click ⬜Edit Header*
2. *Design Ribbon Tab →Options Group →Click ▢ Different Odd & Even Pages.*
3. *Click Next Section 🔲 Next.*
4. *Select the Page Number Button in the Header & Footer Group. Point to the Top of Page option and select Accent Bar 1 from the gallery.*
5. *Click Next Section 🔲 Next.*
6. **Now that we have Different Odd and Even Headers this choice of page number style is no longer appropriate:** *Select Page Number Button in the Header & Footer Group. Point to the Top of Page option, and select Accent Bar 2 from the gallery.*
7. *Select the Previous Section Button in the Navigation Group to return to the Even Page Header area.*
8. *Select the ▣Go to Footer Button in the Navigation Group to display the Even Page Footer area. Press [Tab] key and type Excel Sporting Goods.*
9. *Select the Next Section Button in the Navigation Group to display the Odd Page Footer area. Press [Tab] key and type Fitness Equipment Show.*
10. *Close the Header & Footer Tools tab.*
11. **View the first two pages in the Print View:** *File Tab →Print → Select in the Zoom Slider to zoom to two pages. Notice that the headers and footers are different on the first, the even, and the odd pages.*

19.6 Setting The Starting Page Number

The **Page Number Format Dialog Box** allows you to select a number format other than the default option of **1, 2, 3**. Options include letters and Roman numerals. It also enables you to add chapter numbers to the page numbers, based on the heading styles. You can also control **Page Numbering** by specifying at what number you wish the page count to begin. You may also want to reset your **Page Numbers** if your document contains a cover page. **Page Numbers** are usually not printed on the cover page of a document.

Practice Exercise 127 - Set Start Page Number

This will set the starting **Page Number**. If necessary, switch to **Print Layout View.** Continue from the previous practice exercise.

1. ***Click Insert Ribbon Tab → Header&Footer Group →Click Page Number → Select Format Page Numbers.***
2. ***Click Number format.***
3. ***Click 1, 2, 3, if necessary.***
4. ***Click ⬭ Start at.***
5. ***Click ▲▼ to 0.***
6. ***Click OK .***
7. *Notice that the page number does not appear at the top of the first page. Scroll to the top of the second page, which is the first of the content pages of the document. Notice that the page numbering in the header of the second page now starts as appropriate on page 1.*
8. *Notice that despite this change to the page numbering format, the Status Bar shows the second page as Page: 2 of 4. Microsoft Word still numbers the pages consecutively from the first page of the document, no matter what page numbering format you use. The document pagination will not show in the document unless you insert it; however, you will need to remember that when printing, for example, page 2, Microsoft Word will print the second page of the document, not the page numbered or formatted as 2 in the content.*
9. **Close document without saving it:** *File Tab →* Close .

Student Project X - Working with Headers and Footers

1. ***File Tab →*** 🗁 Open ***→ Browse →C:\Data\Word365-12\Headers and Footers Practice1.Docx.***
2. **Open the Header area for editing:**

   Insert Ribbon Tab →Header&Footer Group → Header Button → Edit Header.
3. **Change the header so that the first page is different:**
   Header&Footer Ribbon Tab →Options Group →☑ Different first page.
4. **Leave the First-Page Header blank and switch to the First-Page Footer:**

   Header&Footer Ribbon Tab →Navigation Group → Go to Footer Button.
5. ***Insert Ribbon Tab → Quick Parts Button →Select ▭ Field →Scroll down to find the Filename field →Select OK .***
6. ***Insert Ribbon Tab →Text Group → Quick Parts Button →Field → Filename.***

7. **Add the Current Date at the right tab position:**
Click on the Tab *key twice → Header&Footer Ribbon Tab →Insert Group → Date&Time Button→Monday, January 20. 2020→* OK *.*

8. **Adjust the tab stops:**
   a. *View Ribbon Tab → Ruler, if necessary.*
   b. *Drag the center tab marker to 3.5→Drag the right tab marker to 6.5.*

First Page Footer
Headers and Footers Practice1.docx   Monday, January 20, 2020

9. *Display the next footer and enter a Page #:*
   a. **Header&Footer Ribbon Tab →Navigation Group →Next Button.**
   b. **Header&Footer Ribbon Tab →Headers& Footers Group → Page Number Button →** Select *Current Position→Plain Number.*

10. **Adjust the tab stops:**
Drag the center tab marker to 3.5→Drag the right tab marker to 6.5.

11. **Switch to the header and add a title:**
Header&Footer Ribbon Tab →Navigation Group →Go to Header Button → Type "All Products" at the right margin.

12. **Adjust the right tab stop to Align to the right margin:** *Drag the right tab marker to 6.5.*

All Products

Header

13. **Reset the starting page number to 0:**
   a. *Header&Footer Ribbon Tab →Headers and Footers Group →Page Number Button→Top of Page →Plain Number 3.*
   b. *Header&Footer Ribbon Tab →Insert Group →Page Number Button→Format Page Numbers →Start at: 0 →* OK *.*

   Tip: The cover page is Page 0 and the document will start numbering on Page1.

14. *Close the Header & Footer Tools tab.*
Header&Footer Ribbon Tab → Close Headers& Footers.

15. **Look at the document in the Print View:** *File Tab →Print. Notice that the cover page does not contain a header and that the first page of the document containing body text is numbered Page 1.*

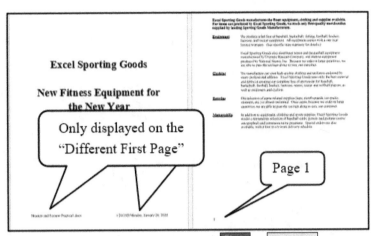

16. **Close the document without saving it:** *File Tab* → Close → Don't Save.

Chapter 20 - Styles

20.1 Using The Quick Styles Gallery

A **Style** is a group of formatting attributes that are saved with a **Style** name. **Styles** make it simple to format text and paragraphs consistently. The symbol next to a **Style** name indicates which type of **Style** it is:

Style Type	Symbol
Character	a
Paragraph	¶
Linked paragraph and character	¶a

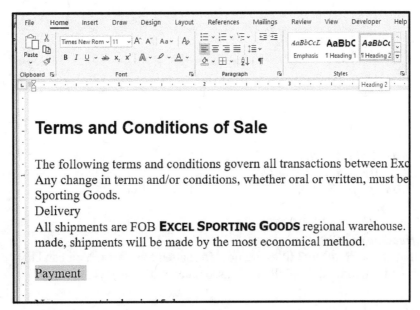

Practice Exercise 128 - Quick Styles Gallery

1. *File Tab→* [📂 Open] *→ Browse→ C:\Data\Word365-12\Styles.Docx.*
2. *Select the title "Terms and Conditions of Sale."*
3. *Select Heading1 Style* [AaBb(Heading 1] *in the Home Ribbon Tab→Styles Group*
4. *Format the titles "Delivery", "Payment", "Minimum Orders" and "Returns" using the* [AaBbC(Heading 2] *Heading2 Style.*
5. *Click anywhere in the document area.*

20.2 Modifying Styles

There are over 200 **Styles** built into **Microsoft Word** and of course, you can create your **Styles** too. Most of the time you will want to use very few of these, but you may also want to apply more rigorous control of their use or have different **Styles** available for different types of documents. The **Manage Styles Dialog Box** is where you can organize the **Styles**.

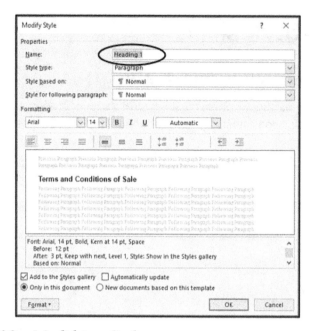

Practice Exercise 129 - Modifying Styles

Continue from the previous practice exercise.

1. ***Select "Terms And Condition of Sale."***
2. ***Right-click on Heading1 →Modify.***
3. ***Change Heading1 to Size 16.***
4. ***Select Delivery.***
5. ***Right-click on Heading2 →Modify.***
6. ***Change Heading1 to Size 14.***

Tip: Notice that all the **Heading2** titles are now formatted to size **14.** You can change the **Style** characteristics and it will modify all the titles associated with the **Style**.

20.3 Creating A Style

The **Quick Styles** gallery provides several **Styles**, organized into **Style** sets, for you to use. These have been designed to offer a wide range of attractive and functional options for you to use in various circumstances. However, you may wish to create a new **Style** in order to present some text in a particular way.

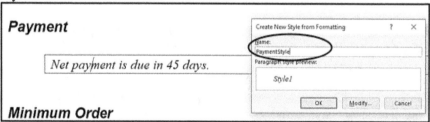

Practice Exercise 130 - New Style

This will create a new **Style**. You can do this by formatting the relevant text and then creating the **Style** based on that formatting.

Continue from the previous practice exercise.

1. ***Click Home Ribbon Tab.***

2. *Drag to select the text "Net payment is due in 45 days" under the heading Payment.*
3. *Release the Mouse Button.*
4. *Click the Border Dropdown List Button* ⊞˅ *in the Paragraph Group on the Home Ribbon Tab.*
5. *Click the Outside Borders option.*
6. *Click the Increase Indent Button* ⧉ *in the Paragraph Group.*
7. *Click the Italic Button* I *in the Font Group.*
8. *Click Down Arrow* ▽ *in the Styles Group on the Home Ribbon Tab.*
9. *Click* A₊ *Create a Style.*
10. *Style Name: PaymentStyle →* OK *.*
11. *Type the words under the "Net Payment due in 45 days".*
    Of "10% Penalty if later than 45 days." (See example below)

> *Net payment is due in 45 days.*
> **10% Penalty if later than 45 days.**

12. *Format the words "10% Penalty if later than 45 days." Using your new Style called PaymentStyle.*

> *Net payment is due in 45 days.*
> *10% Penalty if later than 45 days.*

13. *Select the word "Sporting" under the heading Delivery.*

> **Delivery**
> All shipments are FOB **EXCEL SPORTING GOODS**
> made, shipments will be made by the most econom

14. *Click Down Arrow* ▽ *in the Styles Group on the Home Ribbon Tab.*
15. *Click* A₊ *Create a Style.*

Create New Style from Formatting — Name: Excel Emphasis — Paragraph style preview: STYLE1 — OK | Modify... | Cancel → OK.

16. *Select the first paragraph above and apply the new Style.*

> **Terms and Conditions of Sale**
> THE FOLLOWING TERMS AND CONDITIONS GOVERN
> AND SPECIALTY SPORTS. ANY CHANGE IN TERMS A
> MUST BE APPROVED BY THE MANAGEMENT OF EXCE

Tip: *Another way to create a Style is to Right-click on the selected text →* [Styles] *Button (located in the Mini Toolbar) →* A₊ *Create a Style.*

20.4 Editing An Existing Style

The **Quick Styles** gallery provides many **Styles** for your use, organized into **Style** sets designed to suit different purposes. You can also create entirely new **Styles**. However, there may be times when you wish to adjust or edit an **Existing Style** within a document in order to meet a particular formatting need. This edit will not affect the **Existing Style** but will only adjust the specific text to be modified.

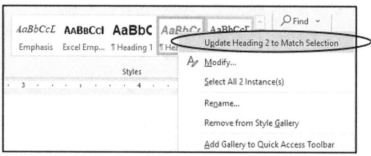

Practice Exercise 131 - Existing Style

Continue from the previous practice exercise.
1. ***Click Home Ribbon Tab.***
2. ***Drag to select the text "Payment", which is formatted as Heading2 style.***

3. ***Release the Mouse Button.***

4. ***Click the Font Color Dropdown List Button*** in the Font Group on the Home Ribbon Tab. Format the Font Red.***

    Tip: The **Heading2** style was not changed, just the text.
5. ***Right-click on Heading2 Style →Click Update Heading2 to Match Selection.***
Tip: The existing **Style** has been updated. Note that all instances of text with this **Style** in the document have been updated.

20.5 Adding A Style To The Quick Styles Gallery

The **Quick Styles** gallery, located in the **Styles Group** on the **Home Ribbon Tab**, provides a rapid method of previewing and applying **Styles** to selected text. **Microsoft Word** populates this gallery with its extensive library of **Styles**, of which there are over 200 to choose from. When you select a different **Style** Set to use with your document, the **Quick Styles** gallery is repopulated with the **Styles** associated with the selected **Style Set**.

You can also add a **Style** to the **Quick Styles** gallery, perhaps one that you use regularly but doesn't appear in the gallery or one that you have created yourself, or one that has been removed and you want to replace.

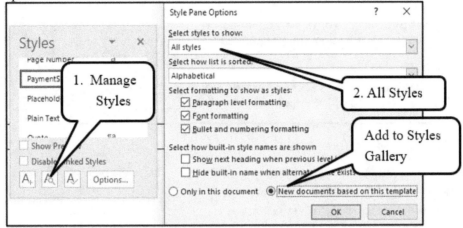

Practice Exercise 132 - Options

Continue from the previous practice exercise.

1. ***Click Home Ribbon Tab →Click Styles*** 🔽 ***→Click*** `Options...` ***Options button.***
2. ***Click Select Styles to show:*** `▾` ***→Click All Styles.***
3. ***Select*** `◉ New documents based on this template`
4. ***Click*** `OK`.
5. ***When you start a new Document, the style will be permanently part of the Style Gallery.***

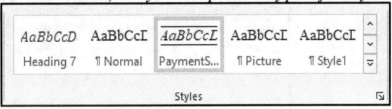

20.6 Clearing Formats And Styles

You can use the **Clear Formatting** command to remove formatting and **Styles** from the text. When you remove all formatting and **Styles** from the text, it adopts the attributes of the **Normal Style**. You can remove formatting and **Style** from a single instance or from all instances of that formatting or **Style**.

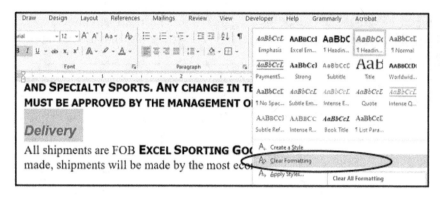

Practice Exercise 133 - Clear Style

Continue from the previous practice exercise.

1. ***Click on the Delivery heading.***
2. ***Click Down Arrow*** 🔽 ***in the Styles Group.***
3. ***Click Clear Formatting.***
4. ***Select the text 45 DAYS at the end of the paragraph under the Payment heading and clear the formatting by opening the Styles gallery and selecting Clear Formatting. Notice that the text adopts the formatting of the surrounding paragraph, not the Normal Style. Deselect the text.***

20.7 Deleting A Style

You may have created a **Style** within a document that you now wish to delete because it has become unnecessary. You will not be able to delete the standard **Styles**, such as **Normal** and **Heading1**, but you can delete any new **Styles** that you have created.

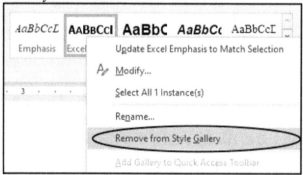

Practice Exercise 134 - Delete Styles

Continue from the previous practice exercise.

1. ***Click Home Ribbon Tab.***
2. ***Click anywhere in Excel Sporting Goods in the first sentence.***
3. ***Click Styles*** 🔲**.**
4. ***Click Down Arrow*** 🔽 ***in the Excel Emphasis Styles Group.***
5. ***Click Delete Excel Emphasis.***
6. ***The Style has been deleted, and the selected text has reverted to the Normal Style.***

20.8 Using Style Inspector

It is sometimes useful to know whether the text has been manually formatted instead of formatted using **Styles**. **Style Inspector** is a convenient way to do this and enables you to clear manually applied formatting easily.

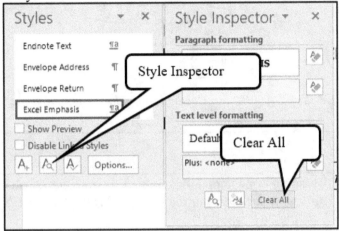

Practice Exercise 135 - Style Inspector

Continue from the previous practice exercise.

1. ***Click Home Ribbon Tab→Click Styles*** ⬚ ***→Click Payment text→***
2. ***Click*** 🎨 ***Style Inspector.***
3. ***Click*** ⬚Clear All ***Clear ALL button.***

Student Project Y - Using Styles

1. ***File Tab→*** 📂 Open ***→ Browse →C:\Data\Word365-12\Styles Practice1.Docx.***
2. **Display the Styles Group on the Home Ribbon Tab:**
   Home Ribbon Tab→Styles Group.

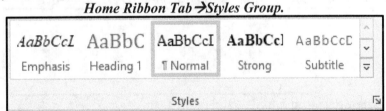

3. **Apply the Heading1 Style to the first paragraph of the document, Excel Sporting Goods, and then center the paragraph:** *Home Ribbon Tab→Styles Group→Click the down arrow to the lower right of the Styles, if necessary→Choose the Heading1 Style.*

Excel Sporting Goods

Summer Equipment Showcase

4. **Create a new Style named ESG Heading:** *Click on the heading "Excel Sporting Goods"→Home Ribbon Tab→Styles Group→Click the* ⬚ *diagonal arrow in the lower-left corner→*

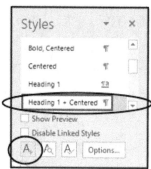

Choose the ![A+] *Create a Style Button (located in the lower-left corner of the Styles pane)* →*Name: ESG Heading* → OK *.*

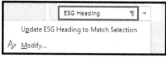

5. **Modify the ESG Heading Style to include double line spacing:** *Home Ribbon Tab* →*Styles Group* →*Click the diagonal arrow under the Change Styles Button* →*Click on the down arrow next to the ESG Heading Style* →

![A] *Modify* →*Choose the Format drop-down located on the bottom of the Dialog Box* →*Paragraph* →*Indents and Spacing tab* →*Line Spacing: Double* → OK → OK *.*

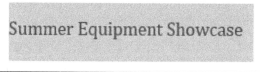

6. **Apply the ESG Heading Style:**
    Select the "Directions to the Central Valley Convention Center" (page 2) →
    Home Ribbon Tab →*Styles Group* →*Choose the ESG Heading Style.*

> ## Summer Equipment Showcase

7. **Create a new Paragraph Style named My List:**
    7a. *Home Ribbon Tab* →*Styles Group* →*Click the diagonal arrow under the Change Styles Button* →*Choose the New Style Button* ![icon] *located in the lower-left corner of the Styles pane* →
    7b. *Name: My List* →*Style based on: Heading 3* →
    7c. *Format Dropdown List* →*Font* →*Font tab* →*Arial, 14 points* → OK *.*
    7d. *Format Dropdown List* →*Tabs* →*Alignment:* ☑ *Left* →*Tab Stop Position: 1.5* →*Set* → OK *.*

7e. *Format Dropdown List→Paragraph → Indents and Spacing tab→Spacing: Before: 6 points→Spacing: After: 6 Points→* OK .

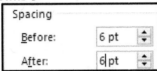

8. **Apply the My List Style to the list beginning with Special offers and ending with Promotional items:** *Select the text "Special offers and ending with Promotional items"→ Home Ribbon Tab→Styles Group→Click the down arrow to the lower right of the Styles, if necessary→Choose the MyList Style.*

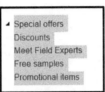

9. **Create a character Style named Emphasis 2, based on the text Morning on page 1. Then, apply the Style to the text Midday and Evening:**
    9a. *Select the text Morning → Home Ribbon Tab→Styles Group →*
    Click the diagonal arrow under the Change Styles Button→
    Choose the New Style Button ![icon] *located in the lower-left corner of the*
    Styles pane→Name: Emphasis 2→Style Type: Character→ OK .

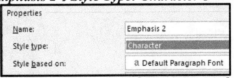

    9b. *Select the word Midday→Home Ribbon Tab →Styles Group →*
        Click the down arrow to the lower right of the Styles Group, if necessary
        →Select Emphasis 2.
10. **Clear the formatting from the text Summer Equipment Showcase:**
    Select the word Summer Equipment Showcase →Home Ribbon Tab→Styles Group→Click the down arrow to the lower right of the Styles Group, if necessary→ A◇ *Clear Formatting.*

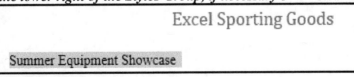

11. **Delete the ESG Heading Style:**
    Home Ribbon Tab→Styles Group→Click the diagonal arrow under the Change Styles Button→choose the down arrow next to the ESG Heading Style→Choose Revert to Heading1 →Delete→ Yes .

12. *Close the Styles Dialog Box, if you have it open, and then close the document without saving it. Click the* ☑ *in the upper right corner of the Styles pane* → *File Tab* → Close → Don't Save.

Chapter 21 - Table Of Contents

This is located at the beginning of a document listing the subject and page number. It is created from the defined styles throughout the document.

21.1 Generating A Table Of Contents

Many **Long Documents** (such as manuals, reports, and books) include a **Table Of Contents** to help readers find information. A **Table Of Contents** lists the topics and subtopics in the document and usually includes the starting page number of each.

A **Table Of Contents** also makes it easier to navigate a long document on the screen. Each heading in the **Table Of Contents** is a hyperlink to the actual source text in the document. Holding the **Ctrl key** as you click any heading automatically takes you to that heading in the document.

The most efficient way to create a **Table Of Contents** is to apply the built-in heading styles, **Heading1** through **Heading 9**, to the topics and subtopics in a document. Each of these heading styles is recognized by **Microsoft Word** as a **Table Of Contents** entry.

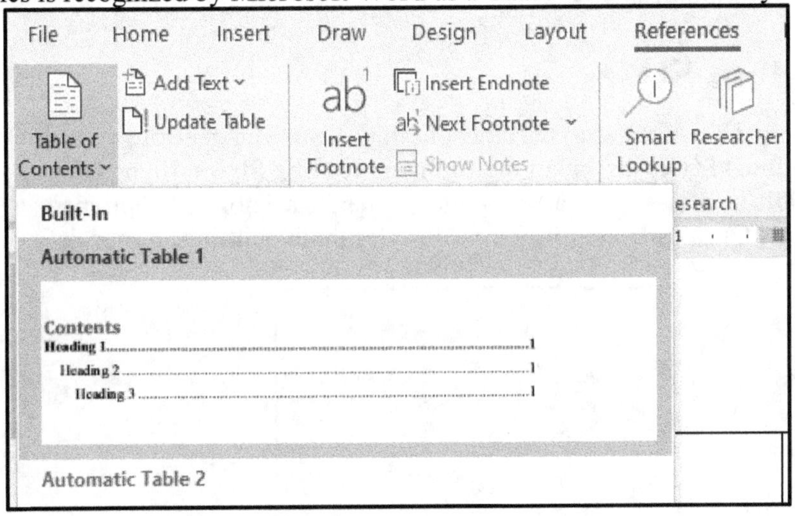

Practice Exercise 136 - Table Of Contents

1. ***File Tab→ Open Open→Browse→C:\Data\Word365-12\Table of Contents1.Docx.***
2. ***Scan through the document and verify the style for the heading "CUSTOMER INFORMATION." It should be Heading1.***
3. ***Scan through the document and verify the style for the heading "Products Distributed by Worldwide Sporting Goods." It should be Heading2.***
4. ***Press Ctrl Home keys, if necessary.***
5. ***Click References Ribbon Tab.***
6. ***Click Table Of Contents***
7. ***Click Automatic Table 1.***

Tip: ***Point to the Benefits of Excel Sporting Goods heading in the Table Of Contents and hold Ctrl key; notice that the mouse pointer changes into a pointing hand. Click the Benefits of Excel Sporting Goods heading; Microsoft Word goes to the corresponding document text.***

21.2 Removing A Table Of Contents

If you are not satisfied with the **Table Of Contents** or, simply wish to **Remove** it, **Microsoft Word** lets you delete a **Table Of Contents** easily.

Practice Exercise 137 - Removing

1. ***Click References Ribbon Tab.***

2. ***Click Table Of Contents***
3. ***Click Remove Table of Contents.***
4. ***Close the Document without saving it.***

21.3 Using Custom Styles

If you have applied user-defined styles to document headings, you can generate a **Table Of Contents** based on the **User-Defined Styles** instead of the **Built-In Heading Styles**. If you have applied both **User-Defined** and **Built-In Styles**, you can use both to generate a **Table Of Contents**.
The **Table Of Contents Options Dialog Box** lists all styles (both built-in and user-defined) in use in the

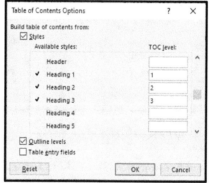

current document and a **Table Of Contents** level numbers are automatically assigned to each **Built-In Style**. You can assign the desired **Table Of Contents** level number to any available style, as well as exclude any styles you do not want to use.

Practice Exercise 138 - Custom Styles

1. *File Tab→* Open *→Browse→C:\Data\Word365-12\Table of Contents2.Docx.*
2. *Go to page 3 and click on the Product Features heading. Display the Styles task pane by clicking the ⌐ launcher arrow in the Styles Group on the Home Ribbon Tab. Notice that the user-defined Feature style has been applied to the heading.*

Close the Styles task pane and return to the top of the document.
3. *Click* Ctrl Home *keys, if necessary.*
4. *Click References Ribbon Tab→Table of Contents Group→*

Click Table Of Contents →*Click Custom Table of Contents.*
5. *Click Options* Options...
6. *Click ☐ Styles, if necessary to select it.*
7. *Click in the box to the right of Features.*
8. *Uncheck the Heading 3 box by removing the number 3.*

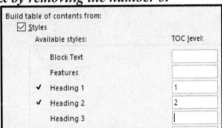

9. *Click* OK *→Click* OK

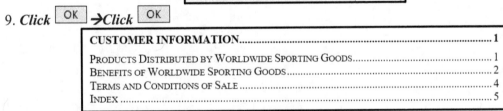

10. *To display the TOC field code, press* Shift F9 *keys.*

21.4 Updating A Table Of Contents

Once a **Table Of Contents** has been generated, additional editing changes can make it incorrect or incomplete. Adding, deleting, or rewording headings can also make the **Table Of Contents** incorrect. After you have made changes to a document, you can quickly **Update** the existing table of contents, rather than having to create and format a new one. You can choose to **Update** the entire table or only the page numbers.

Practice Exercise 139 - Updating

1. *Insert a blank page in front of Customer Information on page 2 (Layout Ribbon Tab→Page Setup Group→Breaks→ Next Page.) Press* Ctrl Home *keys to move to the top of the document.*
2. *Click References Ribbon Tab→Table of Contents Group.*
3. *Click Update Table*

Chapter 22 - Index

Indexing will appear at the end of the document and will list the subject and page number for quick reference. **Indexing** requires two commands:

1. **Mark Entry:** *References Ribbon Tab*→ *Mark Entry.*
2. *References Ribbon Tab*→*Insert Index.*

22.1 Mark Entry

This will **Mark** a word to be added to the **Index**. It will not create the **Index**, but only **Mark** the word for entry. Most people prefer to **Mark Index Entries** after a document has been completed because **Microsoft Word** can **Mark Multiple Occurrences** of the same text. When **Microsoft Word** marks all occurrences of **Index** text, it marks only the first occurrence of the text in each paragraph and will only record one entry of the page number in the **Index**. In other words, it won't display the referenced word as "1,1,1,2,2,2,2,4,4,4,4,4", but it will reference the word as 1,2,4. This is done when the Current Page option is checked in the **Mark**

Entry Dialog Box. As soon as you **Mark Text** for an **Index Entry**, **Microsoft Word** displays the

Formatting Marks ¶ , including the {**XE**} field codes, which are hidden text. You can use options available on the **Display** page in the **Microsoft Word Options Dialog Box** to view only the hidden text if desired.

22.2 Mark All

This will go through the entire document and find all instances of the selected word and **Mark** it to be added to the **Index**.

22.3 Typing Index Entries

In addition to selecting text to **Mark** as **Index** entries, you can type **Index** entries for terms or phrases that do not appear in the document but are implied or understood. For example, the word **backpack** in a document about camping equipment might be **Index**ed by both **pack** and **backpack**.

A {**XE**} field code appears in the document for each **Index Entry** you create.

Practice Exercise 140 - Mark Entry

1. *File Tab→* Open *→Browse→C:\Data\Word365-12\Index.Docx.*
   If necessary, go to the top of the document.
2. *Click in the selection bar to the left of the Sporting Equipment text.*
3. *Click References Ribbon Tab→Index Group→Click* Mark Entry→
   Click Mark .
4. *Mark Clothing on page 1 as the main Index Entry. Leave the Mark Index Entry Dialog Box open.*
5. *Mark the following Index entries by selecting each entry, clicking in the Mark Index Entry Dialog Box to activate it, and selecting the appropriate Mark command.*
   Supplies
   Memorabilia
   Product Features (select the Mark All button to mark all occurrences)
6. *Close* Close *the Mark Index Entry Dialog Box.*
7. *Hide the Formatting Marks.*

22.4 Generating An Index

After you have marked all desired **Index** entries, you can format and compile the **Index**.
You can create one of two types of **Indexes**: indented or run-in. An indented **Index** lists each **Index** level on a separate line and applies the **Index 1**, **Index 2**, and **Index 3** styles as appropriate; **Index 2 Subentries** are indented below **Index 1** main entries, and **Index 3 Subentries** (below).

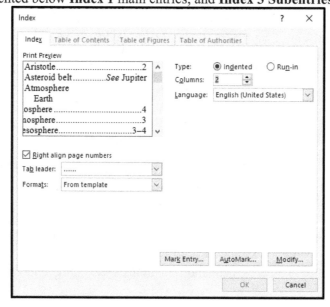

Practice Exercise 141 - Generating Index

Continue from the previous practice exercise.
1. *If necessary, display the References Ribbon Tab.*
2. *Press* Ctrl End *keys.*
3. *Click Insert Index: References Ribbon Tab →Index Group→ Insert Index.*
4. *Click* ◯ *Indented, if necessary.*
5. *Click Columns* ▲▼ *to 2, if necessary.*

6. ***Click Formats*** 🔽.
7. ***Scroll as necessary and click Formal.***
8. ***Click*** ⬜ ***Right align page numbers, if necessary.***
9. ***Click Tab leader*** 🔽.
10. ***Click the second option, if necessary.***

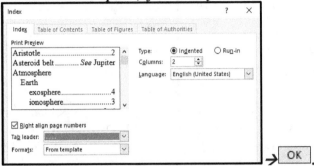

11. ***To Update the Index, click the Update Index button from the ribbon.***

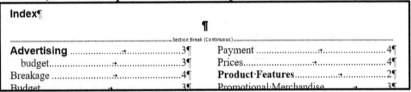

12. ***To turn off the Paragraph Marks: Home Ribbon Tab →***

    Paragraph Group →Paragraph Mark ¶.

Test it: Inspect the **Subentries** and **Cross-referencing Index Entries.**

22.5 Creating Index Subentries

A **Subentry** will be indented under a **Marked Entry** in the **Index**. Identify the **Subentry** by marking it, and the **Index** will be generated using a different command. You can create one or more **Subentries** for the main **Index Entry**, as well as **Subentries** for the **Subentries**, up to a total of three **Index** levels. For example, the main entry **Clothing** could have second-level **Subentries Children, Men,** and **Women**. The **Children Subentry** could have the additional third-level **Subentries** of **Infant** and **Adolescent.**

You can use the **Subentry Box** in the **Mark Index Entry Dialog Box** to create a second-level **Subentry**. To create a third-level **Subentry**, you must type the second-level **Subentry** followed by a colon (**:**) and the text of the third-level **Subentry**.

Practice Exercise 142 - SubEntries

If necessary, go to the top of the document and display the **References Ribbon Tab**.
1. *Locate the Service Features text on page 2.*
2. *Select the text outstanding Service.*

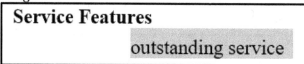

3. *Release the mouse button.*
4. *References Ribbon Tab→Index Group→Click* ▯ *Mark Entry button.*
5. *Press* ▢Tab *key.*
6. *Type Service Features.*

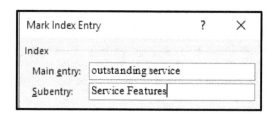

7. *Click Mark* ▢Mark▢.
8. *Continue marking the following and under the Subentries category type Service Features:*
   friendly customer support
   stock control
   cooperative advertising agreements
   semi-annual promotions
   well-trained, knowledgeable sales staff
9. *Click Close* ▢Close▢.

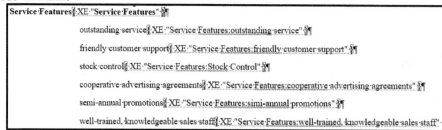

10. *Notice that each Subentry appears in a separate field and includes the main entry.*
11. **Update the Index: References Ribbon Tab→ Index Group→Update Index.**

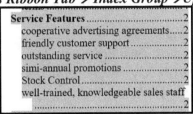

Service Features	2
cooperative advertising agreements	2
friendly customer support	2
outstanding service	2
simi-annual promotions	2
Stock Control	2
well-trained, knowledgeable sales staff	
	2

22.6 Automark

This will **Mark All Words** in the document from a text file. Add words to a text file and then merge the file in order to add words to the **Index** with page numbers.

File Tab→ [Open] *→ Browse → C:\Data\Word365-12\Annual Report w Tables.Docx.*

File Tab→ [Open] *→ Browse →C:\Data\Word365-12\Concordance File.Docx Review the contents.*

References Ribbon Tab →Index Group →Insert Index →Automark →Open Automark file →
C:\Data\Word365-12\Concordance File.Docx.

Student Project Z - Creating an Index

1. *File Tab→* [Open] *→Browse →C:\Data\Word365-12\Index Practice1.Docx.*
2. **Mark the Creating a Document heading as the main Index Entry.**

Select the text "Creating a Document" →References Ribbon Tab →Index Group → Mark
Entry button→ Main entry: Creating a Document Subentry: → [Mark] *button→* [Close].

Index	
Main entry:	**Creating a Document**
Subentry:	

3. *Create a Subentry of Creating a Document.*

   3a. *Select the text "Naming the Document" →References Ribbon Tab →Index Group →*
   Mark Entry button→
   Main entry: *Creating a Document*
   Subentry: *Naming The Document* → [Mark] *button→* [Close].

Index	
Main entry:	**Creating a Document**
Subentry:	Naming The Document

   Tip: Another technique is to mark "Naming the Document" and Cut/Paste
   "Creating a Document" in the code as follows:
   Naming the Document{·XE·"Creating·a·Document:Naming·the·Document"·}

4. **On page 3, mark the Allow Widows and Orphans, Automatic Page Breaks, and Backup Before Edit Document headings as Subentries of the text Modify Document Defaults.**
   4a. *Select the text Allow Widows and Orphans →References ribbon tab →*

   Index Group → Mark Entry button→
   Main entry: *Modify Document Defaults*
   Subentry: *Allow Widows and Orphans* → [Mark] *button→* [Close].

Index	
Main entry:	Modify Document Defaults
Subentry:	Allow Widows and Orphans

*4b. **Select the text Automatic Page Breaks →References ribbon tab →***

Index Group→ 🗏 *Mark Entry button →*
Main entry: *Modify Document Defaults*
Subentry: *Automatic Page Breaks →* | Mark | *button →* | Close |.

Index	
Main entry:	Modify Document Defaults
Subentry:	Automatic Page Breaks

*4c. **Select the text Backup Before Edit Document→References Ribbon Tab***

→Index Group→ 🗏*Mark Entry button →*
Main entry: *Modify Document Defaults*
Subentry: *Backup Before Edit Document →* | Mark | *button→* | Close |.

Index	
Main entry:	Modify Document Details
Subentry:	Backup Before Edit Document

5. If you generate an Index it would look similar to the following:

Page down to the last page of the document→References Ribbon Tab →Index Group → 🗏*Insert Index→* ☑Right align page numbers*OK*

Creating a Document	 1	Modify Document Details		
Naming the Document	 1	Allow Widows and Orphans	....	3
Valid Document Name	 2	Automatic Page Breaks	....	3
		Backup Before Edit Document	....	3

Tip: The significance of step 2 above is a page reference number will be created.
In step 4, we did not create a separate reference to the Main entry.

6. **Position the insertion point in the line above the "Backup Before Edit Document" heading and enter the main Index Entry by "Saving a File Copy": Cross-reference the Saving a File Copy entry to Backup Before Edit Document and then, mark the entry:**
Type in the text "Saving a File Copy" just before the words "Backup Before Edit Document"→Select the text "Saving a File Copy" →

References Ribbon Tab →Index Group → 🗏 *Mark Entry button →*
Main entry: Saving a File Copy
Cross-reference: see Backup Before Edit Document→
| Mark | *button →.* | Close |.

Index	
Main entry:	Saving a File Copy
Subentry:	
Options	
◉ Cross-reference:	See Backup Before Edit Doc

7. **Press** Ctrl End **keys to go to the end of the document:**
Press the Ctrl End *keyboard key.*

8. **Generate a Modern, two-column Index:** *References Ribbon Tab →*

Index Group → 🗏*Mark Entry button →* 🗏*Insert Index→*
   Formats: Modern
   ☑*Right align page numbers*
   Tab Leader: ....

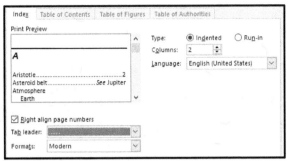

Tip: This will create the following in the **Index**:

> Saving a File Copy .... *See* Backup Before Edit Document

Tip: The code will look similar to the following:

> Saving·a·File·Copy{·XE·"Saving·a·File·Copy"·\t·"*See*·Backup·Before·Edit·Document"}¶
> Backup·Before·Edit·Document·{·XE·"Modify·Document·Details:Backup·Before·Edit·Document"·}

9. **View the {INDEX} field code and then, view the Index text again.**

   Home Ribbon Tab→Paragraph Group→ ¶ *Show/Hide paragraph marks.*

   INDEX

C		M	
Creating a Document		Modify Document Details	
Naming the Document	1	Allow Widows and Orphans	3
Valid Document Name	2	Automatic Page Breaks	3
		Backup Before Edit Document	3
D		**P**	
Document Screen Layout		Page Break key	
Format Line	4	F2 3	
Status Line	4		

10. **Go to page 1 and select the word filename in the first paragraph below the <u>Naming the Document</u> heading. Mark all occurrences of the filename as the main Index Entry.**
    Select the text filename below the title <u>Naming the Document</u> →

    > <u>Naming the Document</u>
    >
    > <u>Multimate</u> gives you the ability to type a document name or filename up to 20

    References Ribbon Tab→Index Group→ 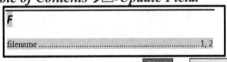 *Mark Entry button→*
    Mark All *Mark All button→* Close .

11. *Press* Ctrl End *to go to the end of the document, then update the Index.*

    11a. *Press the* Ctrl End *keyboard key.*

    11b. *Right-click on the Table of Contents→* *Update Field.*

    > **F**
    >
    > filename 1, 2

12. **Close the document without saving it:** *File Tab→* Close *→* Don't Save .
13. *The final Index follows:*

Chapter 22 - Index

Chapter 23 - References

There are many different ways and techniques to reference information in your document.

Practice Exercise 143 - Open File Annual Report

File Tab→ Open *→Browse→C:\Data\Word365-12\Annual Report.Docx.*

23.1 Bookmarks

Bookmarks are used for navigation purposes. They are visible in the document but invisible when you print.

Practice Exercise 144 - Bookmark

1. **Bookmark the title Talent:** *Select the word "Talent" (page 4)→ Insert Ribbon Tab→Link Group→ Bookmark→Bookmark Name: Talent→ Choose* Add *Add.*
2. *Navigate to Page 1.*
3. **Goto Bookmark:** *Insert Ribbon Tab→Links Group→ Bookmark→Select Talent→Go to button.*

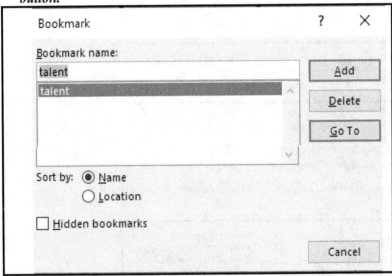

4. **Practice the concept:** *Select the word "Infrastructure" on page 4→ Insert Ribbon Tab→Links Group→ Bookmark→ Bookmark Name: Infrastructure→Choose* Add *Add.*
5. **Delete the Infrastructure Bookmark:** *Insert Ribbon Tab→Links Group→Bookmark→Select Infrastructure→* Delete *Delete button→Close.*
6. *Configuration: File Tab→Options→Advanced→ Show document content→ ☑ Show Bookmarks→* OK *.*

It should look similar to: ┃Talent┃:

23.2 Links

This is a **Link** to a web page, document, or related information that is external from the main document.

Practice Exercise 145 - Links Bookmark

Continue from the previous practice exercise.

1. **Select the text "New Relocation Team" on page 3.**

New Relocation Team: Because
last year, we decided to create a n

2. **Insert Ribbon Tab→Links Group→ Link→ Place in This Document→Bookmarks→Talent→ OK .**

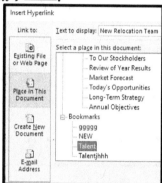

3. **Test It:** *Click on the Link.*

New Relocation Team: Because
last year, we decided to create a

Practice Exercise 146 - Links - Place In Document

Continue from the previous practice exercise.

1. *Select the text "To Our Stockholders" on page 1.*

Insert Ribbon Tab →Links Group → Link → Place in this Document →

Select "Todays Opportunities" → OK .

2. **Test It:** *Click on the Link.*

To Our Stockholders

Practice Exercise 147 - Links - Web

Continue from the previous practice exercise.

1. ***Select the "Milestones" title on page 1→Insert Ribbon Tab→*** 🔗***Links Group→Link→*** 🔲
   Existing File or Web page→www.elearnlogic.com→ OK .

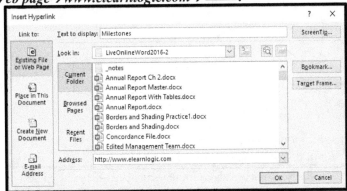

2. **Test It:** *Click on the Link.*

23.3 Footnote

This is a **Reference** to a **Quote**, comment, or text that provides more information listed at the bottom of the page.

> Text in document[i]
> _____
> [i] Footnote end of page

Practice Exercise 148 - Footnote

Continue from the previous practice exercise.

1. ***Locate the Residential title on Page 2.***

> **Market Forecast**
>
> **Residential:** In the South, private housing continues leading the pack. Of course, all of this activity is at the expense of the North. This region hasn't seen significant growth for a long time and the outlook remains bleak. This ongoing trend is a unique opportunity for the Company providing we are flexible enough to channel our resources properly into the Southern offices. [1]

2. ***Click the end of paragraph→References Ribbon Tab→Footnotes Group→*** 📝 ***Insert Footnote→Enter the following:***
   "This information was obtained from the Census Bureau June 2010."
3. ***The following will be displayed at the end of the page:***

> [1] This information was obtained from the Census Bureau June 2010.

Tip: If you insert a **Page Break** at **Market Forecast**, the **Footnote** will move to the next page.

23.4 Endnote

This is a reference to a quote, comment, or text that provides more information listed at the bottom of the document.

```
Text in document[i]
_____
[i] Endnote end of document
```

Practice Exercise 149 - Endnote

Continue from the previous practice exercise.
1. ***Locate the "Relocation" Title on page 3.***

> **Relocation:** With the Northeast continuing to purge both blue- and white-collar jobs, the majority of employment opportunities are still flowing southward. Current forecasts predict population in this burgeoning region will increase at a 15% rate over the next decade. This is why we've decided to focus our relocation efforts, and consequently our staffing efforts, in the Boston and Atlanta offices. With the Boston office "sending" displaced workers and the Atlanta office "receiving" them, leveraging our various Southern satellite offices, we will be poised to take advantage of this employment exodus trend for the foreseeable future.[i]

2. ***Select the end of the paragraph→References Ribbon Tab→***
3. ***Footnotes Group→ Insert Endnote.***
4. ***Type in the following: Located at 123 Test Street.***
5. ***The following will be located at the end of the document:***

```
_____
[i] Located at 123 Test Street
```

23.5 Citation

This credits the reference to a source such as a book, article, or other material. You can either Add a **New Source** or **Add a New Placeholder** that contains a **Citation**.

> Add New Source...
>
> Add New Placeholder...

New Source - Use the **New Source** option if you have the information you need to create a **Citation**. **Add New Placeholder** - Use this if you do not have the necessary information and it will create a **Placeholder** until you receive it.

Practice Exercise 150 - Citation

Continue from the previous practice exercise.
1. ***Select the text "Connor v. OGC, 314 US 252 (2008)" on page 1.***

> **Legal Issues:** On the legal front, Connor v. OGC, 314 US 252 (2008) and Smith v. OGC, F2d 201 (2009) have been dismissed. The primary reason for dismissal in both decisions

2. ***References Ribbon Tab→Citations & Bibliography Group→***

3.  *Insert Citation→ Add New Placeholder→Placeholder1→*

   → OK .

4. *Select the text "Smith v. OGC, F2d 201 (2009)" on page 1.*
5. *References Ribbon Tab→ Citations & Bibliography Group→*
6. *Insert Citation→ Add new placeholder→Placeholder2→* OK .

> **Legal Issues:** On the legal front, (Placeholder1) and (Placeholder2) have been dismissed. The primary reason for dismissal in both decisions was the lack of evidence on the part of the prosecution. However, this does raise and interesting question. Has the Company come to a point in its growth where it now needs a dedicated legal staff? Rachel Martin, a managing partner in a firm that does not currently represent the Company, has proposed that the Company purchase her firm outright.

23.6 Manage Sources

This will allow you to enter the content of your **Citations**.
1. *References Ribbon Tab→ Citations & Bibliography Group →*
 Manage Sources → Select Placeholder1 →Edit→Enter the following:

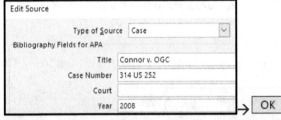

2. *References Ribbon Tab→ Citations & Bibliography Group →*
 Manage Sources → Select Placeholder2 →Edit→Enter the following:

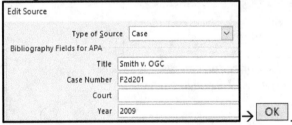

3. **Tip**: If you receive the following message, choose Yes to the following prompt:

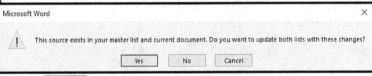

4. *When finished choose* Close .
5. *The result will update the words Placeholder with information*
 in the Placeholder:

> **Legal Issues:** On the legal front, (Connor v. OGC, 2008) and (Smith v. OGC, 2009) have been dismissed. The primary reason for dismissal in both decisions was the lack of evidence on the part of the prosecution. However, this does raise and interesting question. Has the Company come to a point in its growth where it now needs a dedicated legal staff? Rachel Martin, a managing partner in a firm that does not currently represent the Company, has proposed that the Company purchase her firm outright.

23.7 Style

This lists all the different **Citation Styles** available.

Practice Exercise 151 - Citation

Continue from the previous practice exercise.

1. ***Page down to "Today's Opportunities" on page 3→Click after "Today's Opportunities"→***

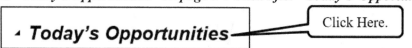

2. ***References Ribbon Tab→Citations & Bibliography Group→Style: Chicago Fifteenth.***

 *Edition*

3. ***References Ribbon Tab→ Citations & Bibliography Group→ Insert Citation→ Add New Source→Enter the following:***

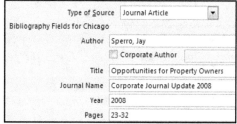

4.

4. **Test It:** *Each Style may provide a different set of requirements. Change the style to different values such as ADA, Harvard, ISO, etc. Try to identify any differences.*

23.8 Bibliography

This is a list of references to source material located at the end of the document. It contains enough information to find the source for further research.

Practice Exercise 152 - Bibliography End Of Document

Continue from the previous practice exercise.

1. ***Page down to the end of the document→References Ribbon tab → Citation & Bibliography Group→ Bibliography drop down → Insert Bibliography.***

2. ***Type in a title of Bibliography:***

Bibliography

Connor v. OGC, 314 US 252 (2008).
Smith v. OGC, F2d201 (2009).

3. **Tip**: If the **Bibliography** changes: ***Right-click →Update references.***

23.9 Captions

This is a text string that describes the object. It is usually located under a picture, graphic, or table.

Practice Exercise 153 - Insert Caption

Continue from the previous practice exercise.
1. ***Select the Organizational Chart on page 3.***
2. ***References Ribbon Tab→ Captions Group→***  ***Insert Caption→ Enter the following:***

23.10 Cross-References

Cross-References are similar to links but refer to a different page on the document. It may refer to text, graphics, tables, and/or pictures.

Practice Exercise 154 - Cross References

1. ***File Tab→Options →Advanced →Show Document content→***

   Field Shading→Always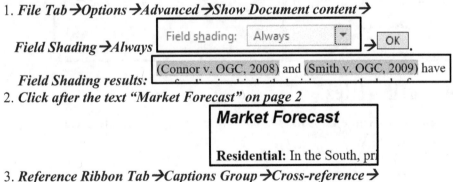

   Field Shading results:
2. ***Click after the text "Market Forecast" on page 2***

Market Forecast

Residential: In the South, pr

3. ***Reference Ribbon Tab→Captions Group→Cross-reference→***
4. ***Reference Type: Heading→Choose "Long term strategy"→***

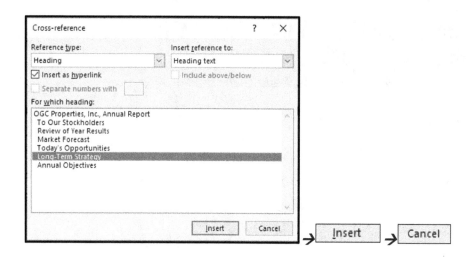

23.11 Table of Figures

This will list the **Figures** or objects that have captions and provide a page number for reference. It is similar to a **Table Of Contents** and will allow the reader to find information easily.

Practice Exercise 155 - Table of Figures

Continue from the previous practice exercise.
1. *Add a blank space just under the title on Page 1.*
2. *References Ribbon Tab →Captions Group →* 📄 *Insert Table of Figures →* OK .

23.12 Table of Authorities

This generates a list similar to a **Table Of Contents** but is designed for legal references.

Practice Exercise 156 - Table Of Authorities

Go to Legal Issues Page 3 bottom.
1. *Select Connor v. OGC, 314 US 252 (2008)*
2. *References Ribbon Tab →Table of Authorities Group →Mark Citation →Cases →*
   → Mark All → Close .
3. *Select Smith v. OGC, F2d 201 (2009)*
4. *References Ribbon Tab →Table of Authorities Group → Mark Citation →Cases*
   → Mark All → Close .

5. *Select just under the Figures on page 1→References Ribbon Tab→*

Table of Authority group→ 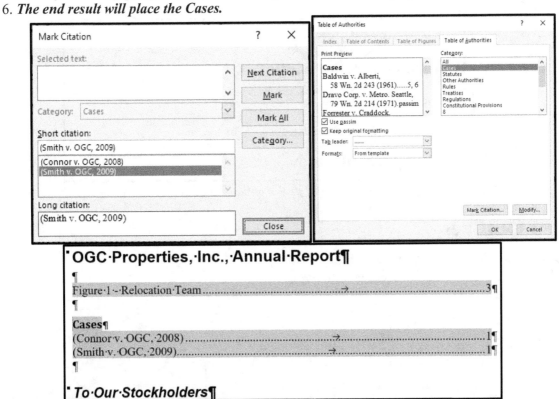 *Insert Table of Authorities →Category: Cases→* OK.

6. *The end result will place the Cases.*

23.13 Master Document

This is a document that provides a link to other documents or subdocuments.

Practice Exercise 157 - Master Documents

1. *File Tab→* 🗁 Open *→Browse→ C:\Data\Word365-12\Annual Report Master.Docx.*
2. *View Ribbon Tab→ Views Group→ Outline.*
3. *Outlining Ribbon Tab→ Master Document Group→Show Document.*
4. *Select the document in order to see the Insert command→*

   Outlining Ribbon Tab→Master Document Group→Insert→

   C:\Data\Word365-12\Shareholder Insert.Docx→ Open .

5. *Outlining Ribbon Tab→Master Document Group→Insert→*

   C:\Data\Word365-12\Results.Docx→ Open .

6. *Outlining Ribbon Tab→Master Document Group→Insert→*

   C:\Data\Word365-12\Forecast.Docx→ Open .

7. *Outlining Ribbon Tab→Master Document Group→Insert→*

   C:\Data\Word365-12\Opportunities.Docx→ Open .

8. *Outlining Ribbon Tab→Master Document Group→Insert→*

C:\Data\Word365-12\Strategy.Docx → [Open] .

9. *File Tab→Save As → C:\Data\Word365-12\Annual Report MasterV2.Docx.*

10. *Collapse Subdocuments.*

⊞ ⊕ **To Our Stockholders**
⊞ ⊕ **Review of Year Results**
⊞ ⊕ **Market Forecast**
⊞ ⊕ **Today's Opportunities**
⊞ ⊕ **Long-Term Strategy**

11. *Click on the ⊞Link (located in the front of the collapsed name).*

23.14 Outlines

An **Outline** can be created to expand and collapse paragraphs easily.

View Ribbon Tab→Views Group→ ▤ Outline.

Chapter 24 - Quick Parts

Each of the concepts in this chapter can be added to the **Quick Parts Gallery**.

24.1 Quick Parts

The **Quick Parts** library is located on the **Insert Ribbon Tab**. It allows you to manage the objects stored in the gallery.

Insert Ribbon Tab→Text Group→▤*Quick Parts→Building Blocks Organizer.*

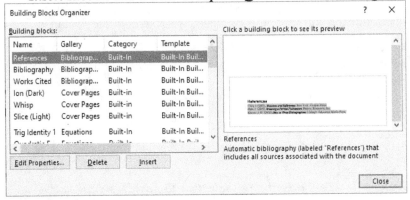

24.2 Cover Page

A **Cover Page** will be located on the first page of the document and usually contains a graphic image or a colorful look and layout. *Insert Ribbon Tab→Pages Group→*▤*Cover Page→Save Selection to Cover Page Gallery.*

Practice Exercise 158 - Cover Page

1. *File Tab→* `📁 Open` *→ Browse→C:\Data\Word365-12\Annual Report with Tables.Docx→* `Open` .

2. *Insert Ribbon Tab→Pages Group→* ▤ *Cover Page→*
   Cubicles or any other desired Cover Page.
3. *Type the company name: OGC Properties*
4. *Type the document title: OGC Properties Inc. Annual Report*
5. *Type the subtitle: Annual Report*
6. *Type Username: (Your Name)*
7. *Year: 2013*

8. **Insert a blank page on Page 2:** *Layout Ribbon Tab→Page Setup Group→*▤*Breaks→*▤*Page.*

24.3 Watermarks

This is a transparent text or graphic image located behind the main text. It could contain words such as **Draft** or **Confidential**.

Design Ribbon Tab→Page Background Group→▤*Watermarks.*

Tip: In previous versions, this was in **Page Layout Ribbon Tab.**

24.4 Header

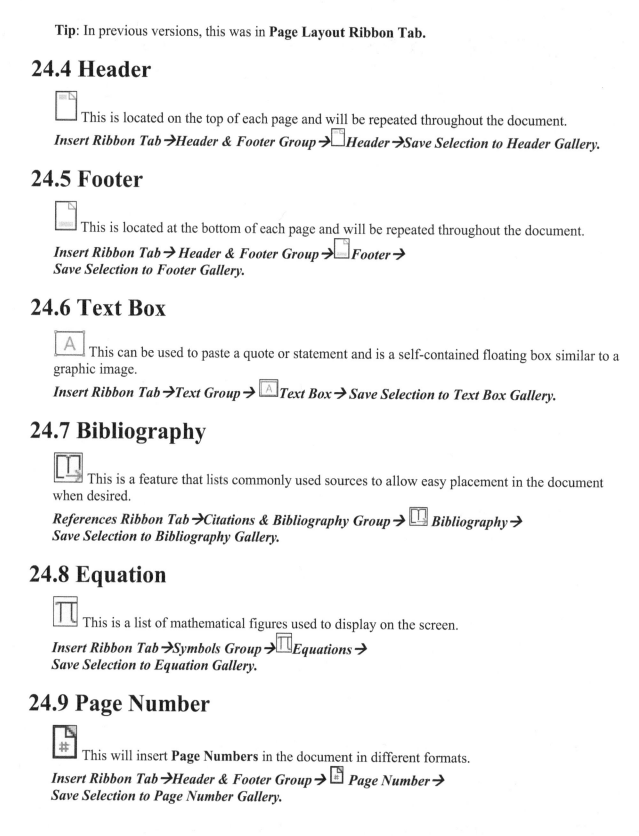

This is located on the top of each page and will be repeated throughout the document.

Insert Ribbon Tab→Header & Footer Group→Header→Save Selection to Header Gallery.

24.5 Footer

This is located at the bottom of each page and will be repeated throughout the document.

*Insert Ribbon Tab→ Header & Footer Group→Footer→
Save Selection to Footer Gallery.*

24.6 Text Box

This can be used to paste a quote or statement and is a self-contained floating box similar to a graphic image.

Insert Ribbon Tab→Text Group→ Text Box→ Save Selection to Text Box Gallery.

24.7 Bibliography

This is a feature that lists commonly used sources to allow easy placement in the document when desired.

*References Ribbon Tab→Citations & Bibliography Group→ Bibliography→
Save Selection to Bibliography Gallery.*

24.8 Equation

This is a list of mathematical figures used to display on the screen.

*Insert Ribbon Tab→Symbols Group→Equations→
Save Selection to Equation Gallery.*

24.9 Page Number

This will insert **Page Numbers** in the document in different formats.

*Insert Ribbon Tab→Header & Footer Group→ Page Number→
Save Selection to Page Number Gallery.*

24.10 Table Of Contents

This will list the commonly used **Table Of Content** layouts. *References Ribbon Tab→Table of Contents Group→Table of Contents→Save Selection to Table Of Contents Gallery.*

24.11 Table

This lists commonly used **Table Layouts**.
Insert Ribbon Tab→Tables Group→Table→Save Selection to Table Gallery.

24.12 AutoText

This will place commonly used text phrases in the document.
Insert Ribbon Tab→Text Group→Quick Parts→AutoText→Save Selection to AutoText Gallery.

Appendix A - Final Project Long Documents

This **Comprehensive Exercise** will cover all long document concepts in **Microsoft Word**. Add additional formatting as needed. The following is an overview of the concepts covered:

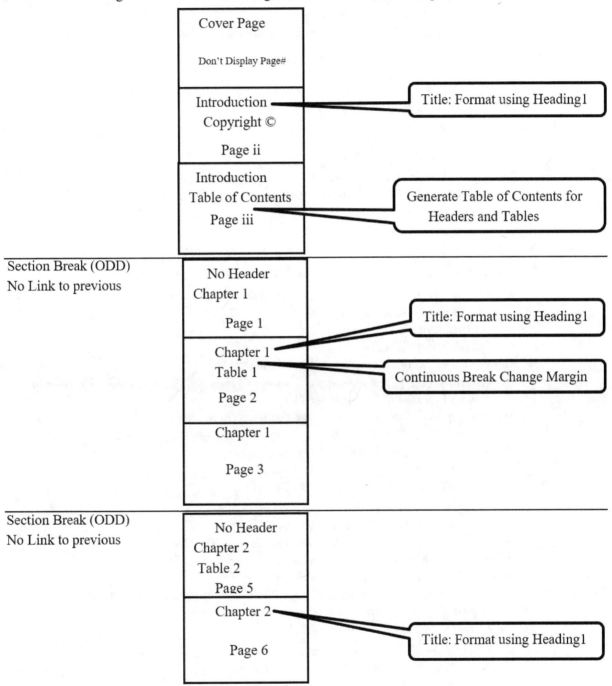

4

Final Project A1 - Page Numbering And Page Breaking

Open document "C:\Data\Word365-3\Long Doc Start Document".

1. **Page 1 - Cover Page**
   1a. **Choose a cover page and include the following:**
      Mike's Sporting Goods
   1b. **Type in the following and use the automatic date update:**
      (Your Name)
      Insert Date here (Insert Ribbon Tab→Text Group→
      Date&Time→Choose date→ ☑ Update Automatically.
   1c. **Insert a ▢Page Break at the end of the page.**
2. **Page 2 - Copyright statement**
   2a. **Use the following information on page 2:**
      Hint type: (c) or Insert→Symbol
      Copyrights © 2014 eLearnLogic. All rights reserved.
      The information in this document is for the sole use of Students.
   2b. **Insert a ▢ Page Break at the end of the page.**
3. **Page 3 - Table of Contents**
   3a. **Format the title "Table of Contents" to be Style of Heading1.**
   3b. **Insert an ▦ "Odd Page section break" after the Table of Contents.**
   3c. **View Ribbon Tab→View Group→▤Draft→Double click on the ▦Odd page break→Layout tab.**
      ☑ Different Odd & Even.
      ☑ Different First Page.
   3d. **Add the Page Number to the Even Page Footer:**
      Insert Ribbon Tab→ Headers & Footers Group→▦ Page Number→Bottom of Page→Left side (Plain number 1).
   3e. **Add the Page Number to the Odd page Footer→Go to Odd page:**
      Insert Ribbon Tab→ Headers & Footers Group→▦ Page Number →Bottom of Page→Right side(Plain number 3)
   3f. **Insert ii Page numbering to the above section (page 1-3)**
      View Ribbon Tab→Views Group→▤ Draft
      Select Page 1 to 3 (Just before the ▦Odd page break)
      Insert→ Page Number →Format Page Number
      Format→Number format = iii, ii, Start at : i
   3g. **If the page numbers are wrong, select new ones and force them to be the desired page. To see the results: View→Print Layout.**
      Select Page Number→Insert→Page Number→Format Page Numbers.
4. **Insert Chapter Page Numbering (Starting at Chapter 1)**
   4a. **View Ribbon Tab→ Views Group→▤Draft**
   4b. **Select below the ▦Odd Page Break.**
      Note: The status bar on the bottom will display Page 5 due to the Odd Page Break.
   4c. **Design Ribbon(Insert→Footer→Edit Footer):**
      ☑ Different Odd & Even
      ▢ Different First Page
   4d. **Add the Page Number to the Even Page Footer:**
      Select the Footer section→Design→Page Number→Bottom of Page→Left side.
   4e. **Add the Page Number to the Odd Page Footer:**

Select the Footer section→Design →Page Number→
Bottom of Page→Right side.

4f. *Insert 123 Page numbering in the above section (page 1-3):*
View Ribbon Tab→Views Group→▤Draft
Select Page 1 to 3 (Just after the ▥Odd Page Break).
Design→ Page Number→Format page number
Format→Number format = 1,2,3, Start at : 1.
If the page numbers are wrong select new ones and force them to be the
desired page: Select Page Number→Insert→Page Number→
Format Page Numbers

5. *Page 1 - Chapter 1 Invitation (Convert text to a column)*
   5a. *Format the title to be Style of Heading1 (Home→Heading1).*
   5b. *Select the text above the table to be converted to columns.*
   5c. *Change the text to 2 columns (Page Layout→Columns→*
   More Columns→Two, ☑ Line Between).
   Tip: A continuous break was automatically inserted.
   5e. *Insert a continuous break before and after the table:*
   Page Layout→Break→Continuous Break.
   5f. *Modify the margin of the table and move it to the left:*
   Page Layout→Margin→Custom Margin→Left: .4.

6. *Page 2 - Chapter 2 Experts*
   6a. *Insert ▥Odd Page Break before Chapter 2.*
   6b. *Format the title to be Style of Heading1.*
   6c. *Place Bullets in front of the Bullet List.*
   6d. *Convert the text Morning, Midday, Evening to a table:*
   Select text→Insert→Table→Convert text to table
   Number of Columns: 2
   Separate Text at: ◉ Tab
   6e. *Select the table on Page 2.*
   6f. *Format the table as desired (Select table →Design →Table Styles).*

7. *Page 3 - Chapter 3 Directions*
   7a. *Insert ▥Odd Page Break before Chapter 3.*
   7b. *Format the title to be Style of Heading1.*

8. *Page 4 - Form Fields*
   8a. *Insert ▥Odd Page Break before "Form Fields."*
   8b. *Format the title to be Style of Heading1.*
   Add the form fields.

Last Name	Aa Rich Text Content Control
First Name	Aa Rich Text Content Control
Company	Aa Rich Text Content Control
Phone Number	Aa Rich Text Content Control
Number of Copies	Aa Rich Text Content Control
Fitness Equipment Brochure	Option Box (ActiveX control) ◉ Yes ◉ No
Workshops Availability	Combo Box: Leadership Skills, Effective Communication, Supervisor Skills
New Product Lines Brochure	Dropdown Box Computer Training, Soft Skills, Technical Training, Project Management.

Final Project A2 - Headers And Footers

Enter the following **Headers** and **Footers**:
Insert→Header→Edit Header
1. ***First Page Header - Section 1***
   No Text
2. ***First Page Footer - Section1***
   No Text
3. ***Even Page Header - Section 1***
   Center the title "Mike's Sporting Goods."
4. ***Even Page Footer - Section 1***
   File Name:(Insert Ribbon Tab → Text Group →QuickParts → Field→Filename).
5. ***Odd page header - Section 1***
   Center the title "Fitness Equipment."
6. ***Odd page footer - Section 1***
   Date field "12/4/02." (Insert→Date&Time)
7. ***Odd page header - Section 2***
   No Text

   Tip: If you do not want the **Odd Page**
     Header to appear in section 2 then turn off the option in the
     Note: To see the **Section** labels:
   Insert→Header→Edit Header.
Page Setup Options

Page Layout→More Options

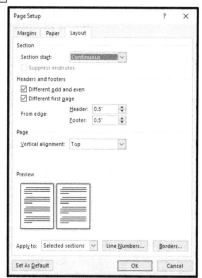

      Header/ Footer Toolbar of **"Link to Previous.**"
8. **Odd page footer - Section 2**
   (Type the **Microsoft Word** "Page" in front of the page number right justified)
       Example: Page 1
9. **Even Page Header - Section 2**
       No Text
10. **Even Page Footer - Section 2**
   (Type the word Page in front of the page number Left justified)
       Example: Page 2
11. Continue typing the word "Page" in front of all remaining pages if necessary.

Final Project A3 - Table of Contents

1. *Make sure all Chapter titles are formatted as Style of Heading1.*
2. *Go to the "Table of Contents" page and delete the old TOC.*
3. *Place cursor under "Table of Contents" title.*
4. *References →Table of Contents →Insert Table of Contents.*

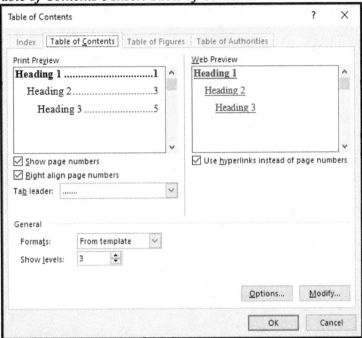

5. *Choose defaults → OK.*
6. *The Table Of Contents will look similar to the following:*

Table of Contents

Final Project A4 - Index

1. *Chapter 1 - Page 1 select "Fitness Equipment Showcase" text→References →Index Group→* *Mark Entry→Mark →Close.*
2. *Chapter 1 - Page 1 select "Equipment Sales"*
   Hold `Alt` `Shift` `X` *keys→Mark →Close.*
3. *Chapter 1 - Page 1 select "Product Training "*
   Hold `Alt` `Shift` `X` *keys→Mark →Close.*

4. *Chapter 1 - Page 1 select "Workshops"*
   Hold `Alt` `Shift` `X` *keys→Mark All→Close.*

5. *Go to the last page of the document→Insert a* Page Break→Type "Title of: Index."
6. *Format the title of Style Heading1.*
7. *References →Index Group→Insert Index.*
8. *Choose defaults→* `OK` *.*
9. *Update the Table of Contents →Right-click on Table of Contents →*
   Update field.

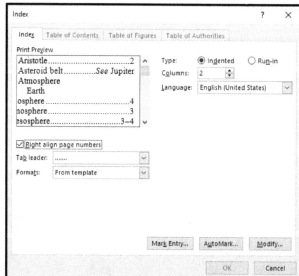

Final Project A5 - Footnotes

1. *Go to Page 2 Experts.*
2. *Place the cursor after "over 50 experts."*
3. *References →Insert Footnote.*
4. *To configure the footnote: References →More Options*
 Example Screen Shot of Footnote page
5. *Type in the following text: Located in the USA.*
6. *Place the cursor after the words "Equipment Manufacturers."*
7. *References →Insert Footnote.*
8. *Type in the following text: Located in the USA.*
9. *The footnotes will look similar to the following:*

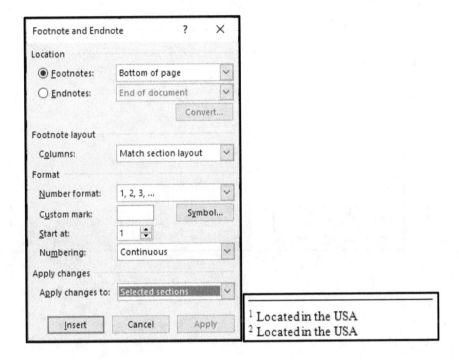

Final Project A6 - Table of Figures

1. *Delete the name Table 1 on Page 1 Chapter 1.*
2. *Select the table title "Product Line."*
3. *References →Insert Caption. Fill out the caption form as follows:*
4. *References →Insert Caption.*
   Fill out the caption form similar to the above form.
5. OK .
6. *Type in the following just under the Table of Contents:*
   "Table of Figures" and format it as a style Heading1.
7. *References →Insert Table of Figures →* OK .
8. OK .
9. *Delete the name Table 2 on Page 2 Chapter 2.*
10. *Select the Chapter 2 table title "Specialist."*

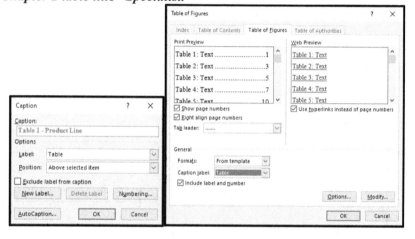

Final Project A7 - Word Forms

1. ***File Tab→Options→Custom Ribbon→☑ Developer tab.***
2. ***Developer Ribbon Tab→Controls group.***

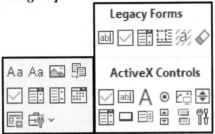

3. ***Select the Last Name form field box on the forms page.***
4. ***Select the "Plain Text Content Control"***

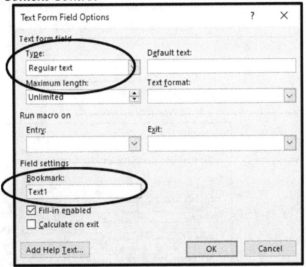

5. ***Repeat this process for each form field.***
6. ***Right-click on the "Fitness Equipment Brochure" R-Click→ Properties.***
7. ***Fill in the form with the following information:***

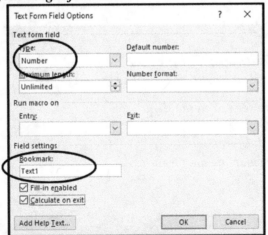

8. ***Repeat this process for all number forms on the bottom.***
9. ***Right-click on the "Total Brochures Requested" form field→Properties.***
10. ***Change the properties to calculate.***

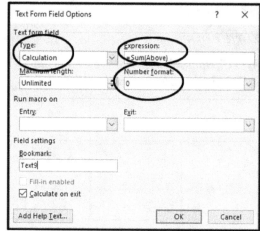

11. ***Protect fields* and Test it:** ***Developer→Protect Group→Restrict Editing***

2. Editing restrictions

☑ Allow only this type of editing in the document:

Filling in forms ▼

Yes, Start Enforcing Protection

12. *The forms page will look similar to the following:*

Forms Page

For more information please fill out the following form

Last Name	Hutchinson
First Name	Jeff
Company	Excel Networks
Phone	801-407-6388
	Number of Copies
Fitness Equipment Brochure	1
New Product Lines Brochure	2
Workshops Availability	4
Total Brochures Requested	7

Final Project A8 - Optional Topics

Optional Topics:
Use Alt F9 *keys to see text in the field.*
Quickparts→Field→Ref
Use to display typed information.
Press F9 *key to recalculate the formulas.*

Appendix B - Forms

Form fields can be used to automate entering information into a document.

Practice Exercise 159

File Tab→  *Open → Browse → C:\Data\Word365-12\New Client Forms.Docx*

B.1 Quick Access Toolbar

This will add the **Insert Form Fields** and **Form Field Options** in the **Quick Assess Toolbar** (located on the top of the interface).

1. *File Tab→Options→Quick Access Toolbar→ Choose commands from:*

   All Commands→Select Insert Form Fields→ `Add >>` *→* `OK` .

2. *File Tab→Options→Quick Access Toolbar→Choose commands from:*

   All Commands→Select Form Field Options→ `Add >>` *→* `OK` .

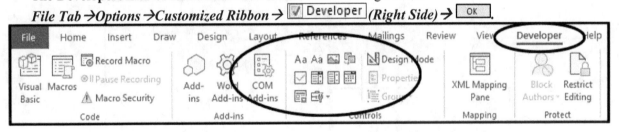

B.2 Developers Tab

The **Developers Tab** contains additional features for creating Forms.

File Tab→Options→Customized Ribbon→ `☑ Developer` *(Right Side) →* `OK` .

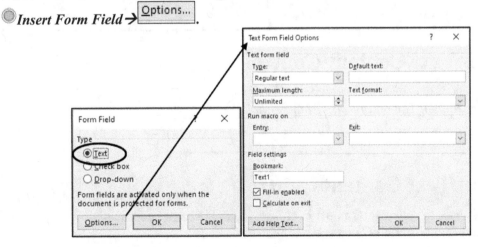

B.3 Form Field Text

Select the blank box under the Title→Quick Access Toolbar→

⊚ *Insert Form Field→* `Options...` .

B.4 Form Field Checkbox

Select the blank box under the Title →Quick Access Toolbar →
◎Insert Form Field→Options....

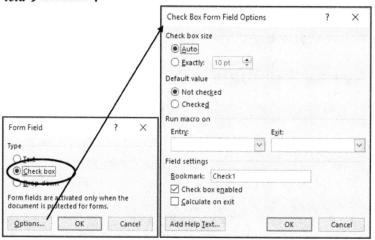

B.5 Form Field Drop-down

Select the blank box under the Title →Quick Access Toolbar →
◎Insert Form Field→Options....

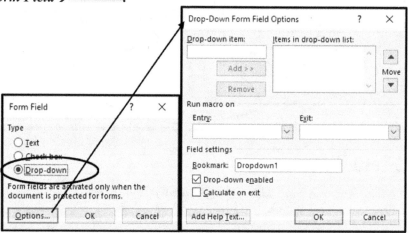

B.6 Rich Text Content Control

Aa This is used to collect text, numeric, or date values.
Developer Ribbon Tab→Controls Group →Click the Aa button.

B.7 Plain Text Content Control

Aa This is used to collect text, numeric, or date values but can't be formatted. It looks very similar to the **Rich Text Content Control box.**

Developer Ribbon Tab→Controls Group →Click the Aa *button.*

Click here to enter text.

B.8 Picture Content Control

This is a control box that allows you to enter a picture.

Developer Ribbon Tab→Controls Group→Click the ▦ *button.*

Picture

B.9 Building Block Gallery Content Control

This allows you to add objects from the **Quick Parts Library.**

Developer Ribbon Tab→Controls Group→Click the ▦ *button.*

Quick Parts

Choose a building block.

B.10 CheckBox Content Control

This is used to select several choices by clicking the checkbox.

Developer Ribbon Tab→Controls Group→Click the ☑ *button.*

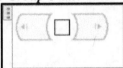

B.11 Combo Box Content Control

This is similar to the **Dropdown List.**

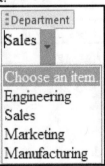

Department

Sales

Choose an item.
Engineering
Sales
Marketing
Manufacturing

Developer Ribbon Tab→ Controls Group→Click the ▦ *button.*

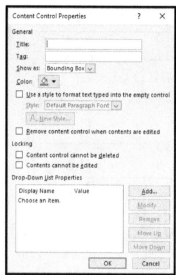

Right-click on Form→Properties.

B.12 Drop Down List Content Control

This is used to select a single answer from a fixed **Dropdown List**. An example would be: Mr, Miss., Mrs. Or Dr.

Right-click on Form→ Properties.

Developer Ribbon Tab →Controls Group → Click the 📋 *button.*

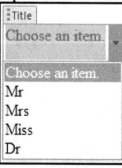

B.13 Date Picker Content Control

This provides a **Drop-down Calendar** to enter the **Date**.

Developer Ribbon Tab → Controls Group →Click the 📅 *button.*

2. *Right-click on Form→Properties*.

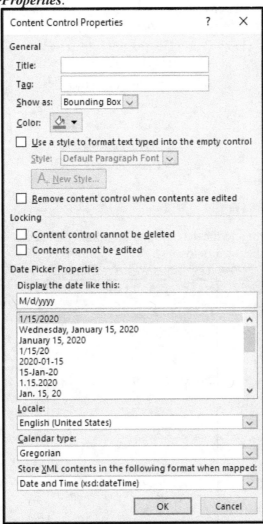

B.14 Repeating Section Content Control

Once you add the **Repeating Section Content Control,** add other controls and they will be repeated.

Developer Ribbon Tab →Controls Group →Click the button.

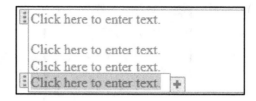

B.15 Legacy Tools

These are older-style tools that contain ActiveX control tools. These have interfaces to the Windows operating system.

Developer Ribbon Tab→Controls Group→Legacy Tools→Legacy Forms→Dropdown→Controls→Properties.

Text Form Fields

CheckBox Form Fields

DropDown Form Fields

Insert Frame

Insert Frame

Form Field Shading

Reset Form Fields

B.16 Protect A Form

This will **Protect The Form** and the data around the form from accidental modification and will allow one to enter data in the form fields.

Developer Ribbon Tab→Protect group→Restrict Editing.

B.17 Calculation Fields

See Final Project Word Forms

Practice Exercise 160 - New Client Form

Build the following form by creating a table and then adding the different form fields.

˙Residential:·New·Client·Form¶

Name¤	TITLE¤	FIRST¤	LAST¤		¤
	¤	¤	¤		¤
Street¤	¤				¤
City¤	¤				¤
State¤	¤		Zip·Code¤	¤	¤
Phone¤	¤		Email¤	¤	¤
Service·of·Interest¤	¤		Property·Type¤	¤	¤
Price·Range¤	¤		Features¤	¤	¤
Comments:¤	¤				¤
Action·Taken¤	¤				¤

Appendix C - Macros

Macros will allow you to automate routine tasks at the push of a button.

C.1 Security Level

This will define the **Security Level** when opening a file that contains **Macros**.

Practice Exercise 161

> ***File Tab→Options→Trust Center→Trust Center Settings→Macro Settings.***
> ***The most popular feature is:*** ☑ ***Disable All Macros with Notification.***

Macro Settings

⚪ Disable all macros without notification
◉ Disable all macros with notification
⚪ Disable all macros except digitally signed macros
⚪ Enable all macros (not recommended; potentially dangerous code can run)

C.2 Developers Tab

The **Developer's Tab** contains additional features and the **Code Group** contains the **Macro** creation tools.

Practice Exercise 162

> ***File Tab→Options→Customized Ribbon→*** ☑ Developer *(Right Side)→* OK .

C.3 Macro Creation

When you create a **New Macro**, several questions will be asked.
To create a **New Macro**: *View Ribbon Tab→Macro→Record Macro or Developers Ribbon Tab→Code Group→*⊡*Record Macro.* We will describe those questions and provide some comments concerning each one:
Macro Name - This is a single word name and cannot contain spaces. It can only contain dashes and underscore characters.

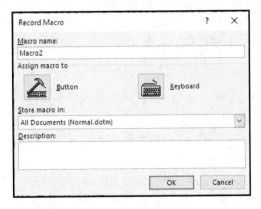

Assigning a Macro To:

 Button - Assign a **Form Button** or **Graphic Image**.

Keyboard - This will assign a **Shortcut Key** to run the Macro. If you use $\boxed{\text{Ctrl}}$ $\boxed{\text{B}}$ keys (a predefined key), it will temporarily reassign the key to the Macro. When you delete the **Macro** or reassign the key, the Bold will return. It is suggested that you assign the **Macro** to a $\boxed{\text{Shift}}$ $\boxed{\text{Ctrl}}$ key combination to avoid using popular pre-assigned keys. To add a **Shortcut Key** at a later time:

Store Macro In:

    All Documents (Normal.dotm) - This is available in every document.

    File Name - This is the currently opened document.

Description - This is the description of the **Macro**.

Tip: To modify this parameter after it is created:

    View Ribbon Tab → Macro →View Macros →(Select Macro) →Options.*

Practice Exercise 163 - Start Recording

This will create a **Macro** to open a file.

1. *Open Blank Document: File Tab →New →Blank Document.*
2. *View Ribbon Tab →* Macros →Record Macro →*

    Macro Name: OpenFile →Store macro in: All Documents → OK .

3. *File Tab →* Open *→Browse →*

    C:\Data\Word365-12\Mail Merge1.Docx → Open *Button.*

4. *View Ribbon Tab →* Macros →Stop Recording.*
5. **Run the Macro:** *File Tab →Close →View Ribbon Tab →* Macros →*

    View Macros →Select: OpenFile → Run *button.*

Practice Exercise 164 - Zoom Macro

Create a **Macro** to **Zoom** 200% in a document.

1. *View Ribbon Tab →* Macros →Record Macro →Macro Name:Zoom200*

    → OK .

2. *View Ribbon Tab →* Zoom Button → ⦿ 200% →* OK .
3. *View Ribbon Tab →* Macros →Stop Recording.*
4. **Run the Macro:** *View Ribbon Tab →* 100% Button →View Ribbon Tab →*

    Macros → View Macros →Select: Zoom200 →* Run *button.*

Practice Exercise 165 - Create A Today Macro

Create a **Today Macro** to place the current date anywhere.

1. *File Tab →New →Blank Document.*
2. *View Ribbon Tab →* Macros →Record Macro →Name: Today →*

    Store Macro In: All Documents → OK .

3. *Insert Ribbon Tab →* Quick Parts →Field →Date →* OK .
4. **Stop Recording the Macro:** *View Ribbon Tab →* Macros →*

    Stop Recording.*

5. **Test It:** *File Tab →New →Blank Document →View Ribbon Tab →* Macros*

    → View Macro →Today →* Run *button.*

Practice Exercise 166 - Format

Create a **Macro** to format an area that is selected. Select a small area on **Word**.
1. *(Select some text in the document)*
2. *View Ribbon Tab →*  *Macros → Record Macro →*
   Macro Name: FormtArea →Store Macro in: All Documents → OK
3. *Home Ribbon Tab →Font Group →* 20 *Font Size:20 →Paragraph Group*
   → Shading: Blue →View Ribbon Tab → Macros → Stop Recording.
4. **Test it:** *Select a different area →View Ribbon Tab → Macros →*
   View Macros → FormatArea → Run *button.*

C.4 VB Overview

Macros are recorded in **Visual Basic +**. You can review the code created and make minor changes if necessary.
The following are characteristics of recording a Macro:
    Key commands are recorded in VB code.
    Each module can contain more than one Macro.
    Comments appear in the code.
    Personal Macro Workbook is available to all workbooks.
    Some Macro names are reserved.

Practice Exercise 167 - Edit Macro

View Ribbon Tab → Macros → View Macros →(Select Macro) → Edit *button.*

C.5 Form Buttons

This will create a **Form Macro Button** used to execute a **Macro**.
Tip: The formatting of the Form Button is limited.

Practice Exercise 168 - View Code

1. *Developer Ribbon Tab →Controls Group →Legacy Tools* → *Command Button* .
2. *Right-click on Button →View Code →(cut n paste VB code).*

C.6 Quick Access Toolbar

Macros can be assigned to the **Quick Access Toolbar** located in the upper left corner of the screen.

Practice Exercise 169 - Add to QAT

Quick Access Toolbar drop-down →*More Commands → Choose command from:*
Macros →(Select desired macro) → Add >> → OK .

C.7 Create Macro Tab

Word 2010 added the capability of adding new ribbon tabs on the top of the screen.

Appendix C - Macros

Practice Exercise 170 - Customized Ribbon

File Tab→Options→Customize Ribbon→Choose Commands from: Macros→Select the View Tab→Right side choose `New Tab` *→Right-Click→Rename→Display Name: Macros→Select Group→Add Macro.*

Practice Exercise 171 - Printer Setup Macro

This will create a **Macro** to set up your printer layout.

1. *Developer Ribbon Tab→Code Group→ Record Macro.*
2. *Macro Name: Print setup.*
   All Documents.
   Keyboard: Shift Ctrl P *keys.*
3. *Change the print setup.*
   Commands to use - Set print area→ Landscape.
4. *Stop Macro.*
5. **Test it:** *Change orientation to Portrait.*
6. *Create a Print Setup Button.*

Appendix D - Collaboration

There are many ways to share information with others using external sources and within **Word**.

Section 1 - Sharing Documents

Practice Exercise 172

File Tab→ Open →*Browse*→*C:\Data\Word365-12\Management Team.Docx.*

D.1 Document Properties

Properties are used to define the document such as Author and Title.
File Tab→*Info*→*Properties*→*Advanced Properties*

Older versions of Word use: *Show Document Panel.*

D.2 Personalize

This is used to define the owner of the **Microsoft Word** program.
File Tab→*Options*→ *General*→ *Personalize your copy of Microsoft Office*→*User Name.*

D.3 Share A Document

(Word 2013 Only Feature)
This will allow you to **Share** the **Document** with others on the **Microsoft cloud**.
File Tab→*Share*→

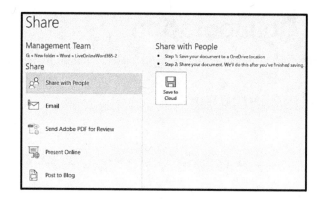

D.4 Compare Documents

This will two **Documents** and display the differences. It can be used to compare an old version with a new version.

Practice Exercise 173 - Compare

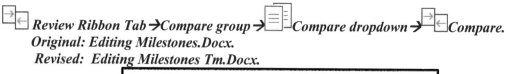 *Review Ribbon Tab→Compare group →* 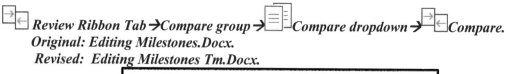 *Compare dropdown →* *Compare.*
        Original: Editing Milestones.Docx.
         Revised: Editing Milestones Tm.Docx.

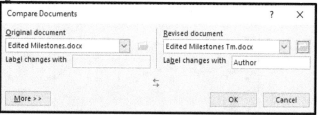

D.5 Combine Document

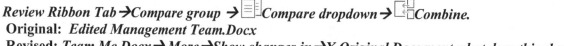 This will **Compare** and **Combine** two **Documents**.

Practice Exercise 174

   Review Ribbon Tab→Compare group → *Compare dropdown →* *Combine.*
    Original: Edited Management Team.Docx
     Revised: Team Mc.Docx→ More →Show changes in →X Original Document what does this show

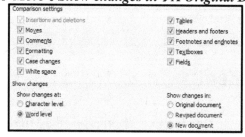

Test using Original:
Edited Management Team.docx and Revised: Team Sr.Docx.

Section 2 - Track Changes

D.6 Track Changes

This will allow you to **Track Changes** to a document. It is especially important if changes to a document might concern legal issues.

D.7 Lock Track Change

This locks the **Track Change** feature so it can't be turned on or off.

Practice Exercise 175

Review Ribbon Tab→Track Changes→Lock Change→

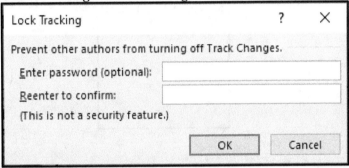

It is now password protected and can't be turned on or off.

D.8 All Markups

This will display a simple **Markup** style, All **Markups**, No **Markups**, or an original layout.

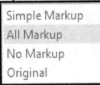

D.9 Show Markups

This will display several types of **Markups**.

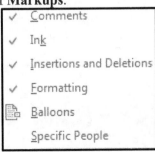

D.10 Simple Markup

(Word 2013+ Feature)
This displays a bar in the left column that hides a **Track Change** comment.

> Open the PDF file in Adobe Acrobat.

Practice Exercise 176 - Simple Markup

> ***Review Ribbon Tab→Track Changes→Track changes→Add a word to the document→The track change bar appears on the left→Click on the bar to see the word highlight.***

D.11 Reviewing Pane

This will **Review** the changes made to a document in a **Vertical** or **Horizontal Pane**.

D.12 Accept

This will **Accept** a single **Markup**.

D.13 Reject

This will **Reject** a single **Markup**.

	Reject and Move to Next
	Reject Change
	Reject All Changes Shown
	Reject All Changes
	Reject All Changes and Stop Tracking

D.14 Previous

⬑ This will **Forward** to the next **Markup**.

D.15 Next

⬏ This will return to the previous **Markup**.

Practice Exercise 177 - Track Changes

File Tab → [🗁 Open] *→Browse→C:\Data\Word365-12\Review Management Team.Docx.*

View Ribbon Tab→Views Group→ [📖] *Read Mode→Jump to* [Screen 1 of 1 ▾]
  →Navigation Pane
Review the Navigation Pane.
Remove comment by the user (Remove Justine Altaman).
View Options →Show Comments & Changes →Reviewers →Justine Altman.

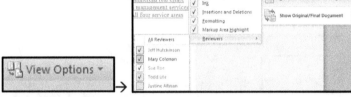

You will no longer see the comments.
Accept Changes:
  Review Ribbon Tab→Change Group→Accept View→Print Layout.

Practice Exercise 178 - Review A Document

File Tab → [🗁 Open] *→ Browse →C:\Data\Word365-12\Milestones.Docx.*
Change username: *Review tab →Tracking group →*
  Track Changes drop-down →Change username.
Change Default colors: *Review→Tracking group →*
  Track Changes drop-down →Change Tracking Options.
  Marking section →Insertions →Color →Green.
  Marking section →Deletions Dropdown List →Color Dropdown List →Red.
  Marking section →Comments Dropdown List →Turquoise.
  Balloons section →Use Balloons (Print and web layout) → Only for comments/formatting.
Review Ribbon Tab →Track Changes →Track Changes
  Continued Strong = Booming
  Six = eleven
Review Ribbon Tab →Comments →
New Comment=It's almost an eleven-fold increase
    3ʳᵈ bullet = $10.7 million.
    Review →Comments →New Comment →Is this correct?
Save the document as My Milestones.Docx.

Section 3 - Comments

D.16 Comments

This is used to have a conversation with team members from any location in a Word Document. A Team member can **Reply** to a comment by entering a reply text and pressing the Reply button.

To do this:

1. *Right-click in a cell→ New Comment.*
2. *Review Ribbon Tab →Comments Group→ New Comment.*
   Initial Comment:

   Jeff Hutchinson A few seconds ago

   Reply   Resolve

3. **Reply to a Comment:**

   Jeff Hutchinson A few seconds ago
   This is a test
      Jeff Hutchinson A few seconds ago

   Reply   Resolve

   Press the Reply button.

Practice Exercise 179

Place insertion point at the end of the comment→Review→Comment→Delete comment.
This modifies the comment:
   Triple-click on the comment and modify it.

D.17 Review All Comments

Review Ribbon Tab → Show Comments.

D.18 Resolve Thread

This will prevent additional comments from being added.

D.19 New Comment

This will add a **Comment** at any point in a document. It can be used to document a graphic image or add additional information to a document.

Practice Exercise 180 - New Comment

Place insertion point at the end of the comment→Review→Comment→Delete comment.
This modifies the comment:
> **Triple-click** on the comment and modify it.

D.20 Delete

This ![icon] **Deletes** a **Comment**.

D.21 Previous

This will move to the ![icon] Previous markup.

D.22 Next

This will move forward to the ![icon] Next markup.

D.23 Reply Comment

(Word 2013 Only Feature)
The **Reply Comment** function allows you and your collaborators to share comments on any changes made, or to be made, in your documents.
Exercise: ***Review Ribbon Tab→New Comment→Message 1→Choose the reply below.***

The **Reply Comment** function allows you and your collaborators to share comments on any changes made, or to be made, in your documents.
Exercise: ***Review Ribbon Tab→New Comment→Message 1→Choose the reply below.***

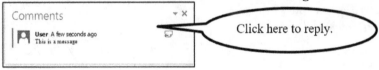

D.24 Comment Complete

(Word 2013+ Feature)
If comments are used for review, they can be **Marked** as **Complete**.

Section 4 - File access

D.25 Link To Excel Worksheet

This will **Link** the **Microsoft Word** document to an **Excel** worksheet.

In Excel: *File Tab →* 🗁 Open *→Browse → C:\Data\Word365-12\Monthly Sales Data.xlsx.*

In Word*: File Tab →* 🗁 Open *→ Browse →*
   C:\Data\Word365-12\Monthly Numbers Memo.Docx
In Excel: *Copy Cells A3 to E6.*
In Word: *Move Down→ Paste Special→Paste Link.*
In Excel: *Modify Excel.*
In Word: *Update Link.*
Embedded Object Create New:
   In Word: *Insert→Object→Object→Create New→Excel Worksheet*
   Cut n Paste data into the embedded worksheet.
Embedded Object Create from file:
   In Word: *Insert→Object→Object→Create from File Tab →*
   Monthly Sales Data.xlsx.
   Cut n Paste into a Word Table:
   Open Excel and cut n paste in Microsoft Word

D.26 Send To Powerpoint

This **Sends** a **Microsoft Word** document, in outline mode, to **Microsoft PowerPoint.**

Practice Exercise 181 - Send To PowerPoint

File Tab → 🗁 Open *→ C:\Data\Word365-12\Stockholder Report.doc.*
Quick Access Toolbar→All Commands→Send to MS Powerpoint.
View→Document Views group→Outline.
Outline tab→Outline Tools Group→Show Level 3.
Send to Powerpoint button→Review slides.

D.27 Send Via Email

Open any file→File Tab→Save and Send→Send using Email→Send as an attachment/Send a PDF.

Appendix E - Mail Merge

E.1 Using The Mail Merge Wizard

Mail Merge is often used to send out the same or similar letters to a large number of recipients. **Mail Merge** enables you to write one letter only and then merge the letter with a **Data Source**, thereby creating customized, individual letters including information specific to each recipient (such as names, addresses, and other details). The result is a professional-looking letter that is tailored to each recipient.

In addition to letters, you can use **Mail Merge** to print mailing labels and addressed envelopes or to create a directory. **Mail Merge** can produce documents in many formats; printed letters, files stored to disk to be printed at a later time, fax documents, and e-mail messages.

Practice Exercise 182 - Start Mail Merge

1. *File Tab→* `🗁 Open` *→Browse→C:\Data\Word365-12\Mail Merge1.Docx.*
2. Start a Mail Merge:
   Note: The steps in this lesson are specific to merging an existing letter with a new **Data Source**. With the guidance provided by the **Mail Merge** task pane, however, you will be able to apply what you learn in this lesson to other circumstances, whether you are working with a new main document, an existing **Data Source**, or any combination of such files.

Click Mailings Ribbon Tab →Start Mail Merge Group →Click Start Mail Merge `Start Mail Merge ˅` *→ Step by Step Mail Merge Wizard.*

E.2 Selecting Document Type (Step 1 of 6)

Before you can perform a mail merge, you must identify the type of the main document you want to use. The main document contains the information common to all merged documents.
The following types of documents are available in mail merge:

Document Type	Definition
Letters	Creates standard **Form Letters** that can be sent to a group of people.
E-mail messages	Creates **E-mail Messages** that can be sent to a group of people.
Envelopes	Creates print addressed **Envelopes** for a group mailing.
Labels	Creates address **Labels** and other types of **Labels**.
Directory	Creates a single document containing a catalog or printed list of addresses.

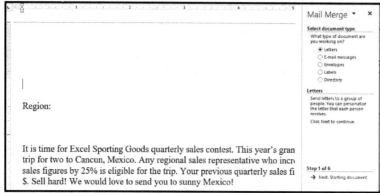

After you have identified the type of the main document, the next step is choosing whether to use the current document or to create a new one.

Practice Exercise 183 - Identify The Main Document

1. **Click ⦿ Letters, if necessary.**
2. **Click Next: Starting document.**

E.3 Select Starting Document (Step 2 of 6)

The next **Mail Merge** step is to identify the starting document.

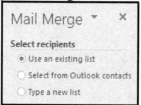

Practice Exercise 184 - Identify The Main Document

1. **Click ⦿ Use the current document.**
2. **Click Next: Select recipients.**

E.4 Creating A Recipient List (Step 3 of 6)

The next **Mail Merge** step is to create or identify the **Data Source**. A **Data Source** is a file that contains the information to be merged into the document, typically the recipients of a letter or an e-mail message. The **Data Source** must contain the variable information that will be inserted into the **Merge Fields** in the main document. A **Data Source** can be a **Microsoft Word** document (save the file as a **Microsoft Office Address List**), a spreadsheet (such as an **Excel Workbook**), a database (such as a **Microsoft Access database**), or a **Microsoft Outlook** contact list.

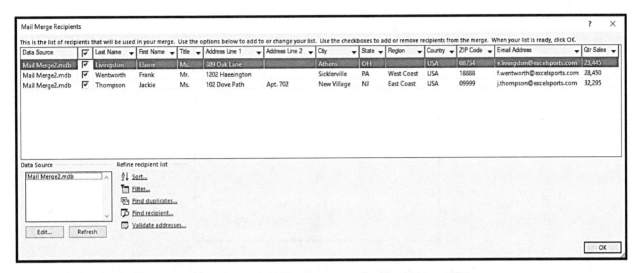

Practice Exercise 185 - Create A Data Source Or Recipient List

1. **Click ⦿ Type a new list.**
2. **Click Create** Create...
   Leave the New Address List Dialog Box open.

E.5 Customizing Columns In A Recipient List (Step 3 of 6)

When creating a **Data Source**, **Microsoft Word** provides a variety of pre-defined fields. Each field is identified by a label called a **Field Name**. You can select which of these fields you want to include in your **Data Source**. Your **Data Source** can be customized by adding, deleting, or renaming fields. **Microsoft Word** also allows you to rearrange the order of the fields.

Practice Exercise 186 - Customize The Columns In A Recipient List

1. *Use the Add, Delete, Rename, Move-Up and Move-down to organize the field names:*
2. *When done, press OK.*

E.6 Entering Records Into A Recipient List (Step 3 of 6)

After you have saved the recipient list, you are ready to enter the variable information into each record of the **Data Source**. You cannot enter multiple lines in a field in the **Edit Data Source Dialog Box**; you must enter one whole record at a time.

Practice Exercise 187 - Enter Records Into A Recipient List

1. Complete the first record with the information shown in the following table, leaving the **Address Line 2** field blank.

2. *Click New Entry* New Entry *to add a new record.*

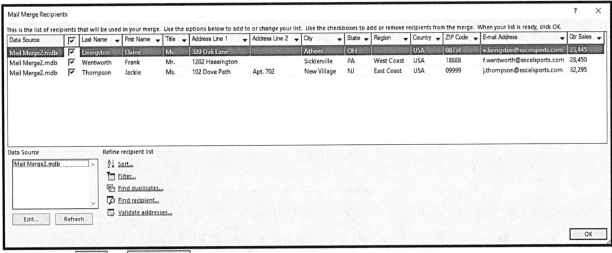

3. *Click* OK → Yes .

4. *You will now be asked to save the data source.*
   Save the file in C:\Data\Word365-12\Mail Merge2.mdb.

Tip: if you already created a data source, click on the data source name below:

Leave the **Mail Merge Recipients Dialog Box** open.

5. *Click* OK *when finished.*
6. *Click Next: Write your letter.*

E.7 Inserting Merge Fields Into A Document (Step 4 of 6)

The next step in the **Mail Merge** process is to **Insert Merge fields** into the main document.
Merge Fields are **Inserted** at the insertion point. When inserted, a merge field is enclosed in
chevrons such as, **<<First Name>>**. The **Merge Field** will also be shaded if the **Field shading** option
is set to **Always** on the **Advanced** page of the **Options Dialog Box.**
Clicking the **More items button to** open the **Insert Merge Field Dialog Box**, which allows you to
insert an individual merge field. Once you have inserted the **Merge Field**, you must close the dialog
box before inserting another **Merge Field** in a different document location.
It is also a good idea to set the **Field shading** option to **Always**.
File Tab →Options →Advanced →Show Document Content →Field Shading: Always.

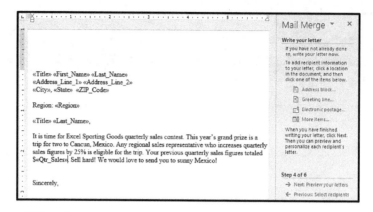

Practice Exercise 188 - Insert Merge Fields Into A Document

1. **Use the More Items** 〔📇 More items...〕 **to add the field codes to the letter:**

«Title» «First_Name» «Last_Name»
«Address_Line_1» «Address_Line_2»
«City», «State» «ZIP_Code»

Region: «Region»

«Title» «Last_Name»,

Tip: Make sure you place spaces and commas at the appropriate places.

2. **Use the More Items** c〔📇 More items...〕 **to add the "Qtr Sales" field to the letter:**

It is time for Excel Sporting Goods quarterly sales contest. This year's grand prize is a trip for two to Cancun, Mexico. Any regional sales representative who increases quarterly sales figures by 25% is eligible for the trip. Your previous quarterly sales figures totaled $«Qtr_Sales». Sell hard! We would love to send you to sunny Mexico!

3. **Click Next: Preview your letter.**

E.8 Previewing Merged Data (Step 5 of 6)

You can **Preview** the main document with the **Merged Data** before you carry out the merge. **Previewing** the **Merged** document is a good idea because you can use the preview to check for format and spelling errors or any unexpected results of the merge.

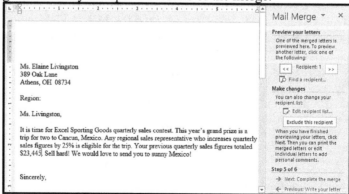

Practice Exercise 189 - Preview The Merged Document

1. **Click Next: Preview your letters.**

2. **To see the next Record: Click the Right Double Arrow** 〔 >> 〕.

3. *To see the previous record: Click the Left Double Arrow*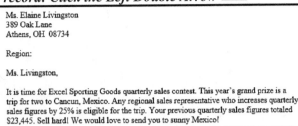

Ms. Elaine Livingston
389 Oak Lane
Athens, OH 08734

Region:

Ms. Livingston,

It is time for Excel Sporting Goods quarterly sales contest. This year's grand prize is a
trip for two to Cancun, Mexico. Any regional sales representative who increases quarterly
sales figures by 25% is eligible for the trip. Your previous quarterly sales figures totaled
$23,445. Sell hard! We would love to send you to sunny Mexico!

4. *Click Next: Complete the mail merge.*

E.9 Merging To A New Document (Step 6 of 6)

After you have previewed the merged records, you can edit the main document or the recipient list as
needed, or you can complete the **Merge**. Editing the main document before you **Merge** will affect all
merged letters while editing a **Data Source** record permanently changes the edited records. When you
Complete the Merge, you can merge letters directly to the printer, or you can merge them into a new
document.

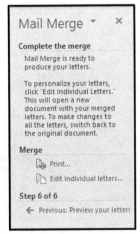

Practice Exercise 190 - Merge To A New Document

1. ***Click Edit individual letters*** Edit individual letters... →*Click ⦿ All, if necessary.*
2. ***Click*** OK.
3. ***Scroll through the new document to view the merged letters.***
4. **Close the document without saving it:** *File Tab* → Close → Don't Save.

Appendix F - Find And Replace

F.1 Using Find

You can use **Microsoft Word's Find** feature to quickly find text in an open document. When **Microsoft Word Finds** the text, it selects it. **Find** appears on the left side of the screen and lists all of the instances it finds.

Practice Exercise 192 - Find

1. **File** *Tab*→ **Open** → **Browse** → *C:\Data\Word365-12\Find Replace.docx.*
2. **Home Ribbon Tab →Editing Group →** **Find button.**
3. **Type "Price" on the left side of the screen.**
4. **Click on one of the solutions found.**

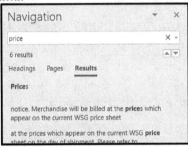

F.2 Using Advanced Find Options

You can select options on the **Find** page in the **Find** and **Replace Dialog Box** to narrow a search. The **Find** and **Replace Dialog Box** must be fully expanded to access these options.

After you have performed a find and closed the **Find** and **Replace Dialog Box**, the arrows on the **Next Page** and **Previous Page** buttons on the vertical scroll bar become

blue and display the **ScreenTips**. **The previous Find/Go To** and **Next Find/Go To**. Instead of scrolling to the next or previous page when clicked, they now move to the next or previous occurrence of the text in the **Find** and **Replace Dialog Box**, even if it is closed. You can use the **Browse by Page** button on the **Select Browse Option** gallery to reset the browse option.

When the **Match case** option is enabled, **Microsoft Word** only finds text that exactly matches the characters in the **Find what** box, including uppercase and lowercase characters.

Find whole words only option ignores text that is part of another word. For example, if the search text is "**inform**" and the **Find whole words only** option is selected, **Microsoft Word** identifies only the word **inform** and not words containing **inform**, such as **information**.

The **Use wildcards** option allows you to use the asterisk (*) and question mark(**?**) wildcards to search for words that fit a pattern. For example, **s?t** finds the words sit, sat, or set, and **s*t** finds those words, as well as the words shirt, shot, and sport.

If words have multiple correct spellings, such as **theater** or **theatre**, you can use the **Sounds like the** option to find the desired text.

With the **Find all word forms** option enabled, **Microsoft Word** finds both singular and plural forms of the search text (if it is a noun) and all possible tenses of the root form of a verb (if the search text is a verb). This option is unavailable if either the **Use wildcards** or **Sounds like** the option is selected.

Practice Exercise 193 - Advanced Find

1. *If necessary, go to the top of the document.*
2. *Home Ribbon Tab→Editing Group→* 🔍 *Find dropdown arrow→* 🔍 *Advanced Find.*
3. *Find What: Returns* | Fi̲nd what: | Returns |
4. *Click* More >> .
5. *Click Search* ⌄ *dropdown arrow→ Search: Down* | Search: | Down ⌄ |
6. *Click* ☑ *Match case.*
7. *Click* << L̲ess .
8. *Click* Fi̲nd Next → Fi̲nd Next → Cancel .

F.3 Finding Special Characters

You can use the **Find** feature to search for special characters (such as an optional hyphen) or formatting marks (such as a paragraph mark or a tab character). You can use **Find** to locate extraneous characters or to check existing ones.

When you are searching for special characters, you can select the desired character from the **Find** and **Replace Dialog Box**.

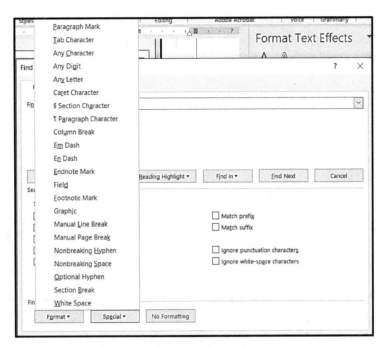

Practice Exercise 194 - Find Special Characters

1. *If necessary, go to the top of the document.*
2. *Home Ribbon Tab →Editing Group→ Find dropdown arrow→ Advanced Find.*
3. *Click More >>, if necessary.*
4. *Click Search dropdown arrow → Search: All*
5. *Click Special ▾ → Click Manual Page Break.*
6. *Click << Less.*
7. *Click Find Next → Find Next → Cancel.*

F.4 Finding A Format

At times, you may want to locate text containing a specific format. You can search for the font, paragraph, tab, language, frame, or style formats, as well as for highlighting. This feature enables you to easily locate formats in order to edit or delete them.

You can search for formats without identifying specific text.

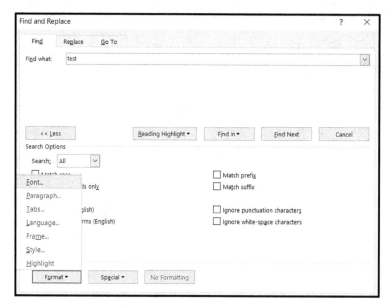

Practice Exercise 195 - Find Format

1. *If necessary, go to the top of the document.*
2. *Home Ribbon Tab→Editing Group→ Find dropdown arrow→ Advanced Find.*
3. **Find What:** *agreement* `Find what:    agreement`
4. *Click* `More >>`, *if necessary.*
5. *Click Search* `⌄` *dropdown arrow →* `Search: All ⌄`.
6. *Click* `Format ▾` *→ Click Font: Arial→Scroll as necessary, and click Arial in the Font list box.*
7. *Click* `OK`.
8. *Click* `<< Less`.
9. *Click* `Find Next` *→* `Find Next` *→* `Cancel`.
10. *Click anywhere in the document to deselect the text.*

F.5 Using Replace

With the **Replace** feature, you can replace found text with alternate text, formatting, or special characters. You can control what is replaced by confirming each replacement.
Microsoft Word can also replace all occurrences of the specified text at one time if you do not want to review each replacement. It is a good idea, however, to use caution when you use the **Replace All** command. You must be precise when specifying the search text so that you do not unintentionally replace the wrong text.

Practice Exercise 196 - Replace

1. *If necessary, go to the top of the document.*
2. *Click* `Replace`.
3. **Find What:** *verbal* `Find what:    oral`
4. *Press* `Tab` *key.*

5. **Replace With:** *verbal* 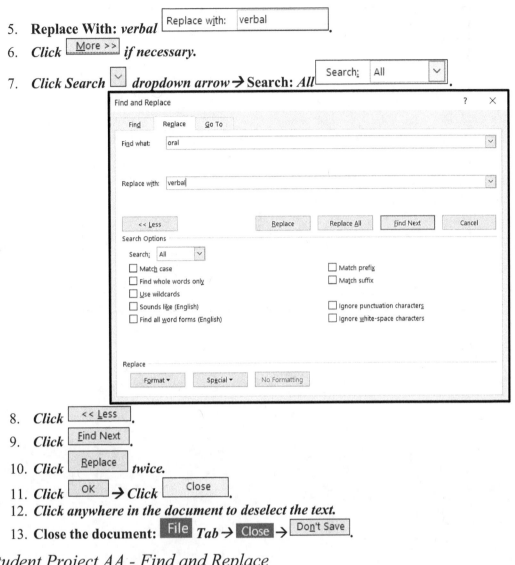 Replace with: | verbal .

6. *Click* More >> *if necessary.*

7. *Click Search* ☑ *dropdown arrow* → *Search: All* Search: | All | ☑ .

8. *Click* << Less .
9. *Click* Find Next .
10. *Click* Replace *twice.*
11. *Click* OK → *Click* Close .
12. *Click anywhere in the document to deselect the text.*
13. **Close the document:** File *Tab* → Close → Don't Save .

Student Project AA - Find and Replace

1. File *Tab* → 📂 Open → 📁 Browse → *C:\Data\Word365-12\Find Replace Practice1.docx.*
2. *Replace all occurrences of the word preview with the word showcase.*
3. *Replace all occurrences of the word free with the word complementary. Be careful to replace whole words only.*
4. *Find all occurrences of the Italic font format and replace them with the Bold Italic font format. (Tip: To find all occurrences of a format regardless of text, delete all text in the Find what and Replace with boxes and deselect any selected options).*
5. *Find a section break. (Tip: A section break is a special character and remembers to first remove all formatting).*
   Then, close the Find and Replace Dialog Box.
6. *Switch to* 📄 *Draft View to see the Section Break.*
7. *Reset the Previous Page and Next Page buttons.*
8. **Close the document:** File *Tab* → Close → Don't Save .

Appendix G - Find and Replace

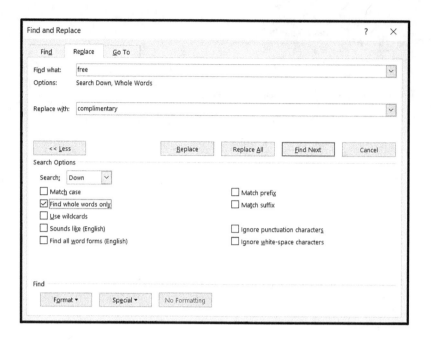

Appendix G - Thesaurus And Smart Lookup

You can use the **Thesaurus** to find the opposite meaning, or antonym, of a word. The **Smart Lookup** task pane uses online services to find information. This may include looking for information about a company in the news, finding information about a person, finding the definition or synonym for a word, finding the meaning of a foreign-language word, or translating a word into another language.

G.1 Using The Thesaurus To Look Up Synonyms

Synonyms are words that have similar meanings. The easiest way to look up a word that appears in your text is to use the **Right-click** on the test and choose **Thesaurus**. This inserts the word in the **Search For** box. **Tip**: In **Word 2007** and **2010**, the **Smart Lookup** was called the **Research Task** pane and it had different searching capabilities.

Practice Exercise 197 – Thesaurus Synonyms

1. **File** *Tab* → 🗁 **Open** → 🗁 **Browse** → *C:\Data\Word365-12\Research.Docx.*
2. *Review Ribbon Tab → Proofing Group →* 📖 *Thesaurus.*
3. *Select the word "Produce" in the first line below the Equipment heading*
4. *You can also type a word into the Search for box. Select the text in the Search for box and enter manufacture. Click the Start Searching button next to the Search for the box to search for synonyms.*
5. *Close the Thesaurus pane.*

G.2 Using The Thesaurus To Look Up Antonyms

You can use the **Thesaurus** to find the opposite meaning, or an **Antonym**, of a word. If the **Thesaurus Pane** is already open, you can find the word (**Antonym**) next to the word in the **Thesaurus Pane**. The easiest way to look up a word that appears in your text is to use the **Right-Click** on the text and choose **Thesaurus**. This inserts the word in the **Search** box.   limited

Practice Exercise 198 – Thesaurus Antonyms

Use the **Thesaurus** to look up **Antonyms**.
Select the word "limited" → Review Ribbon Tab → Language Group → Thesaurus
or Right-click on the word "limited" → Synonyms → Thesaurus.

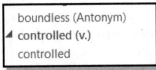

G.3 Translating Text

The **Translation Service** allows you to translate single words and phrases from other languages using bilingual dictionaries. The task pane uses the dictionaries installed locally on your computer to translate words, and if you have an Internet connection, includes online bilingual dictionaries in the search.

Open the Translator pane, then enter the word or phrase you want to translate in the **Selection From** box or by selecting the word or phrase in the document. If you are translating multiple words, you should select all the text desired. While you can use bilingual dictionaries to translate words and phrases, you can also use online services for a machine translation of larger amounts of text, including an entire document. However, you should check a machine translation with a human translator because the **Spelling** and **Grammar** may not be perfect.

Practice Exercise 199 - Translate Text

1. **Select the word "Manufactures"→Review Ribbon Tab→Language Group→
   [icon] Translate dropdown arrow→[icon] Translate Selection.**
2. **Switch the language to: Spanish**
   Test the language French or any language desired.

3. **Close the document:** [File] *Tab* → [Close] → [Don't Save].

Student Project BB - Thesaurus Synonyms

1. [File] *Tab*→ [Open] → [Browse] →*C:\Data\Word365-12\Research Practice1.Docx.*
2. **Review Ribbon Tab→Proofing Group→ Thesaurus.**
3. **Thesaurus:**
   3a. **Select the word experts in the second paragraph and use the Thesaurus to find a synonym for the word expert and choose Specialist.**

   Tip: Choose the dropdown arrow next to *Specialist*→ [Insert].
   3b. **Display additional synonyms for the word specialist.**
   3c. **Replace the word with a synonym.**
4. **Translation:**
   4a. **Select the word demonstrations in the second paragraph.**
   4b. **Use the Translation service to translate the word into any language you have installed. (Tip: Select a language from the To list).**
5. **Close the document without saving it:** [File] *Tab* → [Close] → [Don't Save].

Appendix H - Word Short Cut Keys

You can use the keyboard to execute many **Microsoft Word** commands. Any command listed below that starts with **Ctrl** or **Alt** means you should hold down the **Ctrl** or **Alt** key while pressing the key that follows it. Unless stated otherwise, the shortcut keys are not case sensitive.

H.1 Move Cursor

One character to the right	**Right Arrow**
One character to the left	**Left Arrow**
Beginning of line	**Home**
End of line	**End**
Down one line	**Down Arrow**
Up one line	**Up Arrow**
Down one screen	**PgDn**
Up one screen	**PgUp**
Next page	**Ctrl** **PgDn**
Previous page	**Ctrl** **PgUp**
Beginning of document	**Ctrl** **Home**
End of document	**Ctrl** **End**

H.2 Select Portions of the Document

A word	**Double click**
A sentence	**Ctrl** **Click**
A paragraph (Triple Click)	**Click** **Click** **Click**
Anything	Click at the beginning of the area, **Shift** click at the end
Everything (all)	**Ctrl** **A**

H.3 Other Shortcut Keys

Close the Window	**Ctrl** **W**
Open a document	**Ctrl** **O**
Close Active Document	**Alt** **F4**
Cut	**Ctrl** **X**
Copy	**Ctrl** **C**
Paste	**Ctrl** **V**
Undo	**Ctrl** **Z**
Redo	**Ctrl** **Y**
Bold	**Ctrl** **B**
Italic	**Ctrl** **I**
Underline	**Ctrl** **U**
Change Case	**Shift** **F3**
Left Justify	**Ctrl** **L**
Right Justify	**Ctrl** **R**
Center Justify	**Ctrl** **E**

Full Justification .... **Ctrl** **J**

Single space .... **Ctrl** **1**

Double space .... **Ctrl** **2**

Toggle Spacing Before .... **Ctrl** **0** (zero)

Heading 1 Style .... **Ctrl** **Alt** **1**

Heading 2 Style .... **Ctrl** **Alt** **2**

Heading 3 Style .... **Ctrl** **Alt** **3**

Normal Style .... **Ctrl** **Shift** **N**

Find .... **Ctrl** **F**

Replace .... **Ctrl** **H**

Manual Page Break .... **Ctrl** **Enter**

Line Break .... **Shift** **Enter**

Increase Indent .... **Ctrl** **M**

Decrease Indent .... **Ctrl** **Shift** **M**

Increase Hanging Indent .... **Ctrl** **T**

Decrease Hanging Indent .... **Ctrl** **Shift** **T**

Increase Font Size .... **Ctrl** **]** Select text then press the] square braket key.

Decrease Font Size .... **Ctrl** **[** Select text then press the [square braket key.

Toggle Super^{Script} .... **Ctrl** **Shift** **+**

Recalculate **F9**

Reveal Field Codes .... **Alt** **F9**

Reveal Formatting Pane .... **Shift** **F1**

H.4 Selection Techniques used for Macros

Selects one character to the right .... **Shift** **Right Arrow**

Selects one character to the left .... **Shift** **Left Arrow**

Selects a word from its beginning to its end .... **Ctrl** **Shift** **Right Arrow**

Selects a word from its end to its beginning .... **Ctrl** **Shift** **Left Arrow**

Selects a line from its beginning to its end .... **Home**, and then press **Shift** **End**

Selects a line from its end to its beginning .... **End**, and then press **Shift** **Home**

Selects one line down .... **End**, and then press **Shift** **Down Arrow**

Selects one line up .... **Home**, and then press **Shift** **Up Arrow**

Selects a paragraph from its beginning to its end .... **Ctrl** **Shift** **Down Arrow**

Selects a paragraph from its end to its beginning .... **Ctrl** **Shift** **Up Arrow**

Selects a document from its end to its beginning .... **Ctrl** **Shift** **Home**

Selects a document from its beginning to its end .... **Ctrl** **Shift** **End**

From the beginning of a window to its end .... **Alt** **Ctrl** **Shift** **PgDn**

Selects the entire document .... **Ctrl** **A**

Selects a vertical block of text .... **Ctrl** **Shift** **F8**, and then use the **Arrow** keys

Index - Microsoft Word - Building Professional Documents

Microsoft Office Courseware

Step-By-Step Training Guides and Workbooks
Available on Amazon.com (Search for author, Jeff Hutchinson)

To review a sample book, see sample video clip, Amazon reviews and to purchase: Go To: https://www.elearnlogic.com. These **Step-By-Step Training Guides** focus on specific learning concepts including brief descriptions as well as many short 2-5 minute exercises for practice. The Table of Contents and Index will allow students to look up desired concepts quickly and easily. These guides are invaluable resources used to build and maintain computer skills for industry, as well as for personal use.

Available in Paperback: $14.95 or Kindle eBook: $9.95

https://www.amazon.com /dp/B09FW4BZDF

https://www.amazon.com/dp/ B09FX1ZG5V

https://www.amazon.co m/dp/B09FXGMF44

https://www.amazon.co m/dp/B09J8672X1

Paperback: $14.95, Kindle $9.95

About the Author

Jeff Hutchinson is a corporate computer trainer and consultant. He teaches **Microsoft** and **Adobe** products from beginning to advanced topics. Jeff has a BS degree from BYU in Computer-Aided Engineering and owned a computer training and consulting firm in San Francisco, California for several years. He currently works as an independent computer instructor and these training guides are based on topics most commonly taught.

https://www.amazon.com/ dp/B09WHL9CHY

https://www.amazon.com /dp/B09WH1W2D3

Available in Paperback: $14.95 or Kindle eBook: $9.95

https://www.amazon.com /dp/B091JYRPGY

https://www.amazon.com /dp/B0881Z43R7

https://www.amazon.com /dp/B091NC5MB5

https://www.amazon.com /dp/B07XGFMLF1

Contact Information: Jeff Hutchinson, jeffhutch@elearnlogic.com or (801) 376-6687.
Evaluation copy: http://www.elearnlogic.com/

www.ingramcontent.com/pod-product-compliance
Lightning Source LLC
LaVergne TN
LVHW081753050326
832903LV00027B/1930